Careers in
Fundraising

LILYA WAGNER

John Wiley & Sons, Inc.

This book is printed on acid-free paper. ∞

Copyright © 2002 by John Wiley & Sons, Inc., New York. All rights reserved.

Published simultaneously in Canada.

No part of this publication may be reproduced, stored in a retrieval system or transmitted in any form or by any means, electronic, mechanical, photocopying, recording, scanning or otherwise, except as permitted under Sections 107 or 108 of the 1976 United States Copyright Act, without either the prior written permission of the Publisher, or authorization through payment of the appropriate per-copy fee to the Copyright Clearance Center, 222 Rosewood Drive, Danvers, MA 01932, (978) 750-8400, fax (978) 750-4744. Requests to the Publisher for permission should be addressed to the Permissions Department, John Wiley & Sons, Inc., 605 Third Avenue, New York, NY 10158-0012, (212) 850-6011, fax (212) 850-6008, E-Mail: PERMREQ@WILEY.COM.

This publication is designed to provide accurate and authoritative information in regard to the subject matter covered. It is sold with the understanding that the publisher is not engaged in rendering legal, accounting, or other professional services. If legal advice or other expert assistance is required, the services of a competent professional person should be sought.

Library of Congress Cataloging-in-Publication Data

Wagner, Lilya.
    Careers in fundraising / Lilya Wagner.
      p. cm.
    Includes bibliographical references and index.
    ISBN 0-471-40359-8 (pbk. : alk. paper)
    1. Fundraising. I. Title. II. Series.

   HG177.W34 2001
   658.15'224'02373—dc21

               2001045364

Printed in the United States of America.

10 9 8 7 6 5 4 3 2 1

Beyond Fund Raising: New Strategies for Nonprofit Innovation and Investment
Kay Sprinkel Grace, CFRE
ISBN 0-471-16232-9
Inspirational yet practical, this book teaches you how to "put away the tin cup" and take fundraising to a new level. An experienced fundraising consultant and volunteer, Grace shows you how to establish a true relationship between philanthropy, development, and fundraising. You will also get forms, checklists, and flow charts to help you understand, visualize, and incorporate this new philosophy into your own nonprofit organization.

Careers in Fundraising
Lilya Wagner, Ed. D., CFRE
ISBN 0-471-40359-8
Careers in Fundraising provides expert guidance on professional opportunities in the field of fundraising, including topics on professional development, on-the-job issues, and the significance of fundraising as a career. This comprehensive resource covers all aspects of the profession, and also addresses the personal mission and commitment necessary for success in the field.

The Complete Guide to Fund-Raising Management
Stanley Weinstein, ACFRE
ISBN 0-471-24290-X
This book is a practical management, how-to tailored specifically to the needs of fundraisers. Moving beyond theory, it addresses the day-to-day problems faced in these organizations, and offers hands-on advice and practical solutions. The book and accompanying disk include sample forms, checklists, and grids to help the reader plan and execute complicated fundraising campaigns.

Critical Issues in Fund Raising
Dwight F. Burlingame, Ph.D., CFRE, editor
ISBN 0-471-17465-3
This book examines the most pressing issues facing fundraising professionals today. Extensive chapters cover donors, innovative fundraising, marketing, financial management, ethics, international philanthropy, and the fundraising professional. Written by a team of highly respected practitioners and educators, this book was developed in conjunction with AFP, the Council for the Advancement and Support of Education, the Association for Research on Nonprofit Organizations and Voluntary Action, and the Indiana University Center on Philanthropy.

Cultivating Diversity in Fundraising
Janice Gow Pettey
ISBN 0-471-40361-X
Cultivating Diversity in Fundraising offers an overview in cultivating successful fundraising and an enhanced understanding of philanthropic motivation in four selected racial/ethnic populations—African American, Asian American (Chinese, Filipino, Japanese, Korean, and South Asian), Hispanic/Latino (Cuban, Dominican, El Salvador, Mexican, and Puerto Rican), and Native American. By understanding the rich philanthropic traditions of the individuals they are working with and soliciting funds from, fundraisers will be better equipped to serve their communities and their organizations.

Direct Response Fund Raising: Mastering New Trends for Results
Michael Johnston
ISBN 0-471-38024-5
This guide offers fundraisers, managers, and volunteers an excellent understanding of how to plan and execute successful direct response campaigns. The success of a nonprofit direct response program requires staying on top of recent trends in the field. These trends include appealing more effectively to aging baby boomers as well as tapping into powerful new databases, the Internet, CD-ROMs, diskettes, and videos. The book includes a CD-ROM, with all the full-color, complete examples from the book, as well as many more.

Ethical Decision-Making in Fund Raising
Marilyn Fischer, Ph.D.
ISBN 0-471-28943-3
This is a handbook for ethical reasoning and discussion. In her provocative new book, Dr. Fischer provides conceptual tools with which a nonprofit can thoroughly examine the ethics of how and from whom it seeks donations. With the book's Ethical Decision-Making Model, the author explains how fundraisers can use their basic value commitments to organizational mission, relationships, and integrity as day-to-day touchstones for making balanced, ethical fundraising decisions.

The Fund Raiser's Guide to the Internet
Michael Johnston
ISBN 0-471-25365-0
This book presents the issues, technology, and resources involved in online fundraising and donor relations. A practical "how-to" guide, it presents real-world case studies and successful practices from a top consulting firm, as well as guidance, inspiration, and warnings to nonprofits learning to develop this new fundraising technique. It also covers such important factors as determining your market, online solicitation pieces, security issues, and setting up your Web site.

Fund Raising Cost Effectiveness: A Self-Assessment Workbook
James M. Greenfield, ACFRE, FAHP
ISBN 0-471-10916-9
A comprehensive, step-by-step guide that will help nonprofit professionals ensure that their department and campaigns are as efficient and cost-effective as possible. It combines a thorough explanation of the issues critical to fundraising self-assessment with easy-to-use worksheets and practical advice. The accompanying disk contains all the sample worksheets, plus software for downloading a nonprofit's fundraising data from major software products into charts, graphs, and P&L-like spreadsheet templates.

Fund Raising: Evaluating and Managing the Fund Development Process
James M. Greenfield, ACFRE, FAHP
ISBN 0-471-32014-5
Covering initial preparation in 15 areas of fundraising and the ongoing management of the process, this book is designed for fundraising executives of organizations both large and small. Included are numerous examples, case studies, checklists, and a unique evaluation of the audit environment of nonprofit organizations.

International Fundraising for Not-for-Profits: A Country-by-Country Profile
Thomas Harris
ISBN 0-471-24452-X
The only comprehensive book of its kind, it examines and compares the fundraising environments of 18 countries around the world. Each chapter is written by a local expert and details the history and context of fundraising for the country, local and global economic factors, legal and fiscal practices sources of funding, and what fundraising practices are considered acceptable by the culture and government.

The Legislative Labyrinth: A Map for Not-for-Profits
Walter P. Pidgeon, Jr., Ph.D., CFRE
ISBN 0-471-40069-6
Currently, only a fraction of the nonprofit community takes advantage of the legislative process in representing their members and furthering its missions. Nonprofits are missing a significant way to fulfill their mission of gaining visibility and attracting new members and funding sources. This book answers the questions of nonprofits thinking of starting a lobbying program.

The Nonprofit Handbook: Fund Raising, Third Edition
James M. Greenfield, ACFRE, FAHP
ISBN 0-471-40304-0
The third edition of this invaluable handbook provides a complete overview of the entire development function, from management and strategic planning to hands-on, practical guidance for the various kinds of fundraising. Written by leading fundraising professionals, edited by James M. Greenfield, this invaluable resource brings together over 40 contributors who are vanguard experts and professionals in the field of fundraising.

Nonprofit Investment Policies: Practical Steps for Growing Charitable Funds
Robert P. Fry, Jr., esq.
ISBN 0-471-17887-X
Written in plain English by an investment manager who specializes in nonprofit organizations, *Nonprofit Investment Policies* explores the unique characteristics of nonprofit investing. Covered topics include endowment management, planned gift assets, socially responsible investing, and more. This book includes charts and graphs to illustrate complex investment concepts, tables and checklists to guide nonprofit managers in decision making, and case studies of organizations of various sizes to show how to successfully develop and implement investment policies.

The NSFRE Fund-Raising Dictionary
ISBN 0-471-14916-0
Developed by NSFRE experts, this book provides clear and concise definitions for nearly 1,400 key fundraising and related nonprofit terms—from development and accounting to marketing and public relations. It also offers additional resource material, including a suggested bibliography.

Planned Giving Simplified: The Gift, the Giver, and the Gift Planner
Robert F. Sharpe, Sr.
ISBN 0-471-16674-X
This resource, written by a well-known veteran of planned giving, is a down-to-earth introduction to the complex world of planned giving, a sophisticated fundraising strategy that involves big money, complex tax laws, and delicate personal politics. This book shows charities, and in particular the charities' planned givers, how to understand the process—both the administration of planned gifts, as well as the spirit of giving.

The Universal Benefits of Volunteering
Walter P. Pidgeon, Jr., Ph.D. CFRE
ISBN 0-471-18505-1
Volunteering is good for nonprofits, individuals, and corporations because it builds strong interpersonal and professional skills that carry over into all sectors. A concise, hands-on guide to maximizing the use of business professionals in the nonprofit volunteer context, this workbook is a vital resource for all those in-volved in volunteering efforts. Included is a disk with all the worksheets and model documents needed to establish effective, successful, and ongoing volunteer programs.

THE AFP/WILEY FUND DEVELOPMENT SERIES

The AFP/Wiley Fund Development Series is intended to provide fund development professionals and volunteers, including board members (and others interested in the not-for-profit sector), with top-quality publications that help advance philanthropy as voluntary action for the public good. Our goal is to provide practical, timely guidance information on fundraising, charitable giving, and related subjects. AFP and Wiley each bring to this innovative collaboration unique and important resources that result in a whole greater than the sum of its parts.

The Association of Fundraising Professionals

The AFP is a professional association of fundraising executives that advances philanthropy through its more than 25,000 members in over 159 chapters throughout the United States, Canada, and Mexico. Through its advocacy, research, education, and certification programs, the AFP fosters development and growth of fundraising professionals, works to advance philanthropy and volunteerism, and promotes high ethical standards in the fundraising profession.

2001–2002 AFP Publishing Advisory Council

John Wiley & Sons

Susan McDermott
Editor (Professional/Trade Division), John Wiley & Sons, Inc.

AFP Staff

Richard B. Chobot, Ph.D.
Vice President, Professional Advancement, AFP

Jan Alfieri
Manager, AFP Resource Center, AFP

This book is dedicated to all those who have been in my classes, workshops, seminars, conferences, conference sessions, and other meeting places and who went beyond just sitting there. Because you shared experiences, asked for my advice, incorporated the knowledge I was able to convey, told me about your achievements and your disappointments, and in many cases befriended me, my life in fundraising has been richly blessed. My best wishes continue to go with you.

Acknowledgments

No book such as this one can be the work of just one person. My sincere thanks go to scores of people who generously gave their time and expertise during the development of this book, and therefore contributed to making it a reality and a contribution to the profession.

In particular, I thank the following:

Martha Cooley, formerly of John Wiley & Sons, Inc., for her advice and encouragement when this project was developing.

Susan McDermott, of John Wiley & Sons, Inc., for picking up where Martha left off and being accessible and helpful.

Dorothy Hearst of Jossey-Bass Publishers, whose feedback guided me in the initial process of developing the proposal for the book.

Jamie Levy, Cathlene Williams, Dwight Burlingame, and John Wagner for reading the manuscript carefully and making timely and valuable suggestions for improvement.

Bonnie McKinney for her overall assistance, especially in conducting interviews, securing quotations, and finding references.

Tim Seiler for his excellence as a role model in collegiality, teaching, training, and fundraising practice.

Each of the professionals who contributed sidebars and quotations for each of the chapters.

Contents

Foreword

BY PAULETTE MAEHARA

W hen does a profession actually become a profession? At what point does a job cease being a daily, paycheck-oriented, killing-time-until-the-next-thing-comes-along occupation, and become a life-long aspiration with professional practitioners dedicated to skill mastery and knowledge sharing with other colleagues?

Typically, five criteria make up a profession: an established body of knowledge, educational standards and opportunities (whether formal or informal), continuing research, standards of professional practice, and self-regulation. One can easily argue that fundraising meets each of these five criteria and should be considered a profession. But this definition is a touch too academic, I believe, for the average person. So how else can we determine when a true profession actually comes into being, and if fundraising qualifies?

It would be nice if little kids dreamed of being fundraisers; then we would probably know for sure. But those lucky professions—doctors, police officers, firefighters, astronauts—have pretty much remained the same over the years, and it doesn't look as if kids will be playing "fundraiser" anytime soon.

The dreams of young kids might not be a good indicator, but the aspirations of high school graduates, college students, and other young adults are. Although exact numbers are difficult to come by, it's clear that there is increased interest in the nonprofit sector in general, and in fundraising in particular. The number of schools and universities offering not just courses, but degrees and certificates, in these areas is increasing dramatically (and points to the body of knowledge, education, and research criteria I mentioned earlier). That more and more young people, with their whole lives ahead of them, are considering spending much of their professional lives as fundraisers is a testament to the establishment of fundraising as a true profession.

Another indicator of *profession* status is the growth of fundraising. A good example is my own organization, the Association of Fundraising Professionals (AFP), which represents individual fundraising practitioners. Over the last 10 years, AFP has more than doubled its membership to nearly 25,000 members. This growth signals that there is a growing community of fundraisers who want to learn from and share with fellow colleagues their common issues, problems, achievements, and challenges. The top reasons for joining AFP:

- Our Code of Ethical Principles and Standards of Professional Practice
- Networking with fellow colleagues
- Continuing education opportunities (items that satisfy the five criteria I mentioned in the beginning).

A large and growing group of practitioners dedicated to ethics, standards, and education seems strong evidence of a true profession.

Finally, the publication of this book, *Careers in Fundraising,* says a lot about fundraising and its evolution. Ten to fifteen years ago, one would have found numerous volumes with titles such as *Careers in the Nonprofit Sector.* But books specifically on careers in fundraising? Difficult, if not impossible, to find. The scope of this book, with sections on everything from the history of fundraising to diversity and interviewing skills, reveals the depth and intricacies of fundraising. From this volume alone, it is clear that fundraising is not your typical daily, paycheck-oriented, killing-time-until-the-next-thing-comes-along job.

Of course, none of this is to say that the dreams of young adults or the publishing of a book immediately qualify fundraising as a profession. But it seems clear to me that at some point over the last 10 to 15 years, fundraising became a true profession. The exact moment that this happened cannot be pinned down (and it might well have been earlier, although I do not think there was the critical mass of practitioners needed); as with many things, it was more of an evolution than any particular event.

Regardless of when fundraising became a profession, it is clear that it is an exciting time to be in the profession. Charitable giving is increasing, and various legislatures are looking at ways to provide additional incentives for people to give. Magazines are not simply publishing lists of the wealthiest people, but also the most generous givers. Fundraising is in the public spotlight as never before. Concurrently, e-mail and the Internet are providing charities with innovative methods of reaching out to new potential donors, while the growing internationalization of philanthropy offers additional opportunities for enterprising fundraisers and their organizations.

All of these factors are combining to create a huge need for professional fundraisers. The market for fundraising knowledge remains very strong, and ads for fundraisers are appearing at a dizzying rate. According to recent AFP surveys, fundraisers spend an average of three years at a position before moving on to bigger and better opportunities. At the same time, compensation for fundraising professionals has risen 30 percent over the last three years, and we expect these increases to continue. So whether you are new to the profession or an experienced practitioner, the time is now.

Given the frenetic pace of the profession, the publication of *Careers in Fundraising* couldn't come at a better moment. Every profession needs a guidebook, and this book comes as close as I have ever seen. Take a step back and appreciate the rich and diverse facets of fundraising in this very comprehensive volume. Inside you'll find practical how-to knowledge, historical data, philosophical discussions, and inspirational material written by practitioners who have helped shape the face of fundraising. Whether you are thinking about stepping into the profession, considering a new position, debating about whether to ask for a raise, looking to recharge your professional batteries, or just wanting to see what fundraising is really all about, there is something here for everyone.

Winston Churchill said, "We make a living by what we get, but we make a life by what we give." I would add that we also make a life by helping others to give—to educate and involve them in the philanthropic process. Fundraising is an exciting, fulfilling, and noble profession. Although not the stuff of a child's dreams, fundraising does help create the dreams of our society and our world—of improving the quality of life for every individual. It is the fuel that drives our hopes and visions for a better tomorrow. And what could be more enriching and fulfilling than that?

Paulette Maehara, CFRE
President and CEO
Association of Fundraising Professionals

Foreword

BY TIMOTHY SEILER

This book is overdue.

Fortunately, no fine accompanies the overdue notice. Rather, a widespread readership will delight in the availability of this book and recommend it to others. There will be ample copies of this book—in libraries, bookstores, college courses, and in the briefcases of fundraisers, board members, executive directors, and others interested in this burgeoning arena known as fundraising.

Following by half a decade the pioneering *Fundraisers: Their Careers, Stories, Concerns, and Accomplishments* by Margaret A. Duronio and Eugene R. Tempel, *Careers in Fundraising* takes a crucial place at the top of the reading list in the exploding literature of fundraising. While Duronio and Tempel profiled those already in fundraising, describing the usually circuitous routes the majority of today's fundraisers took to get into fundraising, Lilya Wagner's book serves as a guidepost for persons deliberately planning to enter fundraising. The field has not had anything like this before, and the book is a substantive contribution.

I am one who initially tried fundraising as a career opportunity "through the back door" or mostly by accident. Except for a trusted friend whose experience and advice I valued, I had no career counseling or list of important questions to ask before taking my first fundraising position. Wish that I had! You who read this book are lucky; take advantage of the experience, wisdom, and counsel contained in these pages.

Lilya Wagner brings to you in these pages her own experiences, knowledge, and sound advice from a variety of career perspectives. She has been a fundraiser, university administrator, teacher, trainer, author, editor, staff person, boss, board member, volunteer, and team player. And she has even had from time to time one of those dreaded positions we all hope never to experience—one that militates against success. She has learned, and offers in this book, how to ask the right questions before accepting a position in order to maximize your chances for getting the right position. Through all her experiences, occasionally bad but overwhelmingly positive, she has recognized fundraising not as a job but a career.

Adding to her own experiences, Lilya enhances this book through stories from the experiences of many other accomplished fundraisers and affiliated professionals. This book contains the voices of many of the best advisers you will find today, offering direction and suggestion for charting a fulfilling career in fundraising. The accumulated wisdom in these pages will serve you well in career decisions.

The book is exciting because it brings together the academic and the technician; it bridges theory and practice. As fundraising emerges into a recognized profession, this bridge becomes more important. As never before, today it is possible to prepare deliberately and academically for a career in fundraising. The time is coming when getting into fundraising "through the back door" will be unacceptable. Academic preparation, along with professional credentialing, will become the coin of the realm, and those with the most promise for a career in fundraising will be those who have studied, read, and prepared to be effective fundraisers. This is a book I would have relished at the beginning of my career. Today I welcome it as a much-needed contribution to the exploding literature about fundraising and how to prepare for a career in fundraising.

I applaud Lilya Wagner for writing this book, and for using the word *fundraising* in the title. As Duronio and Tempel describe who fundraisers are today, Wagner offers a guidepost for who fundraisers will be tomorrow.

Timothy L. Seiler, Ph.D., CFRE
Director, Public Service and The Fund Raising School
The Center on Philanthropy at Indiana University

Introduction

According to Aristotle, "To give away money is an easy matter and in any man's power. But to decide to whom to give it, and how large and when, and for what purpose and how, is neither in every man's power—nor an easy matter. Hence it is that such excellence is rare, praiseworthy, and noble."[1] Fundraising professionals have a significant role to play in the excellent, praiseworthy, and noble decisions by donors to give of their means. Therefore the fundraiser's work is equally significant.

Fundraisers are "people whose jobs involve the acquisition of revenues from private sources for nonprofit organizations."[2] Fundraising is a job of helping others, of making a difference for those living in undesirable conditions. It is also a means of fulfilling people's aspirations and the development of talents, and to enrich and provide enjoyment through many experiences. Fundraisers are stewards of funds entrusted by the public they serve. As Jim Greenfield pointed out, "Money is raised from those who can spare it to help address basic human needs, to improve the quality of life, to even out the differences, or to permit access to improvements of the mind and a lifting of the spirit."[3]

Some people avoid using the term *fundraising* and object to it because its practice is at times held in low esteem. Many others, however, believe that philanthropic fundraising is a noble act, a work of value, and is therefore deserving the respect of a profession. Euphemisms abound—*advancement, development,* and derivations of both these words. Fortunately, negative perceptions are lessening as professionalization reaches new heights, and as fundraising personnel strive to perform their tasks with ethical behavior and a high quality of performance.

There are sufficient reasons to consider philanthropic fundraising as a profession. It is not only a career, with the requisite salary, benefits, and perquisites, but it is also a profession that calls for a sense of excellence, service, and accountability.[4] Nonprofit organizations are served by fundraisers. Therefore, their work deserves appreciation and respect. Not only that, but as Robert L. Payton, founding director of the Center on Philanthropy at Indiana University, stated, "To be committed to philanthropy as volunteer and professional is to work harder—if not more efficiently—than most people."[5]

Pejorative labels are, unfortunately, applied to fundraising professionals, sometimes because of wrong perceptions or myths about what fundraisers do, other times because of unethical practice or because of the ineptitude of the so-called professional. These terms demean the practice and prevent optimal effectiveness by the professional and the organization.

Fortunately, the climate for acceptance of fundraising as a professional practice is changing. This is due to increased public awareness of its importance and value, a renewed focus on philanthropy in the United States as well as internationally, and education and training that promotes excellence in practice.

As recently as 15 years ago, professionals "backed into" or "fell into" their careers. Few formal training courses existed (the exception being The Fund Raising School, established in 1974) and higher education rarely engaged in teaching people to work in the nonprofit sector.

Even as few as 10 years ago the literature available to the aspiring professional was scarce. It was easy to keep up with books and other printed materials issued by professional associations or publishers brave enough to venture into the nonprofit arena. That has changed considerably, making it possible to find excellent texts on any subject in fundraising, as well as the nonprofit sector. One topic, however, that has been minimally addressed is fundraising as a career. A few sources have been available, but finding one volume that compiled the range of information needed in order to venture successfully into fundraising as a career was impossible. This book fills that gap.

PURPOSE OF THE BOOK

This book is a detailed guide for the reader on how to enter the field of fundraising, what type of education or training is possible and recommended, personal and professional traits that lead to success as a fundraising professional, and types of positions available for the person seeking a career in fundraising. Included are topics on professional development, on-the-job issues, and the significance of fundraising as a career.

It is a timely treatment of the topic because of increased interest by young people in fundraising as a profession of choice, because of the increasing demand for professionalism among practitioners in general, because people seeking more meaning in their lives and therefore also seeking career changes increasingly look to the nonprofit sector, and because the field is achieving more credibility and therefore increasing the demand for literature and research. This book provides readers with a resource that not only covers all aspects of the profession but also addresses the personal mission and commitment necessary for success in the field.

Because fundraising does not happen in isolation but is a significant part of the success of nonprofit organizations, a context is provided. An overview of the nonprofit sector and types of institutions that hire fundraising professionals is important, as are considerations of volunteers and the fundraising team.

Professionalism in fundraising builds on the successes as well as the mistakes made along the way. Therefore, each chapter includes sidebars from colleagues and students that will enhance and illustrate the content of each chapter. The collective wisdom of those who engage in fundraising enhances and illustrates the core material. Relevant books are listed in bibliographies at the ends of many chapters for further reading. In addition, addresses of collegial institutions that promote fundraising, philanthropy, and the nonprofit sector are listed in several locations.

AUDIENCE

This book will be valuable for many readers, ranging from those who are seeking careers or career changes, to those who wish to find a course of study (degree or continuing education), to those who simply want to understand more about what fundraising really is.

College and university students making career choices can be apprised of a noble profession that positively influences the human condition. In addition, they will learn how to find information about undergraduate and graduate programs focusing on nonprofit management, philanthropy, and fundraising.

Midcareer fundraising professionals will find the book useful because of information on career development, professional advancement, and salaries or wages.

Students of all types, including those who wish to understand the profession but not enter it, will appreciate the overview of the profession and its context, the nonprofit sector and the philanthropic environment. Professionals switching careers can better understand the profession and make intelligent choices as to their suitability and personal passion for such demanding work. Advisors and mentors can use this book as a detailed resource for counseling their students.

For librarians, this book serves as a major reference volume. Scholars and academicians can use it as a way of positioning research so that it is relevant and conducive to the development of the profession.

And, perhaps, there are those who will read this just for fun or out of curiosity! Those readers are welcome as well. Because fundraising is often not understood (my own parents used to say to me, "What do you REALLY do?") this book wishes to inform and educate the general public about the excellent and noble profession of fundraising.

OVERVIEW OF THE CONTENTS

The rationale for the arrangement of chapter sequence and content is that the reader approaches the topic from a broad professional perspective and then follows the steps to the technical aspects of practice. Each section and chapter is written in such a way that a reader can select a section or chapter out of sequence and find it understandable as a treatment of the designated topic, while introductions to the sections tie the various components of the book together.

Part One provides an overview of the nonprofit sector, the traditions of philanthropy, and the beneficial relationships with other organizations and other sectors, such as business and government. The reader will gain an understanding of why philanthropy is significant in U.S. culture and society, and what role philanthropy has played and currently serves in the third sector. This allows for a broader view of how fundraising fits into services provided by the nonprofit sector. Such an understanding prevents readers from functioning as technicians and moves them into a professional level of thought and practice. Also included is a brief survey of each sector and the interdependence of the sectors in meeting human needs.

Also significant in Part One is a brief description of fundraising as a profession, beginning with age-old informal practice and moving through periods of development, and finally focusing on the formalization of professional practices. For the new professional, this section provides a context for the practice of fundraising. Novices often don't have a sense of a tradition or roots of a profession and therefore lack perspective. For the seasoned professional, this section may provide either a review of the development of fundraising practice or fill in the gaps in understanding the traditions of philanthropy and fundraising in the United States.

Part Two addresses the fundraising professional's role in a nonprofit organization and in the sector. The value and importance of fundraising for a successful nonprofit organization are discussed in Chapter 3. It provides an overview of how fundraising serves the mission of the organization. Chapter 3 also addresses sources of income for nonprofits and how fundraising is significant in carrying out a mission and providing services to clients of the organization. Therefore, it becomes evident that the fundraiser, rather than being a mere technician, becomes a valuable member of a team.

Chapter 4 describes fundraising positions, the possible positions that a fundraising department or program may have, and the function of each position. Readers will gain an understanding of the various roles of the professional so they can select the positions that best suit them.

Equally important is a consideration of other careers and positions that can utilize fundraising skills and experience. Chapter 5 looks at fundraising as a valuable skill to acquire as part of professional development, leading toward a variety of careers. It is a vital skill for a manager, executive director, president, board member, board chair, or volunteer. Fundraising expertise is a significant part of leadership.

Part Three considers preparation for a career in fundraising. Chapter 6 provides an overview of academic programs that focus on nonprofit leadership and fundraising; also included is an appendix that lists current centers and programs available and a description of the content and focus of study, as well as recommendations for selection of courses. Because there is a wealth of professional opportunity in this area of education and training, guidelines are provided in Chapter 7 that assist the reader in selecting the best offerings. The range and scope of training will be included; that is, a description of what persons or organizations may offer training and how to evaluate the benefits.

Formal education and training is not for everyone. Therefore, Chapter 8 discusses on-the-job training and mentoring. This chapter gives advice on how to maximize such an experience, secure and select a mentor, and how to chart a professional career path in a possibly unstructured learning environment. In Chapter 9, there are also suggestions for the mature professional wishing to change careers. Although the numbers of young people seeking a career in fundraising are growing significantly, an equal number of mid-career professionals also find fundraising to be a viable and desirable career option. In fact, a significant number of persons employed by the corporate or government sectors are turning to nonprofit organizations for meaning and fulfillment of life and career goals.

As an enhancement to Part Three, Chapter 10 contains stories of successful professionals who have either sought fundraising as a career or have made the transition from another profession. The reason for such stories is to give real-life context for the information in the section.

Part Four deals with aspects and issues of a fundraising position. Chapter 11 presents an overview of what the reader can expect to be paid for the various positions discussed in Part Two. Included are suggestions for how to ask for the salary that is appropriate and how to seek a raise. Possibilities for promotion and career advancement are considered in Chapter 12, as well as how to qualify for promotion and how to balance personal and professional goals with the goals of the institution.

One of the goals of both institutions and the profession is diversity, and this is covered in Chapter 13. There are many opportunities for minorities. Nonprofit organizations seek diversity in hiring, especially as attention is increasingly placed on cross-cultural fundraising in the United States. Interviews with professionals representing various ethnic groups enlighten the existing status of minorities in fundraising. Also included are suggestions for those entering the field of fundraising, as well as those seeking to hire minorities.

Other vital topics included in Part Four are working with a boss (Chapter 14) and working as a member of a team (Chapter 15), which are perennial challenges for fundraisers. It is highly important for a professional to learn to communicate with the boss, to understand how to motivate a reluctant organizational leader, to provide the right kind and amount of support for institutional development, and at the same time meet the fundraising goals. The concept of "responsibility without authority" is addressed here; suggestions are provided on how to be a respected professional in the larger setting, while at the same time giving appropriate respect to the leadership of the organization.

Fundraising success depends on a team effort that involves the board, other volunteers, leaders of the organization, colleagues, and staff. Relationships and communication with team members are vital. Also included are board relationships and how to work with committees, as well as ideas on what to do if the CEO doesn't allow access to board members and volunteers.

An extra challenge is experienced by the professional in a one-person shop. Chapter 16 presents the challenge of a professional who must carry out fundraising without benefit of a staff, or who has other responsibilities in addition to fundraising. Suggestions for setting priorities, handling difficult situations, finding time for the necessary tasks, and determining realistic goals are included.

In the last decade, increasing attention has been focused on international fundraising, and this is addressed in Chapter 17. It provides an overview of opportunities for working outside of the United States, differences in approaches to fundraising, what a fundraiser should be aware of in other cultures and countries, and the importance of an international outlook during the twenty-first century. The professional is part of a global community whose emphasis on fundraising, philanthropy, and nongovernmental organizations (NGOs) is increasing.

Chapter 18 notes that the fundraising profession is not without pressures and challenges. Burnout and stressful situations are not uncommon in the profession. This chapter offers ideas on how to bring balance to a professional life, how to handle difficult situations and people, and when to seek help. Particularly significant is a listing of the symptoms of burnout.

Part Five considers the job search, and includes an overview and review of the general qualifications desirable for fundraising (besides the training and/or education listed in Part Two), and specific expertise necessary for the various positions in the field (e.g., planned giving). Chapter 19 covers where to look for jobs, and how and where to network. A listing of information sources regarding fundraising positions is provided, as well as suggestions on how to seek out just the right job.

Interviewing is an important skill to acquire, both for receiving the job offer and for acquiring transferable skills that will serve the professional in other settings. Thus, Chapter 20 suggests strategies for a successful interview, focusing in particular on preparation for questions regarding the desirable qualifications for a fundraising professional.

Not all jobs are "winners." Even the best professionals at times forget to ask relevant questions and ignore or don't notice warning signs of a problematic job situation. Thus, Chapter 21 lists the major warning signals that there may be a problem with the position or the organization. Chapter 22 provides suggestions on how to leave a job without leaving any enemies, pointing out that it's important to know why and when to leave a job and move on with a career.

Finally, due to the range of possible audiences for this book, Chapter 23 includes suggestions for those hiring a fundraising professional, as well as tips on how to look for the right match between the organization and the professional.

Part Six contains vital information for maintaining professional quality and equilibrium. Attitudes toward the profession and professionalism when the fundraising professional is faced with myths and perceptions about fundraising that may be less than favorable are important considerations. Chapter 24 examines some of these concepts and offers ideas for how to develop and maintain a winning attitude. Fundraising depends on an enthusiastic and committed approach. Also creating and understanding a personal mission, and making it congruent with the organization's mission, are important for a professional's success. Chapter 25 offers suggestions on an introspective process that includes examination of values and setting of priorities. Using information from literature and research on successful management and leadership, this chapter also lists traits that lead to success. Performing with a passion is an underlying philosophy for success, including how to move from being a technician to being a visionary leader who has great commitment for the cause. This chapter clearly illustrates why this attitude is important for fundraising success.

Finally, the Conclusion ponders the future of fundraising. It covers predictions for the future of fundraising, including changes in donors, environmental factors that affect how we perform, potential challenges, and changing roles.

Albert Schweitzer, the renowned and talented physician who served the underprivileged at a time when it was not popular, said, "One thing I know: The only ones among you who will be really happy are those who will have sought and found how to serve."[6]

This quote exemplifies the highest purpose of this book—to examine how fundraising makes philanthropy possible in the best way and therefore provides an unimaginable range of service to humanity, making this world a better place for many.

NOTE TO THE READER

Due to the rapid changes occurring in the field of fundraising, this book provides the reader with excellent resources for obtaining the most current statistics and facts.

PART ONE

Understanding the Nonprofit Sector and the Working Environment

F undraising is not a set of techniques to be applied. It is a thoughtful process of asking people to invest in causes that enhance a civil society and provide solutions to human problems. It is based on a philosophy that goes deeper than just meeting financial goals and finding better jobs at a better salary. Above all, it involves the practice of good stewardship and accountability as donors entrust the organization with their funds.

The Donor Bill of Rights, a document prepared by leading nonprofit associations in the United States, begins by saying, "Philanthropy is based on voluntary action for the common good. It is a tradition of giving and sharing that is primary to the quality of life."

For the fundraising professional to become a thoughtful, reflective practitioner, an understanding of context is vital. This section presents a framework for the professional whose work is based on a personal mission, values, and a vision for employment that has a positive impact on others.

The first chapter provides an understanding of why philanthropy is significant in U.S. culture and society, and what role philanthropy has played and currently serves in the nonprofit sector. This allows for a broader view of how fundraising fits into services provided by the nonprofit sector. Such an understanding prevents readers from functioning as technicians and moves them into a professional level of thought and practice.

Chapter 2 contains a historical perspective. For the new professional, this chapter provides a context for the practice of fundraising. Novices often do not have a sense of a tradition or roots of a profession and therefore lack perspective. For the seasoned professional, this section provides either a review of the development of fundraising practice or fills in gaps in understanding the traditions of philanthropy and fundraising in the United States.

Although most of this book is of a practical nature, designed to assist persons considering fundraising as a career, Part One is designed to provide a thoughtful understanding of fundraising beyond a process but as part of the complex forces that form a civil society. As Art Frantzreb, a senior consultant with more than 50 years of experience, has said, "Thoughtful giving begins with thoughts on giving." Likewise, thoughtful asking begins with an understanding of why we do fundraising—what purpose does it serve in the larger scheme of a democracy?

CHAPTER 1

Philanthropic Traditions and the Nonprofit Sector

SIDEBARS BY ROBERT L. PAYTON
AND DWIGHT F. BURLINGAME

Fundraising doesn't take place in a vacuum. It is an essential function in the entire scope of the nonprofit sector,[1] which is supported by philanthropy.

Fundraising is a critical element in the preservation of values. These values, inherent in our civic spirit, are fostered by philanthropic action—giving and volunteering.

Fundraising is not a technical exercise. It takes place within the larger framework of an organization and its mission, and therefore is crucial for civil society and the development or perpetuation of democratic values.

Fundraising is part of philanthropy, defined by Robert L. Payton as "voluntary action for the public good."[2] A fundraising professional is the manager of a process that brings together peoples' sense of caring with needs that must be met.

To be an excellent fundraising professional, therefore, means that an understanding of a larger framework consisting of philanthropy, the nonprofit sector, and civil society is highly significant.

Of the three sectors—government, private or profit making, and nonprofit—the nonprofit sector is the least understood.[3] Yet it is the organizations of the nonprofit sector that touch the lives of ordinary and extraordinary citizens in ways that the other sectors are not obligated to affect or simply cannot. Nonprofit organizations (NPOs) aren't in the business of making a profit; therefore, they are often designated as not-for-profit. While successful nonprofit organizations are allowed to make a profit, this is not their primary purpose. They provide for the interests and needs of all Americans—educational, social, artistic, cultural, physical, environmental, and professional. Hospitals, schools and universities, museums, human service agencies, and others provide services and benefits for all citizens. It is a "sector of opportunity," as described by Dennis Young.[4] It is a sector of organizations entrusted by donors and constituents to meet public needs and to address causes.

The legal underpinnings for the *voluntary sector* are established in the U.S. Constitution in the provision allowing free assembly. Not-for-profit *organizations*—that is, corporations, trusts, and associations that exist for a purpose other than returning profit to owners and shareholders—are made possible through state statute. The existence of *charitable* not-for-profits— that is, organizations that are eligible to receive deductible contributions and claim relief from various taxes—are made possible by federal and state tax codes.

To become a not-for-profit organization in the United States, an organization must first incorporate in the state(s) in which it will do business as a "not-for-profit corporation." Application must then be made to the Internal Revenue Service for recognition as a tax-exempt entity. Within the tax-exempt designation, there is a further distinction as a "charitable" not-for-profit. In the United States, there are approximately 1.62 million not-for-profit organizations, of which 734,000 are 501(c)(3) organizations.

Charitable not-for-profits are those that meet the requirements of Section 501(c)(3) of the Internal Revenue Code. This means that 501(c)(3) organizations can receive donations, which may be tax deductible for donors. There are many legally defined categories for tax-exempt status, but approximately 45 percent fall under three categories, 501(c)(3), 501(c)(4), and 501(c)(7), and of these three, only religious, charitable, and educational organizations are eligible for donee status under the 501(c)(3).

Information on the nonprofit sector is abundant. It isn't the purpose of this chapter to chronicle or replicate material that is readily available (see suggested readings at the end of this chapter). What is intended here is to provide the broader context in which a fundraising professional carries out his or her responsibilities. In that sense, then, the following points will be considered:

- The scope of the sector (i.e., the types of organizations, economic impact, growth and evolution of nonprofit organizations)

- Challenges facing the sector and, therefore, the impact and influence that a fundraising professional has on a healthy NPO and sector

- The traditions of philanthropy and the fundraiser's role in maintaining these traditions

Volunteerism has changed U.S. history, but it is not chained to history. The purposes of voluntary organizations have endured. In the United States, nonprofit organizations initiate new ideas and innovations and influence public policy.

Voluntary organizations also support and protect minority and local interests because they can be more sensitive to causes that are often ignored by majority rule in government. In addition, voluntary organizations render services that government is prohibited from providing, such as religious functions. It is often through voluntary organizations that U.S. government is called into accountability.

The philanthropic tradition of American life and culture has shaped who Americans are as a people and nation. Although government is best able to address many societal problems, it cannot address many individual differences in people and their needs. The for-profit or corporate sector and the free enterprise system have produced a greater standard of living for more people than any in history, but business does not bring about social change in responding to unmet human needs. This is not the function of the corporate world. Through voluntary association, Americans have come together; through nonprofit organizations and philanthropy, they have demonstrated care and concern for others, therefore building community within a vastly diverse society.

Philanthropy encourages better performance of civic duty and provides possible outlets for altruistic action. Voluntary organizations can bring together the three sectors—government, private enterprise, and the nonprofit sector. For example, nonprofit organizations often serve as advocates and activists for a cause that is then adopted by government. Government may then institute new laws or work with the nonprofit organizations to deliver a service. Similarly, nonprofit organizations influence business by providing an educated, healthy work force, research to support innovation and products, and services for employees of for-profit organizations.

Americans have been known as people of optimism with an awesome "can do" willingness to solve problems and overcome obstacles. The task of building our society, our nation, our community, our outer and inner circle of relationships is, as John Gardner said, "a journey of endless renewal." How can renewal be generated? Through the fertile mix of religious, social welfare, health, educational, artistic, and cultural interests that are the source of many of our nation's powerful movements. Nonprofits often focus local and national attention to issues of specific importance and concern, such as drunk driving, child abuse, learning disabilities, historic preservation, and homelessness.

The success of thousands of effective organizations, the numerous examples of positive results, the inspirational stories of human endeavor and achievement—all engender hope and awaken a resolve to benefit society. The fundraising professional is a critical part of this renewal and preservation of civil society.

The freedom to associate in order to address societal issues outside of government has been an immutable part of the American experience, and from this has evolved the nonprofit system as we know it today. Our forefathers felt strongly about the rights of assembly, freedom of speech, and other guaranteed rights of the First Amendment. The voluntary nonprofit sector is enabled by these freedoms and is unmatched throughout the world in size, scope, and variety. It is a rapidly growing part of our society. There are more than 1.62 million nonprofit organizations in the United States. Although the majority of Americans work for businesses or government, a significant percentage of employment is in nonprofit organizations.

The range of organizations in the sector is impressive. The most prominent include the large educational institutions, health care facilities, and cultural organizations, but equally impressive are the many small nonprofits that address specific needs across the country. Perhaps that is what causes exceptional good fortune for a person seeking employment in the sector—there is an organization to match every skill, talent, and interest of the fundraiser.

Although various designations or terms are used to describe the third sector—such as *charitable, independent, voluntary,* or *tax-exempt sector*—six prevalent characteristics define nonprofit organizations, regardless of how the sector is identified. These are defined by Salamon (1999).[5]

- They are formally organized, adhering to government laws but managed by a board and organizational leadership.

- They are private, as opposed to governmental, although many do perform services under government contracts.

- They do not distribute profits. Any surplus is funneled back into programs or an endowment to sustain the organization in the future, and no stock in the organization can be held or purchased.

- They are self-governing. The board is the legal entity that has the responsibility of ensuring that the organization functions according to its mission and is accountable to the publics it serves.

- They make use of the energies of volunteers. There is a volunteer governing board, and often program and operations benefit from volunteer service as well.

- Their activities benefit the public. The activities of a nonprofit organization are concentrated on meeting the needs of an identified group of people and not the stakeholders or leaders of the organization.

The IRS has designed 27 different kinds of 501(c) organizations. Of most importance to the fundraising professional are the approximately 734,000 501(c)(3) organizations. Contributions to these nonprofits are tax deductible. Social welfare organizations, the 501(c)(4), number approximately 140,000. There are 354,000 religious organizations. The total INDEPENDENT SECTOR organizations number approximately 1.62 million. Total annual INDEPENDENT SECTOR revenues are in the range of $664.8 billion, and the percentage of the national economy is 6.1 percent. Nonprofit organizations employ 11.7 million people; this is 8.7 percent of the total U.S. work force.[6]

The sector faces many challenges during the first decade of the new millennium. The mix of resources available to support the sector's causes is changing, with government funding decreasing or changing focus. There is an increasing dependence on fees and other income. A shift in fund recipients sometimes leaves less-than-popular social causes struggling for survival.

For several decades, charitable income has been about 2 percent of national income, but currently there is a renewed emphasis on philanthropy. Recently, both *The New York Times* and *Time* featured the realities and benefits of philanthropic action. This attention increases the challenges and opportunities of the fundraising professional in seeking support for nonprofit causes.

Other situations affecting the sector are the growing gap between the rich and poor, that is to say, a growing inequality of income, demographic changes caused by immigration and emerging minority groups, an aging population that is living longer, and emphasis on cultural differences. These changes are necessary for the professional to understand because they shape relationships with donors.

The sector is more visible and vulnerable. Because its work is so important for the good of civil society, increasing attention has been focused on nonprofit organizations. This, in turn, causes a growth of critical reviews and judgments not always favorable to the sector.

As a result of nonprofit sector growth, there are also attempts at increasing regulation and control, while at the same time advocacy roles are being curbed. Of major significance have been issues of credibility and accountability. Aiding the nonprofit sector in practicing good stewardship of philanthropic funds is a major responsibility of the fundraising professional.

Since the founding of the United States, people have given of their time and money to build a nation known for free enterprise, independent initiative, and resistance to centralized control. This independence causes the organizations that are not government related or for-profit oriented to seek financial support. Therefore, as long as there is a need for revenue, there is a need for a fundraising program. Fundraising professionals, as much as anyone, have the responsibility to preserve the traditions of philanthropy.

In the earliest times when immigrants reached American shores, society was localized and inclusive. From the New England farms to the Western settlements, neighbors assisted each other by cooperating with work, trading goods and services, and providing charity for the needy and sick. They needed each other to survive. Early settlers were also aided by charity from some of the native American tribes.

The Protestant tradition and beliefs that brought many to American shores in the first place also shaped the concept of philanthropy. Charity meant to help others, to not be self-centered in acquiring goods and money. The Puritans, for example, adopted a set of practices in regard to the poor and needy, making them recipients of charitable endeavors. Cotton Mather, a prominent preacher of the eighteenth century, also counseled his parishioners and community to do good to people who needed assistance. He not only believed that doing good was a reward in itself, but also that giving wisely was as important as giving generously.

These early beginnings of both the nation and philanthropy focused on personal charity. The shift came with the prominent patriot Benjamin Franklin, who believed in community and its general welfare. Ever the visionary, he thought that society could transform itself until there were no poor and therefore was little or no need for charity. He applied the concept of associations of people who worked and provided for the common good. Philanthropic activities were designated for the benefit of the whole community; therefore, they benefited the poor and destitute of that community by inclusion.

This phenomenon was noted by Alexis de Tocqueville, a French visitor to the United States in 1831, who provided insightful observations regarding the U.S. proclivity to associate and thereby work for the public good. *Charity,* which meant direct and compassionate service to others, had given way to *philanthropy,* which offered more distant and impersonal action, focused on solution of community social problems.

Associations, first formed spontaneously by people with similar interests and goals, began to be established by public policy. Associations became legal entities and proliferated greatly, until by the middle of the nineteenth century there was considerable concern that the individual would be subsumed into a faceless class of people—for example, the unemployed, the hungry, the homeless.

In order to handle the good intentions of generous individuals in an efficient and effective way—and therefore solve social problems that affected the community in general—social welfare agencies began to be established, and professionalism in social work took root. Concurrently, criticism of philanthropy surfaced, along with critics and reformers who found much to comment on in private philanthropy as well as public relief. The social agencies succeeded in spurring communities to build homes for the poor, but failed to support efforts to police them.

The first major war of the independent United States, the Civil War of the 1860s, saw the formation of numerous relief agencies. Before the war ended, about 15,000 societies had been formed to provide soldiers and their families with aid. In 1861, the first umbrella group was founded—the U.S. Sanitary Commission, a private association. It wanted to bring together the many local aid groups into one entity and therefore exert greater positive influence over military camps, prisons, hospitals, and transportation means.

Additional associations formed to help escaped or freed slaves, but this job became too difficult and complex, and the U.S. government stepped in by establishing a government bureau. This is an early and fine illustration of how the nonprofit sector in the United States often provides the initial steps for the resolution of a social problem, which is then carried out and maintained by government—an appropriate transfer of interest and effort. The bureau extended its influence to education, refugees, orphanages, and employment.

After the close of the Civil War, philanthropy became organized into a system of "how to" and "how not to" rules and practices. Begun just after the Civil War, the movement extended to the beginning of the twentieth century and focused on properly organized and efficient practices of philanthropy by a comprehensive set of rigorously applied rules. One of the main effects of this professionalization was the establishment of state boards of charities. Serving on these boards were prominent citizens who investigated public assistance and welfare institutions and made recommendations to improve them.

Toward the end of the nineteenth century, two significant philanthropists emerged and influenced American philanthropy in lasting ways. The first was the industrialist Andrew Carnegie, who believed that philanthropy had preventive power. He believed that the wealthy should do good by improving society and not just remedy society's ills. His ideas provided the basis for a new form of philanthropy—the foundation.

John D. Rockefeller gave the foundation movement a further impetus by believing he should determine how worthy a cause or organization was before giving to it. He (with the help of assistants) systematized his philanthropy by inquiring about the need and the cause more than had been customary. Both Carnegie and Rockefeller established foundations that focused on special issues and causes, and that greatly influenced the proliferation of foundations that currently exist.

At the beginning of the twentieth century, the process of federated solicitation and giving gained solid footing. (See book by Eleanor Brilliant, *The United Way: Dilemmas of Organized Charity.*) The Committee on Benevolent Association of the Cleveland Chamber of Commerce, begun in 1913, was the first to raise money and distribute it to charities it had approved. By

1929 almost 130 charities in the United States had been created. While this was beneficial for further systematizing philanthropy and for promoting professionalism in raising funds, it also put more distance between the donor and the recipient. During this era, professional fundraising consultants came into being. They engendered mixed views. Some thought they were exploiting the philanthropic process, while others thought that they could work miracles with their talents and skills.

Also during the second decade of the twentieth century, the federal income tax was instituted. Under the new U.S. Tax Code (and continuing to this day), personal contributions to philanthropy became tax deductible. On the heels of this major legislation came World War I. This changed philanthropy immeasurably by expanding the role of government. For example, by 1920 states had begun to initiate programs for needy children, the elderly, and some individuals with disabilities, such as the blind. New York offered unemployment relief. These groundbreaking events moved the nation to increased dependency on the federal government for providing relief. By the time Franklin D. Roosevelt became president, the problems of the Great Depression created an environment hospitable to the establishment of the Federal Emergency Relief Administration. Although it lasted only three years, it had a lasting effect on how philanthropy and charity were viewed by Americans.

By the time World War II loomed, the United States had founded a government-based social insurance system, and more than $208 million was spent on public aid in 1932. This system expanded during the 1950s, and again the face of American philanthropy was changed; voluntary giving no longer held the dominant role. Compare, for example, the amount of private aid versus government aid during and after World War II. Although U.S. charities sent more than $500 million to overseas charity efforts, this amount was minuscule compared to government expenditures of about $12.5 billion under the Marshall Plan. Federal spending continued to increase considerably during the 1960s and 1970s. Numbers of individuals who received welfare escalated, and the nature of social services changed as well.

Much of the frenetic activity caused by the Great Depression, World War II, and the postwar assistance came to a head in the 1970s. Several prominent individuals in the world of philanthropy and fundraising became concerned enough about what they perceived to be a chaotic state of affairs that they convened a Commission on Private Philanthropy and Public Needs, known as the Filer Commission. Their report, issued in 1975, promoted more philanthropy by suggesting a revision of the tax code. They also urged more giving by corporations, and they suggested that regulations on lobbying by charities be relaxed. The Commission's report did not reach the implementation stage, however, and versions of these ideas are still being debated.

INDEPENDENT SECTOR, an organization that was to represent the interests of all tax-exempt organizations, was established in 1980. This organization grew in influence as it lobbied on behalf of more than 800 members and conducted research that would verify the efficacy and value of philanthropy as well as influence improvements in the nonprofit sector. The work of this nonprofit continues today; its research on giving and volunteering in the United States is valuable for the fundraising professional.

As we enter the new millennium, we are seeing attention on returning philanthropy and social assistance to local communities. Charity and philanthropy, which have become increasingly distant from recipients of aid, may once again become a more personal endeavor.

According to a publication issued by the American Assembly, philanthropy and the nonprofit sector perform important functions for society.

1.   They provide a vehicle for individual expression.
2.   They create networks that build *social capital,* meaning the joining together of people with common vision to accomplish public purposes.
3.   They improve democracy by reaching and empowering people who could not otherwise participate.
4.   They have the ability to alleviate human suffering and help realize human potential.

It is the privilege of the fundraising professional to be an integral part of these functions.

The nonprofit sector is about the heart as well as the head. It is replete with values and feelings. Nonprofits and philanthropy enable Americans to demonstrate their care and concern for others and build an authentic community within a vastly diverse society. Over and over again, Americans come together in voluntary association to solve their perceived and real community, cultural, religious, and social needs. As a people and society, we are enriched because of what our nonprofit sector allows us to develop and implement—new ideas, programs, answers, visions.

■ FURTHER READING

The Ninety-third American Assembly. *Trust, Service, and the Common Purpose: Philanthropy and the Nonprofit Sector in a Changing America.* New York: The American Assembly, April 23–26, 1998; 475 Riverside Drive, Suite 456, New York, NY 10115; 212-870-3500.

With the co-sponsorship of the Indiana University Center on Philanthropy, The American Assembly convened leaders of all sectors in 1998. This publication summarizes three days of discussion on dramatic changes occurring in the philanthropic and nonprofit sectors.

Bremner, Robert H. *American Philanthropy.* 2d ed. Chicago: The University of Chicago Press, 1988.

This book concentrates on rediscovering the philanthropic tradition by providing a social history of philanthropy in U.S. society. Discussion includes well-known figures in the history of philanthropy such as Mather, de Toqueville, Carnegie, and Rockefeller. The author explores our nation's distinct proclivity for doing good. The book includes a chronological listing of important dates in philanthropy from 1601–1991.

Bremner, Robert H. *Giving: Charity and Philanthropy in History.* New Brunswick, NJ: Transaction Publishers, Rutgers State University, 1994.

This work offers a historical survey of attitudes toward charity and philanthropy, relying almost entirely on literary sources—religious texts, poetry, published philosophical reflections, short stories, and news accounts.

Brilliant, Eleanor L. *The United Way: Dilemmas of Organized Charity.* New York: Columbia University Press, 1990.

A study of federated giving and its role in U.S. philanthropy.

Burlingame, Dwight F., ed. *The Responsibilities of Wealth.* Bloomington: Indiana University Press, 1992.

A multiperspective view of wealth within the historical context of philanthropy. Bringing together views of well-known authors in specific fields of study, the book offers insights into morality, individual responsibility, religion, liberal philanthropy, social justice, and corporate social responsibility.

Burlingame, Dwight F., ed. *Critical Issues in Fund Raising.* New York: Wiley, 1997.

Many forces—from demographics to politics to business trends—shape the nonprofit sector and the practice of fundraising, but little attention has been given to the premises underlying many of the decisions that fundraisers make in their daily professional lives. This book examines the impact of different factors on this growing and changing field.

Clotfelter, Charles T., and Thomas Ehrlich. *The Future of Philanthropy in a Changing America.* Bloomington: Indiana University Press, 1998.

This book originated in a conference sponsored by the American Assembly and the Indiana University Center on Philanthropy. Scholars and practitioners considered three key issues—forces that determine the shape and activities of philanthropy and the nonprofit sector; how philanthropy and the sector can be strengthened or weakened by those forces; and how the challenges can be transformed into opportunities.

Cutlip, Scott M. *Fund-Raising in the United States: Its Role in American Philanthropy.* New Brunswick, NJ: Rutgers University Press, 1990 (a reprint of a 1965 work).

A comprehensive investigation of the role of fundraising from the seventeenth century to the present. This book explores the effects of public relations and the impact of the practice on philanthropic giving.

Ellis, Susan, and Katherine H. Noyes. *By the People: A History of Americans as Volunteers.* San Francisco: Jossey-Bass, 1990.

A comprehensive history combined with insights on today's volunteers, which gives a new perspective on voluntarism. This book discusses current issues and reveals progression of the nonprofit organization and the evolution of the volunteer movement.

Hammack, David C. *Making the Nonprofit Sector in the United States.* Bloomington: Indiana University Press, 1998.

Explores the history of religious, cultural, arts, human service, educational, and research organizations in the nonprofit sector. This book includes classic documents in the development of the sector and critiques by recent scholars.

Hodgkinson, Virginia A., and Associates. *The Nonprofit Almanac 1996–1997: Dimensions of the INDEPENDENT SECTOR.* Washington, DC: INDEPENDENT SECTOR, 1996.

Comprehensive statistical profiles of the size, scope, and dimensions of the INDEPENDENT SECTOR. It classifies organizations using the National Taxonomy of Exempt Entities, a new classification for the nonprofit sector. It is an essential reference of accurate statistical data for nonprofit strategic planning and comparative analysis.

Kelly, Kathleen S. *Effective Fund-Raising Management* Mahwah, NJ: Lawrence Erlbaum Associates, 1998.

Although this book primarily explores the critical areas of fundraising management, pages 52–68 focus on the nonprofit sector.

Lohmann, Roger A. *The Commons: New Perspectives on Nonprofit Organizations and Voluntary Action.* San Francisco: Jossey-Bass, 1992.

This ground-breaking book provides an integrated vision of nonprofit organizations and voluntary action that enables scholars, practitioners, and the public to think and talk in a new way about this vital arena of human enterprise. Provides fundraisers with a clearer understanding of the nature of giving practices and why people become involved in philanthropy.

Martin, Mike W. *Virtuous Giving: Philanthropy, Voluntary Service and Caring.* Bloomington: Indiana University Press, 1994.

This philosophical primer examines the virtues related to giving, volunteerism, and philanthropy. It develops a unifying conception of philanthropy and investigates such questions as: Does philanthropy express certain values? Do individuals have a responsibility to engage in philanthropic activity? Do motives matter? How might philanthropy make a contribution to self-fulfillment?

Marts, Arnaud C. *Philanthropy's Role in Civilization: Its Contribution to Human Freedom*. New Brunswick, NJ: Transaction, 1991 (reprint of a 1953 work).

Written by a prominent fundraiser and consultant, this intellectual reading discusses the role of philanthropy in the United States and the significance of freedom, which has allowed Americans to contribute to the national well-being.

O'Connell, Brian. *Civil Society*. Hanover, NH: University Press of New England, 1999.

This book traces the concept and practice of citizens as the primary office holders of government and government's essential responsibility to keep open such freedoms as assembly and association to allow and encourage citizen participation and influence in every aspect of society.

Payton, Robert L. *Philanthropy: Voluntary Action for the Public Good*. Phoenix, AZ: Oryx Press, 1989.

Out of print; can be found on the Internet, http://www.Paytonpapers.org. Written by one of the most distinguished leaders in philanthropy today, this book focuses on the place of philanthropy in U.S. society. Discusses the important problems and explores the issues that affect philanthropy. Payton focuses on ethics, tactics of giving, and the need to look deeper into understanding theory and practice. The book includes a research section by Virginia Hodgkinson.

Salamon, Lester M. *America's Nonprofit Sector: A Primer*. 2d ed. New York: The Foundation Center, 1999.

A broad-based analysis of the nonprofit sector. The first part of the book is an overview of the nonprofit sector, the role of government in the welfare system, and the historical origins of the nonprofit sector. The second half divides America's nonprofits into subsectors and explores the unique dynamics of each area.

Van Til, Jon. *Growing Civil Society: From Nonprofit Sector to Third Space*. Bloomington & Indianapolis: Indiana University Press, 2000.

Van Til explores the role of voluntary action and nonprofit organization in contemporary America. Key to this book is the concept of third space, which provides an important tool for the construction of civil society.

■ INDEXES

Philanthropic Studies Index. Indianapolis: Indiana University Center on Philanthropy (only available online at www-lib.iupui.edu/special/ppsl.html).

Includes citations to periodical articles, books, dissertations, pamphlets, and other relevant materials dealing with the broad range of philanthropy.

The Literature of the Nonprofit Sector (LPNS): Washington, DC: The Foundation Center.

LPNS Online is a searchable database of the literature of philanthropy.

Philanthropy is a right. The word does not appear in the Constitution, but philanthropy as voluntary action for the public good affirms the right of citizens to take the public business into their own hands. When someone has a vision of how the society might be made better, and other people share that vision, they have the right to organize to advocate and advance their ideas. A *right* realizes its potential in action. For organizations to realize their potential in action, they need resources. Philanthropy is a right. Voluntary association is a right. Fundraising is a right. The Supreme Court has understood that the right of organizations to express their ideas is based on their right to mobilize resources. The right to gather philanthropic resources is grounded in the First Amendment. Fundraising is protected speech.

Fundraising is not a marginal notion or an afterthought. Fundraising empowers ideas, whether to change society or to preserve tradition, to advocate or innovate or replicate.

Vision, shared values, organization, and resources: those are the four essentials. Causes must be discovered and given voice; people must listen and respond; individuals must find effectiveness by coming together by unforced agreement, combining their talents and energies in organizations and institutions that multiply their capacity as individuals.

Money by itself accomplishes nothing; vision without followers is an illusion. Vision supported by money, sustained by shared commitment, given focus and efficiency, brought to bear on problems and tasks—these are the elements that transform ideas into reality. Money without mission is impotent. Fundraising committed to mission puts idealism to work.

ROBERT L. PAYTON is Professor Emeritus of Philanthropic Studies at Indiana University and Senior Research Fellow Emeritus of The Center on Philanthropy. He served as first director of The Center on Philanthropy from 1988–1993. Prior to that he was scholar-in-residence at the University of Virginia and also president of the Exxon Education Foundation. He also served as president of C. W. Post College and Hofstra University, was ambassador to the Republic of Cameroon, and was vice chancellor for development at Washington University in St. Louis. He is the author of *Philanthropy: Voluntary Action for the Public Good,* which is available at www.paytonpapers.org (other writings are also available on this Web site). He leads the Jane Addams–Andrew Carnegie Fellows Program, which he founded in 1991.

SIDEBAR   DWIGHT F. BURLINGAME

The nonprofit sector continues to grow in recognition by the American public. During the last two decades, discussion about government and business have been joined by the role of the nonprofit, sometimes referred to as the independent or third sector. The sector consists of over 1.62 million organizations including churches, schools, hospitals, foundations, social service organizations, arts and cultural groups, advocacy groups, mutual benefit organizations, and many more. Nonprofits employ more civilians than all state and federal governments combined— which represents approximately 8.7 percent of the labor force in the United States. In addition, more than 100 million people volunteer an average of 3–4 hours per week. All combined, the sector represents about 6.1 percent of the national income.

Nonprofits are characterized as nongovernmental and nondistributing of profits. They have a formal structure, are self-governing, have a significant volunteer component, and serve a public purpose. Throughout U.S. history, voluntary organizations have played a major role in the life of our society. Most importantly, the INDEPENDENT SECTOR has served and continues to serve as a check for government and business. In addition, it provides a space for experimentation from which the best ideas can be institutionalized by government or business. It provides a means to meet diverse needs and to provide for the general welfare, recreation, and spiritual needs of people.

In the last decade, we have witnessed a global associational movement. Much discussion about the role of NPOs or NGOs in a civil society has emerged. It is not a new revelation that groups and group action can give voice to otherwise silent views in democratic societies. Nonprofits cannot take the place of government in terms of equitably and accountability reach; however, they are an important part of the fabric of civil society.

DWIGHT F. BURLINGAME Ph.D., CFRE, is associate executive director and director of academic programs at the Indiana University Center on Philanthropy, and a professor at the Graduate School, Philanthropic Studies and School of Public and Environmental Affairs. He holds degrees from Moorhead State University, the University of Illinois, and Florida State University. He received the CFRE credential in 1989 and is an active member of the Association of Fundraising Professionals Research Council and ARNOVA. He has authored and co-authored eight books and 38 articles. He is active in the nonprofit community as a frequent speaker and consultant.

PROFESSIONALS SAY . . .

When I invited a Jewish woman to give to a Christian college, she said, "I am so glad you asked. It is so good to give!" She immediately wrote a check for her first gift for three times what I requested.

Doris Webb, Advancement Officer and Director of Admissions & Recruitment, Mount Vernon Nazarene College, Mount Vernon, Ohio

In Studs Terkel's book Working, *he interviews a steelworker who works on high-rise buildings. The worker engraves his name on a girder, and when the building is completed, he takes his son to see the structure and tells him that he had an important role to play in building the facility. We, as fundraising professionals, in one way or another, engrave our names on the facilities we help to build and the programs we help to provide. We should take pride in our accomplishments and the role we play to improve the human condition.*

Emanuel Forster, Partner, Forster-Gilbert Associates, Fundraising Consultants, Los Angeles, California.

CHAPTER 2

Historical Perspectives of the Profession

SIDEBAR BY CATHLENE WILLIAMS

In the last couple of decades, individuals in the United States have been smitten with a desire to discover, acknowledge, and relate to their roots. Perhaps the publication of Alex Haley's book, *Roots,* followed by the 1977 TV miniseries of the same name, spurred the longing to know one's origins.

There are legitimate reasons for wanting to know where we came from. At a young age, political situations forced me to leave my homeland and the place of my birth. Only in 1992 was I able to return and discover my roots, my culture, and the people of my heritage. There is a sense of understanding and belonging, a sense of place, that comes with the discovery of what spawned and shaped us.

The same is true for the fundraising professional in understanding the context of the profession. Practice should be supported and enhanced by history and theory. Fundraising as a function can be traced back to biblical citations (e.g., the building of the tabernacle in the biblical book of Exodus), to classical Greece and Rome, to accounts of the Middle Ages (e.g., comments on almsgiving), and to charitable acts and activities of Elizabethan England. Someone obviously asked someone else for money to support what were considered worthy causes back then.

The United States grew up with the spirit of philanthropy. Private gifts from the wealthy in countries of origin helped develop and sustain not just America's colonies but also early institutions. Native American philanthropy certainly aided the survival of some settlers. Government support was also highly influential, but private generosity built the foundations of a philanthropic tradition in the United States. Some authorities consider the fundraising efforts for the establishment of Harvard College in 1641 as the foundation of professional fundraising; others also point to the College of William and Mary in Virginia. Still others believe that Jane Addams and the establishment of Hull House in Chicago in 1889 signal the beginning of organized philanthropy.

Despite philanthropy having played a significant role in the history of the United States, however, fundraising as an organized and organizational function only dates back to the early 1900s. Even the term *fundraiser* is relatively new.

This chapter provides a look at the evolution of fundraising as a professional function. It is designed to foster in the fundraising career seeker a sense of place, an understanding of how the profession developed, and a commitment to what Harrah-Conforth and Borsos refer to as a "philosophy deeper than merely meeting financial goals."[1]

Barbara Marion states that "fundraisers need the 'how to' of the practice and the 'why to' of the profession."[2] The purpose of this chapter is not to chronicle each detail and event in the evolution of fundraising as a profession. There are several excellent resources for this information listed in the readings for this chapter; in particular, Kathleen Kelly's volume provides a thorough overview. The purpose of this chapter is to provide the career-seeker or the new practitioner a sense of where she or he belongs in the development of the profession and what has shaped it.

The early twentieth century is usually identified as the starting point of the professionalization of fundraising. This was partly due to the growth of paid staff, thereby changing the philanthropic landscape from one directed by volunteers to one of professionals who then directed volunteers. Cutlip, who wrote the most definitive history of fundraising in the United States, said, "Organized philanthropy supported by systematic fundraising is a twentieth-century development in the United States. Philanthropy, in America's first three centuries, was carried along on a small scale, largely financed by the wealthy few in response to personal begging appeals."[3] World War I, according to Cutlip, actually provided the seedbed for organized fundraising. Broce, however, believes that the YMCA movement, which began in the early 1900s, actually provided the roots for modern fundraising.

This chapter chronicles the historical context with major events that molded and fashioned today's practices. Just how the eras of the twentieth century are divided when it comes to fundraising history can be somewhat confusing. Kelly identifies four distinct eras. Harrah-Conforth and Borsos give the generational views. Most respected volumes in fundraising practice ignore the historical context altogether. I have chosen to provide a chronological view because the profession is delineated by both change and continuity. Much of what we consider to be standard practice actually began by the creation of innovative techniques to meet certain needs.

Prior to World War I, fundraising was still quite unorganized and haphazard. Philanthropy was usually the domain of the wealthiest. During this period, the need to reduce the requests to the few identifiable donors caused the federated fundraising agencies to emerge. Eventually fundraising began to involve increasing numbers of citizens, particularly in the area of social welfare where organizations and people (e.g., Black churches, women as volunteers) had already been active. At this time, fundraising was the function of nonspecialists, especially volunteers.

Among those who began to lay the groundwork for formalized fundraising were Lyman L. Pierce and Charles Sumner Ward, who are credited with developing the campaign method for the Young Men's Christian Associations. Others active during this era were individuals who served as leaders of alumni associations, such as William Lawrence, volunteer president for Harvard's association. Included in this era should be evangelists, such as Dwight L. Moody and Frederick T. Gates. The latter was able to solicit John D. Rockefeller for a major gift to establish a major institution—the University of Chicago.

The first commercial firm was established by Frederick Courtenay Barber in 1913, but because he charged a commission, his place in historical annals is usually discounted. The progenitors of today's consulting firms were established in approximately 1919.

Despite ongoing activity prior to World War I, fundraising was mostly recognized as the function in which YMCAs engaged. Only as Ward and Pierce began to tutor others did the understanding of fundraising as a function and service expand. Ward is quoted in Cutlip as having said, "I would leave this work immediately if I thought I were merely raising money. It is raising men that appeals to me."[4]

The American Red Cross War Council was created at the beginning of the war with the purpose of combining fundraising for relief efforts. Ward and Pierce, on loan from the YMCA, were hired, and they raised record amounts of money. Another significant figure emerged during this time, John Price Jones. Coming from a newspaper and public relations background, he was the first to combine this experience with fundraising. The YMCA's form of fundraising—which focused on Christian values, stewardship, and Jones's businesslike approach to fundraising—now joined to provide a foundation for modern fundraising—a combination of vision and mission with commercial overtones.

After World War I, consultants became more predominant in fundraising. In September 1919, the firm of Ward, Hill, Pierce, and Wells was established. This included recognizable and famous names, so business was brisk. Others who had received their experience in either the YMCA or the Red Cross campaigns now became the first wave of fundraising counsel—the pioneers. A major occurrence of this time was the acceptance of the fixed fee, not the commission-based fundraising that had been practiced previously. Also, despite of the name recognition of many who established or worked for firms at this time, the idea that the consultant must remain in the background and the attention should be on the organization came into fashion.

The literature in fundraising received a boost at this time. Harold "Si" Seymour, who was to write one of the first definitive books on fundraising, worked for the John Price Jones company. While with the company, he codified a *Standard Practices* volume that became the first training manual in fundraising history.

This era of fundraising consultants slowed down with the Great Depression. The campaigns, which had taken an identifiable format, faded, although Americans still gave, particularly for relief programs. Philanthropy now ceased to be the domain of the wealthy, and the average citizen joined with government to provide relief. Because these were desperate days, fundraising practices took on some questionable aspects. As a result, the American Association of Fundraising Counsel was established in 1935 to preserve the integrity and promote the dignity of fundraising. These pioneers of fundraising as an organized activity "tried to create an image of fundraising as primarily a philanthropic enterprise, an ideological and moral endeavor that also made business sense."[5]

Fundraising matured greatly between the two world wars. At the beginning of World War II, the Red Cross began a blood donor program. This was the result of increasing government intervention in relief funding, such that the Red Cross's traditional services were no longer required. Because the Red Cross adapted to change and raised great sums of money, Cutlip has called it the greatest fundraiser of modern times.

After World War II, the example of the Red Cross caused many other institutions to begin raising money. For the first time, in-house staff began to be hired. This was particularly true for colleges and universities, who saw the need for more funds and increased goals, as well as the need for professionalism to accomplish these goals. During the post–World War II period, the need for fundraising campaigns soared; organizations began to seriously compete for charitable dollars. Established fundraising firms whose names we still recognize (e.g., Ketchum, American City Bureau, Marts and Lundy) put the experience gained in prewar times into practice. "These and other pioneering companies as well as independent consultants served as seed beds for that remarkable talent that was an emerging professional class,"[6] wrote Hank Rosso, who served with the John Price Jones consulting firm.

Much happened in fundraising, perhaps too much and too fast. There was little understanding of professional fundraising among the public. America's ongoing discrepancy of opinion and feeling—sympathy for causes but antipathy for fundraisers—may have had its roots at this point. Lack of standards caused an understandable mistrust of fundraisers, although the public generally exercised its charitable impulses.

The 1950s saw an increase in federal funding programs. The government poured out funds in greater amounts than philanthropy had contributed, yet when these funding programs diminished due to political change, private donors who had become accustomed to government programs were not ready to close the gap. According to Broce, the nation didn't recover from this "hangover effect," as he called it, until the late 1970s.[7]

In 1960 an influential and significant organization was established to serve the growing number of practitioners—the National Society of Fundraisers, renamed the National Society of Fund Raising Executives in 1978 and again the Association of Fundraising Professionals in 2001. With this group was ushered in the era of staff fundraisers, which continues until today. Nonprofit organizations set up development departments and conducted annual and capital campaigns, many of them multimillion-dollar ones. The practice of placing resident consultants from fundraising firms at institutions began to fade with this influx of permanent staff, and consultants became campaign advisors instead. More associations were also founded during this era, with the most recognizable being the Association for Healthcare Philanthropy, established in 1967. Also at this time Cutlip wrote his seminal work on the history of fundraising (first published in 1965, then again in 1990), and Si Seymour wrote his notable book *Designs for Fund-Raising* in 1966. One final landmark of the 1960s was the Tax Reform Act of 1969, which subjected charitable organization to new regulations.

The 1970s saw an expansion of fundraising strategies, such as telethons and door-to-door methods. The Council for the Advancement and Support of Education was formed in 1974. In that same year, The Fund Raising School was established by Hank Rosso, Joe Mixer, and Lyle Cook. This was probably the first formalized training available for fundraising practitioners. Also in the 1970s there was an increase in government oversight. These highlights of fundraising history show that the knowledge about philanthropy and the organizations that employ fundraisers had increased considerably.

The 1980s brought an influx of fundraisers into the nonprofit arena. Much of this was due to government funding cutbacks. Also at this time public educational institutions began to seek support from private funds, something that many initially resisted. The race to compete became fierce. The fundraising function was internalized by this time, with consultants serving an advisory role. A significant organization was formed in 1980, INDEPENDENT SECTOR, whose members would represent approximately 800-plus foundations, corporations, and leading national nonprofit organizations. It has been successful in representing donors and askers, and has served in an advocacy role since 1980. This marks one of the points in history when donors and fundraising professionals began to work together in the arena of philanthropy.

The 1990s was the era of many changes in fundraising. This list contains just some of these changes:

- Increased professionalism in fundraising. Courses and training programs have proliferated.
- A body of research and literature provides a theoretical and practical base for the profession.
- There is an increasing demand for accountability by nonprofits.

- Philanthropic giving has consistently increased (although never higher than 2 percent of the gross domestic product).

- The number of nonprofit organizations has increased.

- There is growing public interest and visibility in philanthropy and understanding of the nonprofit sector.

- There is growing scrutiny of the sector and its organizations, and therefore increased criticism.

- The number of publications related to the sector, philanthropy, and fundraising has greatly increased.

- There is more balance in how individuals enter the profession; that is, no longer does everyone "slide" into fundraising, as many people over 50 years of age did. Now there are formal ways to enter the profession. Some young people are actually saying, "I want to be a fundraiser."

- Increasing use of technology in fundraising, particularly the Internet, provides new opportunities and challenges.

- The characteristics and behaviors of donors are changing.

Fundraising history provides a context of where we belong, what has caused us to work in the ways we do, and to whom we owe a debt of gratitude for shaping the profession. As Pat Lewis, a former president of the National Society of Fund Raising Executives, said, "Our future will be surer if we understand our past."

Hank Rosso wrote about the "traditions that provided building blocks for the structure in which we work today."[8] We who engage in the noble practice of fundraising are part of those traditions, present and future. According to Romain Gary, history is "a relay race in which each of us, before dropping in his [her] tracks, must carry one stage further the challenge of being [human]."[9] Some of you who are reading this book and sharing it will also go on to influence the future of fundraising. You will be making your contribution to a long, although not well documented, tradition of fundraising and will carry the challenge just a bit further.

▮ FURTHER READING

Broce, Thomas E. *Fund Raising,* 2d ed. Norman, OK: University of Oklahoma Press, 1986.

   A clear and concise volume on the basics of fundraising, which also includes a treatise on the history of fundraising.

Gurin, Maurice G. *Confessions of a Fund Raiser.* Rockville, MD: The Taft Group, 1985.

Written by a nationally recognized fundraiser, this book describes his "break" into fundraising and his personal experiences through vivid anecdotes. The book discusses topics such as importance of innovation, challenging donors, and organization's fundraising objectives.

Kelly, Kathleen S. *Effective Fund-Raising Management.* Mahwah, NJ: Lawrence Erlbaum Associates, 1998.

This book explores the critical area of fundraising management. Fundraising management can be the key to success or the door to demise. An organization that does not understand and effectively manage its fundraising programs will soon be suffering. This work explores what it takes to run an effective fundraising program.

Rosso, Henry A. *Rosso on Fund Raising: Lessons from a Master's Lifetime Experience.* New York: Jossey-Bass, 1996.

Learn from a master. This book explores the lessons learned from the life experience of Henry Rosso, a master. This book provides valuable insight and knowledge that only a lifetime of experience can provide.

Schwartz, John J. *Modern American Philanthropy: A Personal Account.* New York: Wiley, 1994.

This book chronicles the author's 46 years of experience in the not-for-profit world and discusses the evolution and growth of fundraising as a profession. It provides key fundraising tips and a discussion of critical issues facing not-for-profits today.

Seymour, Harold J. *Designs for Fund-Raising*, 2d ed. Rockville, MD: Fundraising Institute (a division of The Taft Group), 1993. Originally printed in 1966.

This "classic" of fundraising how-to books contains timely advice. It has consistently been one of the most effective and informative sources since its publication. Many of the recent how-to manuals are based on Seymour's principles, patterns, and techniques. This book discusses importance of cultivation, case statement, motivation, and volunteer relationships, as well as other fundraising topics.

"The Professionalization of Fundraising." *New Directions for Philanthropic Fundraising*, No. 15 (Spring 1997).

The subject of this volume is whether there are sufficient grounds to consider philanthropic fundraising a profession. The topics include licensure and credentialing, accountability, demographics and the experience of fundraisers, and the education of fundraisers.

Shaw, Sondra C., and Martha A. Taylor. *Reinventing Fundraising: Realizing the Potential of Women's Philanthropy.* San Francisco, CA: Jossey-Bass, 1995.

Reveals the reasons why women have not been taken seriously as philanthropists, identifies model programs focusing on women's giving, and outlines new program models that organizations can tailor to their own female constituents.

von Schlegell, Abbie J., and Joan M. Fisher (eds.). *Women as Donors, Women as Philanthropists.* San Francisco, CA: Jossey Bass, Inc., 1993.

Discusses the ways development officers can effectively employ the behaviors and preferences of women in programs that center on women donors and philanthropists.

We think of pioneers as pathfinders—creative, courageous, and hardy people who see opportunities and are willing to move boldly forward into unknown territory. The earliest fundraisers must have been just such individuals. Until they began to assist organizations as paid consultants there was no fundraising profession—no job description, no career path. There were no theories or standards of practice, no ethical guidelines, no "how-to" books to read or courses to take. It was a wilderness out there!

The earliest professional fundraisers were innovators, authors, teachers, and mentors who learned by doing and shared their experiences, empowering those who followed. Maurice Gurin, who was one of my mentors, talked about some of the early leaders in his book *Advancing Beyond the Techniques in Fundraising*:

> Arnaud Cartwright Marts, founder and president of the fundraising consulting firm of Marts & Lundy, Inc., played a significant role not only as a fundraiser but as a strong proponent of the study of philanthropy and its role in civil society.
>
> Frederick Douglass Patterson founded the United Negro College Fund, the first cooperative fundraising venture in U.S. higher education and a precursor to the first united fund.
>
> Harold J. Seymour, a leading consultant in the 1960s, was the author of one of the most popular books on the basic concepts of fundraising, *Designs for Fundraising,* a best-seller in the field from its first publication in 1966 until well into the 1990s.

More recent pathfinders include Henry Rosso and Joseph Mixer, founders of the Fund Raising School, and Robert Payton, founding director of the Indiana University Center on Philanthropy and advocate for the study of fundraising and philanthropy. The list could go on and on. What these leaders seem to hold in common is energy, vision, and courage to break new ground—the traits that make for successful pioneers in any field of endeavor.

In my 14 years of service to the Association of Fundraising Professionals (formerly the National Society of Fund Raising Executives), I have watched pioneers give credibility to the profession. I have been privileged to see fundraising become more respected and legitimized as these pioneers have worked hard to raise standards as well as they have raised money.

CATHLENE WILLIAMS Ph.D., CAE, is senior director of education and research programs for the Association of Fundraising Professionals (formerly the
National Society of Fund Raising Executives), where she is responsible for planning and recruiting faculty for the association's education courses and annual
conference educational programs. She staffs AFP's Research Council and its activities, and is associate editor of AFP's journal *Advancing Philanthropy*, co-
editor of the Jossey-Bass quarterly publication *New Directions for Philanthropic
Fundraising*, and is a member of the editorial board for the international journal *Nonprofit and Voluntary Sector Marketing*. Her prior positions at AFP include director of external affairs and director of library and research services.
Before joining the AFP staff she was project director and director of information services for the National Association of State Boards of Education.

PROFESSIONALS SAY . . .

*I also believe that nurturing key relationships is fundamental for those
working in philanthropy. It's part of that age-old phrase that says "people
give to people, not causes." Even spending time with those who may seem
a drain on your time can sometimes prove fruitful. I remember dreading a
visit to our office from a group of middle school children. The teacher said
they "just wanted to learn more about our health programs overseas." But
after spending a morning with an enthusiastic group of children, I felt
recharged and believed that I may have planted seeds in them.*

Sara Lewis Espada, MA, Area Program Manager, Latin American
Caribbean, Chapel Hill, North Carolina.

*"Professional Fundraiser" is a misnomer. Those in the heart of the pro-
fession do more than raise and collect money. They build institutions,
nurture ideals, improve and enrich our world. The fundraiser's function is
not exclusive to the nonprofit sector. Fundraisers engage in a process of
community organization that serves to enlist, engage, and invest people
and resources in the development of critical social systems—philanthropy,
spirituality, governance, health and human services, education and the
arts, even commerce. When I was young I couldn't decide what to be. I
found the answer by becoming a fundraiser—engaging in a career encom-*

passing the professional attributes of the minister, missionary, teacher, general, advocate, detective, sociologist, manager, analyst, scientist, politician, psychologist, entertainer, innkeeper. Fundraisers work with philanthropists, in fact, fundraisers are philanthropists. They fit the definition "one who helps mankind."

Skip Henderson, MSW, Fund Raising Counsel, Greenbrae, California.

PART TWO

The Fundraising Professional's Role

N ews stories have put much attention on fundraisers and the organizations that we represent. Some of this coverage is putting us on the defensive. We seem to have to defend our work, our profession, our outcomes, and sometimes explain what we actually do. Even our relatives are either confused or suspicious of us, asking at times, "What do you *really* do?"

Public misunderstanding, or lack of understanding, sometimes places the fundraising professional in an awkward position. While we believe we are working for an organization's mission and therefore holding a valued place in society, we battle with myths and perceptions that we are doing something unsavory, and even doing it for a living.

Although fundraising professionals have been able to do much good for so many worthwhile programs, and thus have had a significant role in helping worthy causes succeed, we also have to explain what we do, why we do it, and how we do it. At the same time, we have to convince ourselves and our publics that we are actually professionals, and not just hired solicitors who "hit up" people and "target" their money.

The good news is that the fundraising professional is vitally important for a nonprofit organization's success. There is a great deal of "fun" in fundraising because, while it is a grueling job many times, it is also enormously satisfying. Few practices provide as great a degree of gratification, and rewards are often unequaled because they come in human terms. Fundraising has elements of a ministry and a job—it combines service with skills.

This section discusses the fundraising professional's role in a nonprofit organization and in the sector.

In Chapter 3, the value and importance of fundraising for a successful nonprofit organization is considered. This chapter focuses on what fundraising really is by addressing some of the myths and perceptions related to it. It also considers whether fundraising is a profession and discusses the importance of fundraising for an organization. Fundraising serves the mission of an organization and therefore is a major factor in the relationship of the organization and its markets. Finally, this chapter takes a look at the fundraiser's importance in an organization.

Chapter 4 outlines the skills and qualities that a person considering a career in fundraising should possess. It also provides an overview of the fundraising positions available and gives information on the function of each position. What challenges each professional faces are also included in this chapter. Readers will gain an understanding of the various roles of the professional, and select the right functions for themselves. This chapter takes a brief look at an overriding concern in fundraising—ethical practice.

Other careers and positions, besides those directly related to fundraising, can utilize fundraising skills and experience. Fundraising is a valuable skill to acquire as part of professional development leading toward a variety of careers. It is a vital skill for a manager, executive director, president, board member, board chair, or volunteer. Fundraising expertise is a significant part of leadership. Chapter 5 takes a look at how valuable training and experience in fundraising can be for success in other careers and fields.

Although it acknowledges some of the negative images and perceptions associated with fundraising, the focus of Part Two is on how fundraising is the positive force that generates philanthropy and therefore makes good works and causes possible.

CHAPTER 3

The Value and Importance of Fundraising for a Successful Nonprofit Organization

SIDEBAR BY JOSEPH R. MIXER

Suppose you saw an ad that read like this:

> Join an Antarctic Expedition! We promise you:
> Low pay
> Poor climate
> Safe return doubtful.

Would you respond to this? In 1915, Ernest Shackleton was planning a voyage to cross the Antarctic from west to east, traveling overland. He believed that many would think it would be a privilege to be part of his adventure, and his hunch paid off. Five thousand people responded to the ad.[1]

Using Shackleford's advertisement for personnel as a model, a prospective professional might find an ad like this one:

> *Wanted:* Highly motivated individual who is willing to work long hours without much recognition but will produce great results. Previous experience may vary greatly, and could be in fields such as banking, law, teaching, advertising, accounting, and public policy. Applicant should be ambitious, industrious, able to motivate others, caring, tough, and adaptable. He or she should be willing to work in a setting where no one knows exactly what is done in this job or why. Above all, the applicant should

be willing to share praise and just as willing to take blame, whether or not deserved.

Why would anyone want to be part of a profession where some of the following comments are made?

"The new development officer is frequently required to solicit funds in a social climate fraught with schizophrenia. . . . we also work in arenas highly charged with competition."[2]

"Many people seem to think that fundraising is nothing but fun and games. They hear about all the special events associated with it and envision a glamorous career filled with elegant soirees and sophisticated society. The reality is that this could not be further from the truth, in most cases. The profession is very demanding, time-consuming, and grueling."[3]

"[F]undraisers are regarded with the same mixture of admiration, loathing, suspicion, and awe which we in America regard money itself."[4]

An article from *The Chronicle of Philanthropy* caused many to wonder if fundraisers actually make a difference. In "Growing Ranks of Fundraisers Haven't Increased a Key Measure of Giving," author Thomas Billitteri discussed the fact that while total charitable contributions have risen, the amount donated by average Americans has changed little. He does go on to address the reasons why this situation might exist, but despite such justification, the stinging title has a negative impact.[5]

Then there was an article on an annual conference of the Association of Fundraising Professionals (AFP), formerly known as the National Society of Fund Raising Executives, which reported that too many fundraisers ignore changes in demographics and advances in technology and how these affect fundraising, leading many to believe that professionals are negligent in their practice and in applying the latest knowledge that would lead to success.[6]

In addition to these barbs leveled at fundraising, the question of professionalism has surfaced time and time again. "In spite of fundraisers' pretensions about being 'professionals' our field has no genuine academic or other requirements for admission."[7] The writer of this article went on to give examples on how easy it is to get into and advance in the career of fundraising, and that this has caused many of the problems in perceptions that fundraising is plagued with. Harrah-Conforth and Borsos also commented on the ease that many "find their way into the field by default, or at least . . . the relative ease with which one can enter the ranks and advance."[8]

Also in *The Chronicle of Philanthropy,* Irving Warner wrote, "Fundraisers are coming under intense public scrutiny, and it is clear that the more people hear about us, the less they are impressed by our profession."[9] Finally, in an article titled "Selling Is My Game," the author points out that "no matter how impressive my title is as a fundraiser, I'm still a salesman,"[10] and he goes on to show how fundraising is very much like sales.

So, why do people respond to fundraising as a career? Because it is a privilege to be part of this adventure. At the same time, it is important to address the question: Is fundraising a hot career or a hot seat or something to be avoided altogether, especially in view of comments like the ones just listed?

Certainly with such invectives and denunciations hurled against fundraising as a career, one might wonder why people increasingly choose to enter the field, either as a first career, as a planned career, or as a choice in second or third careers.

Before we explore why fundraising has much appeal to so many, let's look at the status of fundraising in the professional world.

Profession is sometimes considered synonymous with livelihood, craft, vocation, career, or even trade. Robert Carbone of the University of Maryland, College Park, has done considerable study on the meaning of profession, and whether fundraising is actually a vocation moving along a continuum toward being a profession. After reviewing literature on professions, particularly that produced by sociologists, he compiled a list of characteristics that are associated with professional stature and came up with the following:

- *Clarifying roles and functions.* This should be the concern of practitioners and not just a designation by a small number of people. Also, there should be a voluntary organization to which members belong and that helps them define their roles.
- *Acceptance.* This is a question of understanding and acceptance of the professional role by knowledgeable members of society.
- *Practical knowledge.* There should be a pool of knowledge that has been transmitted by practitioners to their successors, and this knowledge is codified.
- *Self-development.* Practitioners engage in improving their skills and developing their abilities to increasingly higher levels.

- *Social consciousness.* Practitioners should understand that their work has value to society and that they perform their tasks in service and not self-interest.
- *Formal training.* Opportunities are available in various settings for improving knowledge, skills, and attitudes.
- *Licensure.* Admission to the practice is controlled in some way.
- *Ethics.* The behavior of practitioners is guided by codes of ethics, and there exists some means by which adherence to this code is controlled.
- *Protection.* The rights and privileges of practitioners are protected in some way.[11]

In a related study, Hannah Dean studied the various meanings of *professional* in her doctoral dissertation. She offered six common characteristics of a profession:

- *Autonomy.* The individual has the right to practice and make decisions.
- *Commitment.* The person feels a sense of "calling."
- *Collegiality.* Colleagues cooperate, offer mutual support, and share knowledge.
- *Extensive education.* There is a means by which to develop and increase a knowledge base.
- *Service orientation.* The job is "other" centered rather than self-centered.
- *Special skills and knowledge.* The practice is based on understanding what specialized abilities and knowledge are necessary.[12]

Considerable headway has been made in the fundraising field to bolster the argument that it is a profession. There is a growing, credible pool of knowledge on which fundraisers base their practice, professional development opportunities are numerous, the need for special skills is readily acknowledged, collegiality is generally an expected behavior and organizations such as AFP and other professional associations foster this, ethical practice is a qualification for membership in professional associations, and more attention is placed on the service aspect of fundraising than ever before.

The debate on just where fundraising is on the continuum between a vocation and a profession certainly continues. For the person considering it as a career, there is sufficient evidence that it is a worthwhile consideration as a life's work.

Most people enter the fundraising field because it is an environment that serves human needs—needs that are not served by the other sectors, business and government. People want to heal, to educate, to preserve cultures, to shelter the abused, to inspire, or to preserve. But in order to succeed in fundraising as a career, you have to believe in the mission of the organization you serve. Other objectives can certainly be worthwhile—career advancement, involvement in a specific field of interest, or working in a field that has such significant impact on nonprofit causes—but belief in the causes that a fundraising professional serves is of primary importance. Fundraising should touch souls, the professional's as well as those who are served.

It is true that there are hours spent in painstaking research. Preparation goes into every "ask," from proposal writing to one-on-one solicitation, the planning for each successful event, the writing of materials such as fundraising letters, the cultivation steps so vital for each market, the juggling of constituents' wants and demands, the complexities of managing volunteers and working with the board. The list could go on and on, and it can be mind-numbing.

But at the end of each day, the professional has engaged in a journey worth sharing because, whether or not the results of that day's efforts are visible, the professional can take pride in the nature of the work. Fundraising, or *development,* as some prefer to call it, is a fundamental part of the process that makes institutions successful. The genuinely committed professional feels a "calling" to the work of fundraising. The satisfaction is derived from results, often intangible as well as those that are not visible for some time in the future, not from recognition.

An orientation to public service is critical and should be a significant motivation for entering the professional. Idealism and enthusiasm must be balanced with accountability, businesslike behavior, and practical action. Perhaps the authors Watkins and Redfield summed it up well.

"A development officer will always play a unique role in the not-for-profit world. We must introduce people to each other and induce gatherings of colleagues while often remaining outside the group. We must step forward readily to accept the blame for a failed situation if need be and just as readily give away deserved credit for success. We must sustain our dedication in the face of seemingly overwhelming adversity. Worst of all, we must remember names and faces—lots and lots of names and faces. This is a strange, often difficult, but fascinating and frequently exhilarating profession. It can be the best job there is and it will demand your best work."[13]

At the bottom of it all is this reality—most work in the nonprofit sector, whether it is advocacy, healing, educating, entertaining, preserving, or many other types, just will not happen unless someone brings in money. And the more fundraising is integrated into the entire organization, the more successful it will be.

In this integration process, fundraising can play several roles in an organization. Kelly did a qualitative study on fundraising roles that explained how practitioners carry out job responsibilities. She identified four variations in practitioner behavior—liaison, expert prescriber, technician, and problem-solving process facilitator.[14]

The *liaison* role is a traditional one. The practitioner coordinates, facilitates, and interprets when organizational representatives meet with prospective donors. The *expert prescriber* is in an opposite role. This role assumes responsibility for raising money, and does it with great skill. Others are left out of this process. The *technicians* are not part of the management team. They produce and implement the techniques and strategies needed in the fundraising process, such as use of Internet for fundraising. The *problem-solving process facilitator* is a member of the management team and is knowledgeable about, as well as involved in, the organization's management. Although Kelly calls for more research to verify and substantiate these findings, seasoned professionals would acknowledge that a fundraiser must, at one time or other, function in all four roles. Perhaps this is one of the challenges as well as opportunities of fundraising as a career. Various roles are appropriate for various organizations, and a person's strengths can be utilized in more than one way.

So what should fundraising professionals do about the myths, misperceptions, and problems that face us today, some of which were described at the beginning of the chapter? How can a fundraising professional assure constituents and the public in general that we are a valuable part of a nonprofit team? How can the person entering fundraising as a career be a part of raising the public image of fundraising, and therefore its effectiveness?

Fundraising is not distasteful. We are indeed fortunate if we can serve society in this way. We can project enthusiasm and commitment to the mission of the cause we serve. We can educate the public, beginning with our families and friends, but first we must understand the role of fundraising itself. It is not sales, it is not begging, or "hitting up" for funds. It is a genuine effort to bring together organizations and people of similar interests whose joined forces bring about results.

We can also educate our colleagues, including board members. We need to show them the need for fundraising, and how it is affected by and affects the entire organization. We can improve our professional standing by improving our skills and adding to our knowledge. Our practice should be ethical and our organizations, as well as our work, should be accountable to our constituents.

Collegiality allows us to support each other, to give advice and support to each others' efforts. The outside expert is often more listened to than the in-house professional. We can be each other's consultants and advisors. Also as part of collegiality, we can encourage each other.

We have to know what we are doing and explain this to others so that we will not be viewed as miracle workers but as essential employees who bring in funds. We must be able to explain why certain goals are possible to reach and others are not. Our accomplishments must be genuine and verifiable.

The criticisms will always be there, but we can lessen them by how well we do our work as professionals. Charlatans and unscrupulous persons do exist in our midst. But by our example and the results we exhibit, we can promote an excellent and deserving public image. It is a complex assignment. "Development programs in charitable organizations—and the professionals who lead them—must reflect the highest ethics, exacting standards and unwavering principles if they are to meet the challenges each institution faces and to serve the institution's stakeholders."[15]

In short, perhaps Pablo Casals, the renowned cellist, said it best. "The capacity to care is the thing which gives life its deepest meaning and significance."[16] This perhaps sums up the reasons why fundraising is, and can be, an exciting and fulfilling career—it is focused on caring, and in doing so with excellence.

FURTHER READING

Ciconte, Barbara Kushner, and Jeanne G. Jacob. *Fundraising Basics: A Complete Guide.* Gaithersburg, MD: Aspen Publishers, Inc., March 1997.

A fundraising primer that helps new fundraisers learn the basics, from the vocabulary of fundraising to the nuances of major gifts, includes a chapter on selecting fundraising as a career.

Connors, Tracy Daniel. *The Nonprofit Handbook: Management,* 2d ed. New York: Wiley, 1997.

The Nonprofit Handbook: Management *offers proven advice, from experts in the field, on every facet of a nonprofit's daily operations: management and leadership, human resources, benefits, compensation, financial management, marketing and communications, law and regulations.*

Duronio, Margaret A., and Eugene Tempel. *Fund Raisers: Their Careers, Stories, Concerns, and Accomplishments.* San Francisco: Jossey-Bass, 1996.

This book offers an overview of fundraisers—their educational and career backgrounds, their values and concerns, and the challenges and rewards they experience in their work.

Gurin, Maurice G. *Confessions of a Fund Raiser.* Rockville, MD: The Taft Group, 1985.

Written by a nationally recognized fundraiser, this book describes his "break" into and his personal experiences through vivid anecdotes. It discusses topics such as importance of innovation, challenging donors, organization's objectives.

Kelly, Kathleen S. *Effective Fund-Raising Management.* Mahwah, NJ: Lawrence Erlbaum Associates, 1998.

This book explores the critical area of fundraising management. Fundraising management can be the key to success or the door to demise. An organization that does not understand and effectively manage its programs will soon be suffering.

Mixer, Joseph R. *Principles of Professional Fundraising.* San Francisco: Jossey-Bass, 1993.

In his landmark book, Mixer applies concepts and theories of psychology, organizational development and behavior, and management to the practice of professional fundraising—the same theories and concepts once thought to be the exclusive domain of private industry. In addition to practical models for soliciting donations, the book addresses the complex issue of growth and change within charitable organizations, furnishes an analysis of shifting market resources, and offers assessment of alternative revenue strategies.

Olcott, William A. *Make a Note of It: Wit and Wisdom from Fund Raisers for Fund Raisers.* Chicago: Bonus Books, 1998.

This book explores and provides insightful wisdom from some of the greats in the field of fundraising. Not everything can be learned by a book, many things can only be passed on from others. Make a Note of It *passes wisdom from fundraisers to fundraisers.*

Powell, James Lawrence. *Pathways to Leadership: How to Achieve and Sustain Success.* San Francisco: Jossey-Bass, 1995.

Pathways to Leadership *is a practical, nuts-and-bolts guide written for nonprofit chief executives and those on the career path to becoming chief executives. In this book, Powell provides realistic advice and offers illustrative examples for developing the skills necessary to become a successful nonprofit leader. Filled with checklists, case examples, and many other practical resources,* Pathways to Leadership *is a valuable guide for all nonprofit executives who wish to lead with vigor and mastery.*

Rosso, Henry A. *Rosso on Fundraising: Lessons from a Master's Lifetime Experience*. San Francisco: Jossey-Bass, 1996.

This book explores the lessons learned from the life experience of Henry Rosso, a master. It provides valuable insight and knowledge that only a lifetime of experience can provide.

Weinstein, Stanley. *The Complete Guide to Fund-Raising Management*. New York: Wiley, 1999.

Moving beyond theory this book addresses the day-to-day problems faced in organizations, and offers hands-on advice and practical solutions.

SIDEBAR   JOSEPH R. MIXER

The negative attitudes and perceptions about fundraising arise most often around two facets: the persons involved and the processes or methods employed. The first aspect involves individuals acting as solicitors who fear anticipated rejection or who fear the loss of their social standing by appearing as beggars or mendicants. The second aspect relates to objectionable solicitations by telemarketing and direct mail firms. Overcoming these problems requires different approaches.

For individuals, clarifying the values involved in asking can relieve the stress. Giving is a social exchange process whereby the giver receives psychological and social satisfactions from the requesting nonprofit organization that demonstrates the human needs being served and provides recognition and status to the donor. When the joy and benefits of giving become apparent, the solicitor can more easily shed negative feelings. Additionally, the asking organizations can fortify a positive environment by creating a climate for giving, using group dynamics and motivational skills. Recognition of the long history of philanthropy and sharing with others in United States adds to the stature of fundraising as a means for achieving the values the nation holds dear.

Changing attitudes about methods of fundraising requires large-scale organizational efforts by the community of nonprofit agencies. Professional associations have set up codes of ethics for solicitations, reporting procedures for admonishing abusers, and public relations programs to enhance the virtues of donating. Emphasis on philanthropy in meeting human needs adds to the climate of accepting legitimate fundraising. Support for reasonable surveillance, regulation, and reporting by states' attorneys general enhances a positive view of the profession. The costs of fundraising can be put in perspective by showing that a dollar invested in financial instruments returns 6 to 10 percent, while a donated dollar produces 75 to 80 percent return in human services.

JOSEPH R. MIXER, Ph.D., CFRE (ret.) a trainer and consultant to charitable organizations for more than 35 years, founded the development program in 1961 at the University of California, Berkeley, was cofounder of The Fund Raising School, 1974, is author of *Principles of Professional Fundraising*, and was the 1993 and 1997 Outstanding Executive, National Society of Fund Raising Executives.

PROFESSIONALS SAY . . .

Ultimately, the fundraiser's primary responsibility is to the donor—to be overseer of the donor's interests as they mesh with the mission of the organization. If the donor is not satisfied with the stewardship of their gift, they become disaffected and disengaged from the organization, which ultimately could be to the detriment of the organization. By ensuring that the donor feels connected and engaged, the fundraiser also helps ensure the long-term financial viability of the organization.

Paulette J. Persinger, Campaign Director, Indiana State Museum Foundation

Private support provides the margin of excellence that allows a good organization to become a great one. In a time where outside funding for nonprofits seems uncertain, philanthropy allows us to continue dreaming big dreams, and to remain focused on our mission. Fundraising provides the lifeblood for many of our organizations, and it is absolutely essential for our future. Those of us who are privileged enough to have careers in this field have felt the synergy present when donors are linked with meaningful giving experiences. It is this synergy that will keep philanthropy in the center stage within our organizations.

Shannon M. Miller, University of Iowa Foundation, Director of Development, University of Iowa College of Medicine/University of Iowa Hospitals and Clinics

If you do not understand the importance of fundraising for a nonprofit organization, don't become a nonprofit Executive Director. An ED can spend 50+ percent of his or her time developing funds, especially in a small organization that can not afford to hire a full-time fundraiser. You have to understand the process or you and your board will be disappointed with the outcome.

Cheryl Hall-Russell, Executive Director, Indianapolis Coalition for Neighborhood Development

Skills and Qualities of the Aspiring Professional and Fundraising Positions to Match

SIDEBAR BY HOLLY HALL

According to Peter F. Drucker, the renowned expert in management theory, a radical transformation of work and society is taking place. This is the age of social transformation, he states. The dominant, emerging group of employees are the "knowledge workers," who will make up a third or more of the work force in the United States. Knowledge workers require much education and the ability to acquire and apply theoretical knowledge, and they must develop the habit of continuous learning.[1] Drucker foresaw this change in America's work force when he wrote several decades ago that "(k)nowledge workers do not produce a 'thing.' They produce ideas, information, concepts. The knowledge worker, moreover, is usually a specialist."[2] Certainly this concept is true of a fundraising professional, who is a specialist in the nonprofit sector and a guardian of the philanthropic tradition in the United States.

Robert L. Payton, founding director of the Center on Philanthropy at Indiana University, wrote that "(p)rofessionalism is an *ideal:* that is, it projects a vision of perfection that cannot be fully realized in reality. Professionalism is a *regulative ideal:* that is, it serves as a moral action-guide directing the professional toward right conduct." He goes on to say that professionalism is a recent tradition that has evolved over the last 50 years. "To be a professional was to make a claim to be trustworthy, not only in the sense of competence but in the moral sense as well."[3]

In their book *Fundraisers: Their Careers, Stories, Concerns, and Accomplishments,* Duronio and Tempel state that "the work of fundraising has never been more demanding, more challenging, or more important."[4] In order to meet these challenges, the fundraising professional must be able to ask seven questions, as posed by Payton:

- What is going on?
- What is to be done?
- Who cares?
- What business is it of ours?
- What sources are required?
- Why us?
- Who owns us?[5]

Answering these questions and therefore meeting the implied challenges takes a serious, competent professional who has advanced education and training, is a member in an association of peers, adheres to a code of ethics, exercises good judgment, and believes in the service ethic.

Greenfield asks the question, "Why do the professionals work in a field that has so little public acceptance?" He responds to his own question by stating that fundraising is the business of helping others, and that satisfaction comes from seeing ideas and plans come to life, of being part of an institution that carries out programs to benefit a community.[6] Another writer offers this opinion as to why people want to work in fundraising: "Besides the satisfaction of advancing a mission they believe in, fund-raisers say they like working in an environment in which goals are clear, performance is quantifiable, and advancement is based on results."[7] A person can combine ambition, ability, and skills with personal satisfaction.

In view of the above, it can be seen that the demands made on a fundraising professional are many. They include requirements such as education, job skills, and experience, as well as personal characteristics. It is true that the demands are great, but so are the opportunities. In a 1999 issue of *The Chronicle of Philanthropy,* an article decried the shortage of qualified fundraisers and stated that while many people work in the profession (more than

80,000, according to an estimate proposed by Kelly[8]) not all have the skills needed to raise substantial gifts.[9] Another *Chronicle* article written in the mid-1990s proclaimed, "The job market for fundraisers is booming."[10] Tempel concludes, "Organized fund-raising is an important part of the philanthropic tradition of our nation. Today, more than ever, ethical fund-raising is critical to long-term viability of nonprofit organizations."[11]

REQUIRED SKILLS AND QUALITIES

What skills and qualifications are needed to be a successful professional in the field of fundraising? A quick survey of job ads for fundraising positions, as listed in *The Chronicle of Philanthropy* or *NonProfit Times,* provides an overview of what skills and qualities are sought by organizations hiring a fundraising professional:

- Verbal and written fluency and competence
- Attention to detail
- Ability to conceptualize
- Negotiating skills
- Ability to coordinate and manage
- Innovation, the capability of seeing something new, different, and better
- Analytical skills
- Technical expertise (which varies according to position)
- Mentoring, supervising, and teaching ability
- Understanding of budgeting
- Ability to plan
- Volunteer management

Personal characteristics are also significant to consider. These qualities have been identified as pointing to a successful professional:

- Commitment to public service
- Enthusiasm
- Idealism
- Comfort in dealing with people

- Sensitivity
- Tolerance for ambiguity
- Flexibility
- Honesty and integrity
- Perseverance
- Compassion
- Confidence
- Energy
- Wisdom
- And a little humor sometimes helps

FUNDRAISING ROLES

These lists could probably be expanded. Each skill and quality plays a role in the range of fundraising functions. In other words, a person's abilities and personal characteristics come together in the specific fundraising role he or she chooses. The general areas of concentration include the following:

- *Direct mail or direct marketing*—producing and distributing written materials to a targeted audience. Some particular skills and qualifications needed are writing, ability to work with a deadline, seeking advice from other professionals, creativity, and technical expertise. A professional must have the ability to handle lists, sometimes of great quantity, write copy, handle the details of getting a mailing out, and produce reports on the results.

- *Special events*—organizing functions or benefits that meet several goals, from cultivation and creating good will to raising funds. Skills and qualifications needed include organizational ability, management of many details, creativity in selecting a type of event, and working well with volunteers. Certainly a great deal of patience and flexibility are required in this area.

- *Prospect research*—finding appropriate information about prospects and donors, and managing this information. This subspecialty has taken on new dimensions with the growth of technology. The person undertaking research must have technical ability in researching through the Internet and maintaining records on computer software. Other skills include the ability to research from many sources, compile information, record and manipulate data, and support staff, volunteers, and administrators with appropriate information.

- *Major donor solicitation*—working with people who have the capacity to make large gifts to the organizations. A person specializing in this area must be able to identify and qualify major gift prospects, plan a strategy for cultivation and solicitation, often ask for the gift, provide appropriate follow-up, and ensure proper stewardship of the gift. Major gift officers are often expert communicators and have good human relations skills. They are senior staff and work closely with administration or management of an organization. Corporate and foundation solicitation—seeking funds from these markets—involves proposal writing skills, as well as research and team management. Seeking prospects among these two potential funding sources requires the ability to research, produce written material, edit copy, bring together persons with different knowledge and expertise, communicate with prospects, provide follow-up information, develop appropriate recognition procedures, and be accountable for use of grant funds.

- *Planned giving*—the fastest growing area of expertise that requires much technical knowledge, balanced with people skills. Planned giving is a demanding but growing subspecialty that involves learning about the various instruments for giving, tax structures and implications, and benefits to the donor and the beneficiaries. Planned giving professionals often are senior-level employees and work with volunteers and the president or executive director.

- *Data and records management*—keeping track of information and helping others manage the information. Most organizations maintain computer as well as hard-copy records. A professional must know how to enter the information into the database correctly so that it is useful and can be retrieved for specific purposes. Gift receipting and acknowledgment is often a part of this role. An eye for details and patience in following through are critical for this function.

- *Consulting*—working independently in advising nonprofit organizations. Consultants may specialize or be generalists. They may work independently or with a firm. They will need a broad base of fundraising knowledge and have the ability to give advice.

TITLES IN PROFESSIONAL FUNDRAISING

The titles of organizational positions vary and often reflect the function. First, the general descriptive terms need to be identified. Fundraising (opinions vary on how this term should be written; some prefer fund-raising or fund raising) is sometimes referred to as advancement (mostly in higher education) or development. Some believe these terms are euphemisms that grow out of a reluctance to be direct about the fundraising profession. The most common job titles that evolve from these terms and the functions described here include:

- Vice president for institutional advancement (or just advancement)
- Vice president for development
- Resource development officer
- Director of development
- Major gifts officer
- Annual fund director
- Annual giving director
- Fundraising manager
- Planned giving officer or director
- Grants manager
- Corporate and foundation relations specialist or director
- Fundraising coordinator
- Researcher
- Prospect researcher
- Research assistant
- Database manager
- Records manager
- Administrative assistant
- Development manager

These may take on different forms, depending on where a person works. For example, an educational institution or health care organization may have an associate or assistant vice president for advancement, or for a subcategory such as major gifts. Some organizations create foundations that focus on fundraising for the institution; their leadership may assume the title of president or director. Another possible title is executive vice president if the organization is complex.

TYPES OF FUNDRAISING ORGANIZATIONS

There are several ways to classify types of organizations that could employ a fundraising executive. Classification of nonprofits varies from organization to organization. For example, the National Center for Charitable Statistics' taxonomy differs from the Association of Fundraising Professionals' classification. What is important here is to see the range of possibilities where a person's skills and abilities might best fit. The generally accepted breakdown includes the following:

- Religion
- Education
- Health
- Human services
- Youth
- Arts and culture
- Environment and conservation
- Long-term health care
- Consultants
- Political and advocacy groups
- Associations
- Public benefit

DEMOGRAPHICS IN FUNDRAISING

The person looking at fundraising as a career may wonder what he or she will be part of in terms of type of people, gender, age, race, and other general characteristics.[12]

In their book, *Who Are America's Fundraisers?*, Duronio and Tempel surveyed 955 women and 793 men, of which 1,651 staff members responded. They confirmed that the male–female ratio among fundraising professionals has shifted in the last decade and that the number of women has increased significantly. This finding substantiates the research conducted by AFP and CASE. The increase may have leveled off, but women still outnumber men. There are some fears of the feminization of the field, because this may indicate decreases in salary and respect, but most professionals elect to disregard gender and focus on success indicators instead. Others go so far as to say that feminization could actually be beneficial, given the characteristics that lead to success in fundraising, which include sensitivity to the donor, flexibility, and a sense of caring. These are universal characteristics, but are often attributed to women more than men.

In the Duronio/Tempel study, both males and females enter the field at the average age of 33, but it is likely that in the next decade this age will lower as more college and university young people prepare for a career in fundraising instead of making it their second, third, or fourth career. Regardless of the gender makeup of the profession, there are ample opportunities for both males and females, although males still outrank females in salary (this will be discussed in Chapter 11).

WORKING CONDITIONS

Other areas of interest that a career seeker may want to know about are the details of what it is like to work in fundraising. What is the typical work week like? How often do professionals change jobs, and why? What is the demand for fundraisers?

According to both the 1999 NSFRE (now AFP) profile of members and Duronio and Tempel, we can draw the following conclusions about working in fundraising.

First, fundraising professionals work hard. While many experience 60- and 70-hour work weeks, the average is between 45 to 50 hours a week. Naturally, this will differ among types of work. It is conceivable that a person handling records, prospect research, or mailings could limit a week's work to the normal 40 hours; however, a person involved in major gifts, planned giving, capital campaigns, or administration could work far longer due to the differing demands of the position.

Second, the average length of stay in a position has increased. About 10 years ago the average was said to be about 18 months to two years at one particular job. Over a third of those who participated in the 1995 survey had been with only one employer, and only 4.4 percent had been with five employers. According to the 1999 survey, more than half of the respondents had been with their current employers fewer than four years. Only 18.2 percent had stayed in the same organization for 10 years or more. Again, the type of position might dictate this. For example, those working in entry-level positions may have to move to a different organization or even geographic location to receive a promotion, while senior fundraising professionals may be content to stay for a significant length of time, or even retire from a position. Naturally, some situations are untenable or unmanageable, such as in dysfunctional organizations, and these may cause a person to leave a position.[13]

Duronio and Tempel found that most fundraisers they surveyed intended to stay with fundraising, and many preferred to stay with their current organizations indefinitely. This may also be a significant causal factor in the average age and years of experience of professionals in fundraising. The typical fundraising executive is older than a decade ago and has more years of experience in the field. This may be because the field grew so rapidly in the 1980s and these professionals are now maturing.

Third, the demand for fundraisers is high. A *Chronicle of Philanthropy* article titled "Keeping the Best on Board" described how organizations want to hold on to their best and brightest fundraisers. It said,

> Facing the tightest job market in decades, . . . charities are looking hard these days for ways to recruit and retain good employees. From improving training programs and raising salaries to mounting aggressive recruitment-advertising campaigns, nonprofit groups are scrambling to heighten their appeal as places to work."[14]

Fourth, job satisfaction is generally high among fundraising professionals. A 26-year-old Harvard University graduate who co-founded Peace Games believes that jobs in nonprofits can be as rewarding as those in the high-tech world. He is quoted as saying, "What I can offer folks is something they can't get at Microsoft: the ability to help kids be peacemakers."[15] This is true for many people who have changed from the corporate sector to the nonprofit field. The satisfaction of working with human needs, participating in interesting and worthwhile causes, and achieving results that go beyond the bottom line of financial gain has attracted excellent professionals who have made the switch.

NEW CHALLENGES AND ETHICAL ISSUES

In progressing up the ladder of professionalism, both in practice and positions held, the fundraising professional will find a constantly changing set of challenges. In pooling the opinions of current experts, the following might be acknowledged as being significant in this century. Some people might find these challenges daunting, but others relish the opportunity of expending their talents and energies and welcome the rigorous work involved. Whatever the attitude of the career seeker, these challenges are real but also change over time, taking on new characteristics as old issues are resolved and new ones surface. These new challenges include:

- Increased scrutiny of the sector, with judgments on how money is used and why it is needed.

- More demand for accountability or "transparency" by increasingly sophisticated donors who wish to know what their investment is accomplishing.

- Technological advances that both enhance fundraising capability and challenge the small shop in particular.

- Globalization—a world view of civil society and an understanding of the role of fundraising in developing and maintaining civil society. This presents new possibilities for fundraising practice, but also makes it necessary to adapt principles to new cultures and contexts.

- More competition for philanthropic dollars due to steady growth of nonprofit organizations.

- An anticipated transfer of wealth that presents new opportunities but challenges as well, because donors' ways of giving are changing. There is more demand for results and more involvement by donors, and donors seek out causes that interest them rather than wait for organizations to come to them.

- Increasing economic inequality, and therefore greater necessity for action by nonprofit organizations.

- Demographic changes that affect who can give and who needs nonprofit services.

- Blurring of sectors and the continuing challenge to educate the public about the sector and how it affects our communities and lives.

- The move from outputs to outcomes, increasing emphasis on results.

The fundraising professional plays a significant role in the operation of healthy, viable nonprofits that can face the challenges of this decade. It requires the use of skills, abilities, and personal traits that match various roles and responsibilities of the fundraising professional. Above all, the professional will engage in fundraising practice in an ethical, principled way because the fundraiser is the steward of a donor's trust and funds.

One of the most significant documents on the topic of ethics in practice was issued by INDEPENDENT SECTOR, a Washington, D.C.–based national coalition of more than 800 organizations that have an interest in philanthropy and voluntary action. In "Ethics and the Nation's Voluntary and Philanthropic Community: Obedience to the Unenforceable," the authors state that Americans are increasingly concerned about ethical behaviors practiced in all institutions, and they recommend a process that includes constant commitment to ethical behavior.

The committee put together by INDEPENDENT SECTOR[16] to develop this document identified three levels of ethical behaviors. The first was to be concerned about obeying laws. This means an avoidance of committing an illegal act, such as hiring or promotions that deny equal employment opportunity, or reports to governments or foundations that are filed with inaccurate information. The second level concerns unethical behavior. Perhaps a professional knows the right action but is tempted to take a different route. Examples of this may be when grant funding covers more than 100 percent of a director's salary, or when no minority persons are on boards of organizations serving minorities in a community. Finally there is the ethical dilemma, when the decision is not just a contest between good and evil but a decision to be made from differing options. Whether to accept a donation from a donor whose actions are not compatible with the organization's mission may be one example of an ethical dilemma, as is the decision of how many of a donor's demands can be met without compromising an organization's integrity.

The INDEPENDENT SECTOR document presented the following values and ethical behaviors as suggested guidelines for nonprofit organizations and practitioners working for them:

- Commitment beyond self
- Obedience of the laws
- Commitment beyond the law (i.e., obedience to the unenforceable)

- Commitment to the public good
- Respect for the worth and dignity of individuals
- Tolerance, diversity, and social justice
- Accountability to the public
- Openness and honesty
- Prudent application of resources

A book by philosopher Marilyn Fischer provides an excellent resource for developing an ethical stance and set of principles by which to make ethical decisions in fundraising.[17]

Fischer states that for fundraisers, three basic value commitments can be identified:

- The organizational mission that directs the work
- Relationships with the people with whom they interact
- Sense of integrity

She goes on to say, "We bring ethical sensitivity to decision making when we place particular decisions in the context of these three basic value commitments."[18] Her book provides resources by which fundraising professionals can examine situations and help make choices for their organizations.

Occasionally the fundraising professional will be faced with situations that are in conflict with a personal set of ethical standards. Such a conflict should be handled through discussion regarding the right course of action. Resigning in protest may not be the best way to serve the organization. There are no easy answers to ethical dilemmas, and the brief overview presented here should only be a starting point for the fundraising professional to examine ethical viewpoints and processes by which the organization's ethical standards are upheld and personal values are maintained. Ethics are, on the one hand, a set of principles, and on the other hand, they are a set of specific behaviors. There is no universal definition, and disagreements abound.

The fundraising professional should be aware of and adhere to the AFP Code of Ethical Principles and Standards of Professional Practice, reproduced on the next page.

AFP CODE OF ETHICAL PRINCIPLES AND STANDARDS OF PROFESSIONAL PRACTICE

Statement of Ethical Principles

Adopted 1964; amended October 1999

The Association of Fundraising Professionals (AFP) exists to foster the development and growth of fundraising professionals and the profession, to promote high ethical standards in the fundraising profession and to preserve and enhance philanthropy and volunteerism.

Members of AFP are motivated by an inner drive to improve the quality of life through the cause they serve. They serve the ideal of philanthropy; are committed to the preservation and enhancement of volunteerism; and hold stewardship of these concepts as the overriding principle of their professional life. They recognize their responsibility to ensure that needed resources are vigorously and ethically sought and that the intent of the donor is honestly fulfilled. To these ends, AFP members embrace certain values that they strive to uphold in performing their responsibilities for generating charitable support.

AFP members aspire to:
- practice their profession with integrity, honesty, truthfulness and adherence to the absolute obligation to safeguard the public trust;
- act according to the highest standards and visions of their organization, profession and conscience;
- put philanthropic mission above personal gain;
- inspire others through their own sense of dedication and high purpose;
- improve their professional knowledge and skills, so that their performance will better serve others;
- demonstrate concern for the interests and well-being of individuals affected by their actions;
- value the privacy, freedom of choice and interests of all those affected by their actions;
- foster cultural diversity and pluralistic values, and treat all people with dignity and respect;
- affirm, through personal giving, a commitment to philanthropy and its role in society;

- adhere to the spirit as well as the letter of all applicable laws and regulations;
- advocate within their organizations, adherence of all applicable laws and regulations;
- bring credit to the fundraising profession by their demeanor;
- encourage colleagues to embrace and practice these ethical principles and standards of professional practice; and
- be aware of the codes of ethics promulgated by other professional organizations that serve philanthropy.

Standards of Professional Practice

Furthermore, while striving to act according to the above values, AFP members agree to abide by the AFP Standards of Professional Practice, which are adopted and incorporated into the AFP Code of Ethical Principles. Violation of the Standards may subject the member to disciplinary sanctions, including expulsion, as provided in the AFP Ethics Enforcement Procedures.

Professional Obligations

1. Members shall not engage in activities that harm the members' organization, clients, or profession.
2. Members shall not engage in activities that conflict with their fiduciary, ethical, and legal obligations to their organizations and their clients.
3. Members shall effectively disclose all potential and actual conflicts of interest; such disclosure does not preclude or imply ethical impropriety.
4. Members shall not exploit any relationship with a donor, prospect, volunteer, or employee to the benefit of the members or the members' organizations.
5. Members shall comply with all applicable local, state, provincial, and federal civil and criminal laws.
6. Members recognize their individual boundaries of competence and are forthcoming and truthful about their professional experience and qualifications.

(continued)

AFP CODE OF ETHICAL PRINCIPLES AND STANDARDS OF PROFESSIONAL PRACTICE

Solicitation and Use of Charitable Funds

7. Members shall take care to ensure that all solicitation materials are accurate and correctly reflect their organization's mission and use of solicited funds.

8. Members shall take care to ensure that donors receive informed, accurate, and ethical advice about the value and tax implications of potential gifts.

9. Members shall take care to ensure that contributions are used in accordance with donors' intentions.

10. Members shall take care to ensure proper stewardship of charitable contributions, including timely reports on the use and management of funds.

11. Members shall obtain explicit consent by the donor before altering the conditions of a gift.

Presentation of Information

12. Members shall not disclose privileged or confidential information to unauthorized parties.

13. Members shall adhere to the principle that all donor and prospect information created by, or on behalf of, an organization is the property of that organization and shall not be transferred or utilized except on behalf of that organization.

14. Members shall give donors the opportunity to have their names removed from lists that are sold to, rented to, or exchanged with other organizations.

15. Members shall, when stating fundraising results, use accurate and consistent accounting methods that conform to the appropriate guidelines adopted by the American Institute of Certified Public Accountants (AICPA)* for the type of organization involved. (* In countries outside of the United States, comparable authority should be utilized.)

Compensation

16. Members shall not accept compensation that is based on a percentage of charitable contributions; nor shall they accept finder's fees.

17. Members may accept performance-based compensation, such as bonuses, provided such bonuses are in accord with prevailing practices within the members' own organization, and are not based on a percentage of charitable contributions.

18. Members shall not pay finder's fees, or commissions or percentage compensation based on charitable contributions, and shall take care to discourage their organizations from making such payments.

PUTTING IT TOGETHER: SEEKING A FUNDRAISING CAREER

In putting all these characteristics and skills together, from determining a desirable role to finding a suitable organization for a person's talent, the steps for seeking a career in fundraising could be illustrated like this:

1. Understand what fundraising is, how it fits into the nonprofit sector, and its relationship to philanthropy.

2. Develop and accept a mission of service and commitment to fundraising as a profession.

3. Seek knowledge of fundraising and the sector by acquiring education and/or training. Become an overall professional while specializing in a subspecialty.

4. Acquire the first job at an appropriate level of responsibility. This may be in data management, as an assistant director, or proposal writer.

5. Continue professional development and seek career advancement by accepting jobs that are progressively more demanding and challenging. Compensation is a factor in this. Positions at this stage may be director of development, major gifts officer, or planned giving specialist.

6. Develop good leadership skills while continuing to polish and perfect skills and acquire additional knowledge.

▪ FURTHER READING

Anderson, Albert. *Ethics for Fundraisers.* Indianapolis: Indiana University Press, 1996.

This book provides good insight into the relationship of ethics and fundraising.

Briscoe, G. Marriane. *Ethics in Fundraising: Putting Values into Practice.* San Francisco: Jossey-Bass, 1994.

This groundbreaking sourcebook takes a major step toward developing a code of professional ethics for fundraisers. The examination of the fundraising profession in the moral life of a civil society is the topic of the first three chapters. These chapters are meant to give fundraisers a better and more elevated view of their work as much as to help their donors, bosses, and friends understand that fundraising may be difficult work, but it is certainly not dirty work. The remaining five chapters deal with ethics and the practical issues of fundraising, such as personal and professional decision making, the nonprofit board of directors, compensation methods, research, and fundraising management.

Cohen, Lilly, and Dennis R. Young. *Careers for Dreamers and Doers: A Guide to Management Careers in the Nonprofit Sector.* New York: The Foundation Center, 1989.

The first comprehensive career guide of its kind, this book helps the person to assess interests and skills for employment in the nonprofit sector. While published in 1989, some of the concepts are still relevant.

Duronio, Margaret A., and Eugene R. Tempel. *Fund Raisers: Their Careers, Stories, Concerns, and Accomplishments.* San Francisco: Jossey-Bass, 1997.

A thorough study that answers "Who are fundraisers?" The research establishes a baseline of information about fundraisers from how they enter the field to what issues affect their work.

Fischer, Marilyn. *Ethical Decision Making in Fund Raising.* New York: Wiley, 2000.

This book provides conceptual tools with which a nonprofit can examine the ethics of how and from whom it seeks donations. It discusses fundraising dilemmas and examines day-to-day issues. Includes excellent discussion questions and case studies.

Greenfield, James M. *Fund-Raising: Evaluating and Managing the Fund Development Process*, 2nd Edition. New York: Wiley, 1991.

A comprehensive guide to designing fundraising programs and a step-by-step approach to evaluating and managing. Demonstrates effective fundraising methods, measuring results against potential, designing the gift plan appropriate for an organization, and recruiting donors.

Kelly, Kathleen S. *Effective Fund-Raising Management*. Mahwah, NJ: Lawrence Erlbaum Associates, 1998.

This book explores the critical area of fundraising management. Fundraising management can be the key to success or the door to demise. An organization that does not understand and effectively manage its fundraising programs will soon be suffering. This work explores what it takes to run an effective fundraising program.

Koziol, Kenneth G., ed. *Ethics in Nonprofit Management: A Collection of Cases*. San Francisco: Institute for Nonprofit Organization Management, University of San Francisco, 1998.

This is a good selection of cases related to ethics in fundraising and nonprofit management.

National Society of Fund Raising Executives. *1999 Profile of NSFRE Members*. Alexandria, VA: 1999.

Comprehensive career survey, the sixth in 20 years, which covers background, employer, professional activities, compensation, use of technology, and opinions on professional issues. The results represent a sample of NSFRE's members and provide useful information about the profession and individuals involved in raising philanthropic dollars.

Sukiennik, Diane, William Bendat, and Lisa Raufman. *The Career Fitness Program*. Upper Saddle River, NJ: Prentice Hall, 1998.

This book guides you through the vital processes of self-assessment, career exploration, and job search. It contains practical advice and information, charts, and graphs, all designed to help you discover yourself and find your place in the world of work.

Tempel, Eugene R., Sara B. Cobb, and Warren E. Ilchman, eds. *The Professionalization of Fundraising*, no. 15 (Spring 1997), p. 72.

This is a collection of readings regarding the development of professionalization in fundraising, ranging from considerations of how to acquire the appropriate training and education to issues of public trust.

Experienced fundraisers and other experts point to new and continuing trends shaping the fundraising profession and the job market:

Ethical Challenges

One problem that has multiplied, along with the growing number of seven- and eight-figure gifts in recent years, is the donor who wants to call all the shots in exchange for large donations, says Walter Sczudlo, general counsel of the Association for Fundraising Professionals, in Alexandria, Virginia. "Donors want to build a wing in a hospital and use only a certain company's equipment, because they own stock in the company or they're good friends with someone there." Sometimes, he adds, the fundraiser ends up fighting board members who want to give the donor whatever he or she wants, even though it is not in the organization's best interest.

More Foundations

One reflection of donors' desire for control over their philanthropic dollars is the "huge run up" in foundations being created by families and wealthy individuals such as Bill Gates, founder of Microsoft, says Bruce Flessner of Benz Whaley Flessner, a Minneapolis fundraising consulting firm. Over the long run, fundraisers who work with foundations will become much more important, as the wealth in the funds grows and the founders' control wanes with age or death, according to Flessner and other experts.

High Demand

For years now, the need for seasoned fundraisers has been increasing faster than the number of available candidates. The demand has stayed high, regardless of ups or downs in the economy. When times are good, charities look to development officers to help them reap the benefits, by launching capital campaigns, large-scale special events, and other fund-raising efforts. When the economy is bad, the same organizations rely on fundraisers to protect them from declines in giving.

Younger Fundraisers

More and more people are entering the field right after college—a reversal of the more common scenario a few years ago, when development officers joked that no one starts out to be a fundraiser. "I would love to see the age demographics now, because I'm sure it's changed," says Abbie von Schlegell, chief development officer at the Shakespeare Theatre in Washington, D.C. "I see people starting in development who plan to stay all the way through their career." What this means for older people, she notes, is being in competition with younger people who have less experience.

More Scrutiny

Job candidates under 35, however, aren't necessarily getting the higher-level development jobs, particularly at the largest, best-paying institutions, headhunters say. "The younger people are out of luck with my clients," says Steven Ast, a Stamford, Connecticut, executive recruiter who fills top fundraising jobs, particularly at universities. Nonprofit organizations, he says, "are more savvy, and board members are scrutinizing candidates much more carefully now, to make sure they really have the experience of bringing in the money."

Pigeonholing

Most charities do a poor job of training up-and-coming fundraisers in a broad range of skills so they can advance in the organization, says Jay Berger of Morris & Berger, an executive recruiting firm in Pasadena, California. "They're losing a lot of young talent because of this," he says. "People in annual gifts, special events, or even planned gifts get pigeonholed in that area of development," he notes, so it is often hard for them to get the senior management jobs. To get more skills—and the mentoring they need to advance—a few fundraisers have turned to fundraising consultants, paying them out of pocket for coaching on how to get ahead. Rita Fuerst, a Boston fundraising consultant, says she was hired by a development officer who paid for six months of coaching on management skills such as creating strategic plans and case statements so he could advance. "Oftentimes," says Fuerst, "you're on your own in terms of professional development."

HOLLY HALL spent a dozen years covering fundraising and related topics as a writer and senior editor for *The Chronicle of Philanthropy*. Recently, she was recruited to the American Red Cross, where she serves as the editor of the organization's new national magazine, *The Humanitarian*. A former editor with *Psychology Today* magazine, she has also written for a variety of publications, including other fundraising texts and the *Washington Post*.

PROFESSIONALS SAY . . .

A great volunteer once told me and a group of young volunteers why he loved to ask people to give. He said when he asks for a gift the organization wins because it can serve more people. The people we are serving win because we can provide better services. Most importantly the people I ask for a gift win because they have an opportunity to participate in their community. It is this dedication that I believe is important for all of us who work in philanthropy. For people who are working with or intend to work with charitable and philanthropic organizations—especially those who wish to join the noblest of fields, fundraising, I offer these professional points for your career: (1) Work for charitable and philanthropic organizations that, if you could afford to, you would work for free. Love your work. Love your cause. (2) Learn about philanthropy, its history in the United States, and how it is conducted in other countries. Know more about the laws and regulations governing charitable and philanthropic organizations and charitable solicitation than your organization's attorney. (3) Provide a voice for the people you serve. Encourage them to participate in the community. The greatest good we do is bringing about change in society. (4) Treat your staff like volunteers and your volunteers and your organization's clients as if they are your boss. (5) Find people in the field you respect and speak with them frequently. Have faith. One person can change the world.

Rita Fuerst Adams, CFRE, President, Charitable and Philanthropic Management Counsel

When I started my position in 1988, the attitude about the primarily female constituency was that "women don't give." The dean actually offered a free hour of marriage and family therapy from our high-rated program in order to get couples to give equally! In trying to find ways to motivate that constituency, I found that regardless of the group, if the organization's mission is important you can find ways to motivate donors. Educating donors is key. Focusing on mission, impact of gifts, and stewardship turned our program around. In addition, building my knowledge of research has had a huge impact on my career.

Cheryl Altinkemer, Director of Development and Alumni Relations at the School of Consumer Affairs and Family Science at Purdue University, Layfayette, Indiana.

In addition to the requisite technical knowledge, effective fundraisers will also have the ability to create three facilitative conditions essential in the process of soliciting a gift: Empathy—the ability to understand why a person gives from his or her perspective; Genuineness—the ability to be unpretentious, both in thought and speech, with the prospect during all stages of the cultivation process; and Respect—the ability to treat every donor, no matter whether "big" or "small," with equal regard and worthy of being valued.

Jack Boyson, Professor of Communications, Johns Hopkins University and Senior Planner, International Youth Foundation

CHAPTER 5

Value of Fundraising Skills and Experience in Other Careers and Positions

SIDEBAR BY CHARLES H. HAMILTON

W hat do these people have in common?

- Lynn is vice president of an international organization that handles humanitarian aid and funds microenterprise. His former experience includes a high-level position in the United Nations offices in New York.

- Kathy heads up a major association. She is concerned with member services and managing a major conference. In a previous job she organized a museum of medical history.

- Rick is executive director of a zoo in a Southern California city. His past experience was with organizations like World Wildlife Fund.

- Gene is executive director of an association that has member groups from all over the United States. He interacts with other leading organizations in the field of leadership.

- Ellen is head of a women's fund at a community foundation. She comes from a nonprofit leadership background.

- Allan is head of a Hispanic institute for spirituality. He conducts workshops over a wide region, and is an author and leading theologian.

- Marilyn is a university president. She has a stellar career in higher education administration, beginning with a dean's position.

- John heads a corporate foundation. He has the privilege of being a philanthropist with someone else's money, and he travels to many colleges and universities, giving away scholarships.

- Mable runs a women's shelter. She is also a psychologist with a Ph.D. and presents workshops on abuse prevention.

So what do these people have in common? None of them is a fundraising professional, but their professions include fundraising. Securing financial resources for their organization is one of their leadership responsibilities. These people are committed to fundraising, and know it is very important for their organizations' success.

Fundraising is a demanding profession. It requires the development of numerous skills, and is most successful when implemented and developed in a planned and organized way. The complexity of human relations in the fundraising process entails diplomacy, tact, fairness, friendliness, objectivity, warmth, and, above all, interest in the other person. Communication skills are of great importance in a fundraising career path, as is an understanding of basic finance. And it doesn't hurt to have some psychology courses as well as management training as part of professional development in the career of fundraising.

With this array of qualities and credentials that are a part of the successful professional, it is no wonder that fundraising is not only an exciting career in and of itself, but is also a significant part of other professions and careers. Indeed, the ability to fundraise is vital for many professions, and success in fundraising often boosts a person's career advancement.

In this chapter, we'll first consider the prevalent qualities and characteristics that are generally required for professionalism and achievement in fundraising, and how these are also requisites in other careers that may involve fundraising. Then we'll look at how fundraising ability plays a significant role in a sampling of career tracks and goals.

We cannot be successful in the entire process of raising funds unless we develop and enhance certain personal and professional qualities. More often than not, these same qualities are also requirements for success in other professions and occupations. I have selected 10 broad categories, beginning with concrete skills and moving toward more subjective elements.

1. *Professional competence and technical skill.* Fundraising demands proficiency in written and spoken communication. It also requires good time management ability, basic financial acumen, and computer literacy. Materials have to be written well, and communication with volunteers, donors, colleagues, and the general public must take place at the highest level of discourse. Because of the complexity of managing a fundraising program, time management is a critical skill to acquire, if a person is not inherently inclined to being well organized. Much depends on a fundraising professional's understanding of financial accountability and credibility; a basic knowledge of accounting and reporting is important to have. Finally, without computer skills, a fundraising professional is greatly hampered in all of the above, from computing to tracking donor gifts.

   These skills are also important in many other professions, such as program management and administration, public relations, event management, and marketing. Therefore, mastering the qualities necessary for successful fundraising is useful because other career options might become available, if desired.

2. *Ability and motivation to learn.* Fundraising is a dynamic process, and best practices change frequently. The outstanding fundraiser reads, attends workshops, interacts with colleagues and mentors, and is in a constant learning mode. To sit back and do things the way they have always been done is simply not wise or even possible in fundraising.

   This quality is a component of success for almost all careers; therefore, the fundraiser who makes learning a daily task and takes responsibility for updating knowledge and acquiring new information is also prepared to expand with career options, whether in fundraising itself or other nonprofit positions (as well as some jobs in the other two sectors).

3. *Human relations skills.* Knowing how to interact and deal with all kinds of people is a quality that should be ingrained in the successful fundraising professional. This goes beyond just good communication skills. It means acquiring sensitivity toward the needs and desires of others, being able to accept suggestions and even criticism graciously, interacting on a social basis with ease—particularly paying attention to the comfort levels of others—and being diplomatic.

Without a doubt, these skills are vital for almost all other professions. Most job ads, such as in *The Chronicle of Philanthropy,* usually list "good human relation skills" as a criterion for hiring.

4. *Creativity.* Fundraising professionals can't afford to become stagnant. They must always be open to new ideas, to innovative ways of doing things. Otherwise, how will the organization and its fundraising case be memorable? An attitude of "we've always done it this way" just won't do. Creativity is important on a wide scale, from writing a direct mail piece that will receive at least some attention to giving distinctive recognition to a major donor.

    The ability to "think outside the box" is critical for most other professions that may be based on the same skills as those needed in fundraising. In fact, most executive search personnel look for evidence of the ability to think in new and different ways.

5. *Leadership.* Leadership doesn't mean having the top position in an organization, or the power associated with such a position. The fundraising professional can lead from the middle. Managing from the middle is not a new concept; leading, however, is. Although we must continue to manage, we must also recognize that we are uniquely placed to accomplish a great deal. This requires understanding that power is not just positional; it also comes from the ability to influence others.

    We work in service to others' goals and purposes, we often have more expertise than authority, we don't have the final say but we do have important influence, and our most important "clients" are people who often don't understand our function. We share the challenge of working with people and processes that move the organization toward its primary mission. Most of us do this from the middle, not the top, of "corporate" pyramids. We are support or service professionals. This role is important in determining the organization's strategic direction and is essential for getting results. It may be difficult, challenging, rewarding, and growthful. Our ultimate purpose should be to serve in the achievement of others' goals and purposes while simultaneously reaching for our own, both in fulfilling our organization's mission and our personal one.

Leadership is much more than a recognized position at the top of an organization or group. It means being able to motivate and influence others, to provide expertise and advice, to have the knowledge that leads to credibility, and to get things done by achieving consensus—the willingness of all participants to support the decision or action. Such leadership qualities are indispensable for most careers, not just fundraising.

6. *Ability to command respect and self-confidence.* When people trust the fundraising professional and the organization represented with their money, they must have confidence in the credibility and integrity of both. Our own self-esteem and therefore self-confidence projects onto our work. Low self-confidence influences behavior; negative thoughts and feelings translate into self-defeating behavior, thereby creating self-fulfilling prophecies. It also affects our relationships with people.

   Belief in the value of what we do on behalf of our organizations and building credibility through excellence in the profession are important for fundraising success. As has been noted earlier in this book, fundraising isn't without some negative perceptions. We must overcome these and inspire respect and confidence from our donors, as well as all other constituents.

7. *A positive outlook and vision.* American poet Langston Hughes wrote, "Hang on to dreams for if dreams die, life is a broken-winged bird that cannot fly." While keeping both feet on the ground, the successful fundraiser maintains a vision of the future and shares it with donors and all other constituents. This is part of the leadership role that fundraising professionals play in an organization. It is not enough to just work toward reaching this month's or this year's goal. We want our causes to be sustainable and to grow, and we share this vision with others. Adversity does come, but maintaining a positive attitude despite problems and obstacles we confront daily will cause others to want to be part of our causes.

   There is no future in believing that something cannot be done. The future is in making it happen. History is replete with individuals who made dogmatic statements that something could not be done. For example, "Everything that can be invented has been invented," Charles H. Duell, director of the U.S. Patent Office, said in 1899. "There is no likelihood man can ever tap the power of the atom," was said by Robert Millikan, who received the Nobel Prize in Physics in 1923. And Lord Kelvin, president of the Royal Society, said in 1895, "Heavier than air flying machines are impossible." Fortunately, those who knew all the reasons some things couldn't be done were wrong, and others chose not to listen![1]

8. *Honesty and integrity.* It takes courage and character to win at anything, not just fundraising. We must know what is right and wrong, and use standards of ethical behavior in both business and personal lives. A strong code of ethical values, both personal and organizational, will help our donors trust us with their investments of time and money. At a time when headlines are rampant with unethical behavior, ranging from athletics to Wall Street to politics, it is more important than ever to engage in ethical practices in fundraising.

9. *Adaptability, flexibility, and perseverance.* Fundraising—indeed, the nonprofit sector—changes constantly. John Gardner said, "Life is hard. Just to keep on going is sometimes an act of courage. . . . As a rule you have to have picked up some mileage and some dents in your fenders before you understand." He goes on to say, "Life is an endless unfolding and, if we wish it to be, an endless process of self discovery, an endless and unpredictable dialogue between our own potentialities and the life situations in which we find ourselves."[2]

   Being able to adapt to situations, both the positive challenges as well as the severe problems we and our organizations encounter, is a vital trait for fundraising success, as well as all career success. Moving toward our goals with flexibility is an everyday necessity. Organizations and their environments are dynamic.

10. *The courage to fail.* Everything worthwhile and everything new involves the risk of failure; however, failure is not fatal. Also, failure may just be a deviation from a stated goal. Failure must be put into perspective. The fundraising professional doesn't always succeed in getting the major gift, reaching the annual fund goal, or achieving 100 percent board giving. The professional must learn to identify the causes for the *nonsuccess* of the moment (a term preferable to *failure*)

and be able to plan on how to overcome the obstacles and move toward achievement. Notice these distinguished figures from American history and culture and their relationship to failure.

Douglas MacArthur dreamed of attending West Point, but was turned down twice. It wasn't until his third application that he was accepted. He had a stunning military career because he behaved like a leader.

Henry Ford went bankrupt in his first year in the automobile business. Two years later his second company also failed. But you must admit, his third one has done rather well.

Twenty-three publishers rejected a children's book. But the twenty-fourth publisher accepted it for publication, and the book sold 6 million copies. The author? Dr. Seuss!

Charles Schulz failed algebra, Latin, English, and physics in high school—and had his cartoons rejected by the yearbook staff. He once applied for a cartoonist job at the Walt Disney studios, but was turned down.

Emily Dickinson wrote about 1,800 poems, but only 7 were published in her lifetime.

These qualities, while highly critical for a fundraising professional to possess, aren't the exclusive domain of this profession. They are just as vital for many other careers. Therefore, if the professional in fundraising masters these qualities and acquires these characteristics, they can be used in other careers as well. To what careers can the fundraising professional aspire? Of what use is fundraising expertise, along with the development of skills and characteristics that contribute to fundraising success? Here are a few ideas related to career advancement, as well as career and skill transference.

First, the fundraising professional may wish to move up the career ladder within an organization, or move to a different position elsewhere. Mastering these skills and qualities will make career advancement more feasible. Second, the fundraising professional may wish to take on different or additional responsibilities in related fields, or even transfer the skills and traits just discussed to new career possibilities. Fundraising involves the acquiring of characteristics and expertise that serve well in many other endeavors. For example, college and university presidents need to spend considerable time in fundraising. At times, professionals in advancement (as fundraising is often labeled in education) can move toward presidential roles. The same is true for presidents or executive directors of almost all other organizations in the nonprofit sector, such as health care, human service, arts, and cultural causes. Other areas where fundraising skills can be used are in program management in most organizations, such as in youth programs, or deans of universities or colleges, who increasingly are responsible for raising funds. Fundraising is valuable for a leadership position (leadership by title and authority) in every organization.

Then there are those positions that can rely on expertise acquired through fundraising competence. These include marketing, both in not-for-profit and for-profit organizations; training and teaching; advertising; freelance writing (including proposals and business plans); public speaking (it is no surprise that some of the best fundraisers come from the ranks of preachers because of the cross-over of necessary abilities); customer and client relations; and project as well as department management. The list isn't exhaustive. What is valuable to understand is that success in fundraising can also, if desired, lead to success in other professions, in addition to career advancement in the field itself. After all, a person can actually craft a better résumé and job application, and do well in an interview, if the qualities described in this chapter are acquired!

Career changes occur, and they occur with more frequency in our era, in this decade and millennium. Although fundraising is certainly a worthwhile and challenging profession in which one could stay for the extent of a working life, reality indicates that personal preferences and unavoidable circumstances sometimes cause us to seek employment in other professions and places. Fundraising ability is never wasted because it includes adaptable traits and qualities.

You cannot know where you will go in the future, but if you give yourself the best chance of success in the fundraising profession, you also have the best chance of handling the future, regardless of where it takes you. Aim high, and you'll have a winning life and career.

More people volunteer and contribute money than vote. While some would suggest that this is a disgrace, there is another point of view; that this is evidence of the robust nature of what might be called philanthropic citizenship. Americans are generous, and fundraising professionals are at the crux of the connection between people's charitable instincts and their causes. Thus, fundraising expertise is a significant leadership skill for a voluntary society at work.

In the foundation world, having had fundraising experience can be particularly valuable for many reasons. Perhaps most important, you will vividly remember the incredible power differential between grant seekers (fundraisers) and grant makers. Hopefully, you will be wary on two counts. On the one hand, you will know to be very careful about what you say to grant seekers. Since your words carry the promise of funding, a simple statement can unrealistically raise hopes, or a minor suggestion can be heard as a requirement. On the other hand, there seems to be a naturally tendency to flatter foundation executives (there is an old joke that when you become a foundation executive, that is the last time you will have a bad meal, tell a bad joke, or get an honest compliment). Remembering your fundraising experience may help you avoid beginning to believe your views are actually more important or insightful than they really are!

Fundraising experience can guard against the games that are played between grant seekers and grant makers. It is one step in becoming a "servant leader," as Robert Greenleaf describes it. And that is certainly important if, as a foundation executive, you are to make the fullest possible contribution to the voluntary sector.

CHARLES H. HAMILTON is executive director of The Clark Foundation in New York City. He currently serves on the board of The Council on Foundations and is chair of the Council's Committee on Family Foundations. He is editor of *The Cultures of Giving* (in two volumes) for New Directions in Philanthropic Fundraising. He has spoken and written widely on philanthropy. In 2001, he edited *Living the Legacy: The Values of a Family's Philanthropy Across Generations*.

PROFESSIONALS SAY . . .

It is a privilege to be a fundraiser. There is no greater calling than to be in a position which encourages and enables people to achieve their philanthropic goals. Fundraising professionals are vital to a nonprofit organization's success. Individuals who are responsible for raising funds should never be too far removed from the actual service or program for which they are raising funds.

Brad Kruse, Organizational Development Specialist, Initiative Foundation, Little Falls, Minnesota.

As a program director, my fundraising skills have been essential to keeping the program operational during times of transition and climate change. I now make sure all my professional staff understand fundraising basics, including how to write a grant proposal.

Paula Allen, Director, Youth as Resources of Central Indiana, Indianapolis, Indiana.

PART THREE

Preparing for a Career in Fundraising

M any who work in fundraising found their way into the profession in a roundabout way. In fact, the metaphors people use in describing the beginning of their careers are picturesque—"I slid into it," "I backed into it," or "I fell into it." For many years this was true. People entered the profession by accident or had to learn fundraising out of necessity. Although this type of career entry still occurs, more often than not people of all ages plan their career paths more carefully. Of course this has been possible because of the proliferation of higher education courses, centers for the study of nonprofit management and fundraising, workshops and conferences, and other guides and aids for career development. So, while the majority of professionals in fundraising sort of "ended up" in the field, a significant surge has taken place for providing a more organized and planned approach to fundraising as a career—a new generation, so to speak.

Part Three contains chapters that address the various ways a person can be prepared for a career in fundraising. This includes higher education degree programs, as well as training opportunities, workshops and conferences, on-the-job training, and mentoring. These opportunities for becoming competent are available for the high school student as well as the adult professional choosing to change careers—and all other types of would-be professionals ranging between these two extremes.

Chapter 6 outlines available educational programs, including undergraduate and graduate degrees. These have proliferated in the last decade, thereby increasing the potential of serious study almost anywhere in the nation. The chapter provides an overview of academic programs that focus on nonprofit leadership and fundraising and includes a list of centers and programs currently available, plus a sample curriculum.

In addition to formal education, there are numerous training programs such as workshops, seminars, and professional conferences. Because there is a wealth of professional opportunity in this area of career development, guidelines will be provided in Chapter 7 that assist the reader in selecting the best offerings, including how to evaluate the credibility and possible benefits of the program. The range and scope of training will be included. As part of this chapter, there will be a discussion of the certification process and its implications for the field, as well as for career success.

Since the beginning of the formalization of fundraising as a career, the main methods of entering the profession were on-the-job training and mentoring. Today these are still significant ways of becoming proficient, often as part of a more formal career track. Chapter 8 gives advice on how to maximize such an experience, secure and select a mentor, and chart a professional career path in a possibly unstructured learning environment.

Although the numbers of young people seeking a career in fundraising are growing significantly, an equal number of mid-career professionals also find fundraising to be a viable and desirable career option. Chapter 9 gives suggestions for the mature professional wishing to change careers and discusses the issues, concerns, and possibilities in such a career move.

Chapter 10 focuses on the professional stories of several individuals who have either sought fundraising as a career or have made the transition from another profession. The stories are inspiration and factual, and help readers identify with professionals who personify the prototype most similar to their career aspirations, and to give real-life context for the information in the section.

CHAPTER 6

Preparation Through Academic Programs

SIDEBAR BY JAMIE LEVY

In a national survey to which 689 business leaders responded, the consensus was that the quality of work force skills and education is one of today's major challenges. The top five skills needed in any workplace, the respondents agreed, were verbal communication, interpersonal skills, math, written communication, and business skills.[1] Some of these skills can be acquired through short-term training such as workshops, self-study, and mentoring (as will be addressed in other chapters in this section), but for the serious fundraising professional, the development of skills will probably take place within an academic environment, whether or not the degree path will be specific to nonprofit management.

Prior to the availability of formal educational offerings in nonprofit management and fundraising, most persons acquired a bachelor's degree before embarking on a fundraising career. The most likely disciplines leading to fundraising were communications, management, public relations, and, to some extent, social work and psychology. Certainly courses from these areas are worthwhile for success in fundraising, but most career seekers lacked the specific training in nonprofit management, budgeting, fundraising, and philanthropy. In order to meet these needs, some major areas of study, such as social work and health care administration, offered some management education in the specialty areas. In some cases, students were urged to take business courses on the assumption that the nonprofit organization should be, or could be, managed like a business.

As demands for accountability and professionalism in the nonprofit sector have increased, organizations have had to become more businesslike. This means they need expertise in marketing, personnel management, strategic planning, budgeting, and other components of a credible organization.

Because of some scandals and accusations of mismanagement, the nonprofit sector acquired a reputation for being "soft," not sufficiently accountable, and lacking in attention to management detail. Although in many cases this was not true, the myths and perceptions persisted. As a result, an increasing emphasis was placed on providing specialized education to persons seeking employment, or already employed in, the nonprofit sector.

Currently those seeking to hire fundraising personnel still indicate a minimum of a bachelor's degree as a requirement for employment, while some organizations prefer master's or even doctorates among their candidates. This is particularly true, of course, among higher education institutions. What has changed, however, is the availability of specialized degrees, certificates, and courses that offer a professional the opportunity to focus on the eventual career, and not put together his or her educational experience bit by bit, a course here and a workshop there.

As the number of nonprofits has increased nationwide, from 1.38 million in 1990 to 1.62 million in 1998 (latest research figures by INDEPENDENT SECTOR), so have the number and availability of courses of study in colleges and university. This is true for both public and private institutions. In the early 1990s, higher education institutions that offered courses in nonprofit management, including fundraising, were mostly in the East. Now educational possibilities are available in most regions of the United States.

These program offerings include:

- Master's degree programs
- Master in public administration (MPA), with a concentration on nonprofit management
- Undergraduate coursework
- Certificate programs
- Fellowships
- Doctoral programs that allow concentrations in nonprofit management
- Interdisciplinary degree programs
- Summer institutes

A debate among academic institutions continues as to where degree programs and courses should be placed. Some believe that nonprofit management courses should be in schools of business, while others argue for public administration as a home for such study. Others still believe that nonprofit education should be integrated in the major field of study, such as arts administration. A few programs are free standing; these tend to be interdisciplinary. Such a debate is not a problem for the career seeker. It simply means that attention should be paid to the various educational options available.

The most likely curricula for a program of study would include:

- Management of nonprofit organizations
- Accounting and financial management
- Marketing
- Volunteer and personnel management
- Legal issues
- Economics
- Overview of the sector
- Some history and philosophy of the sector
- Research

Some may include tax policies, government and the nonprofit sector, and issues of the sector and its organizations.

Oddly enough, not all programs require fundraising courses or similar "nuts and bolts" education, but often these are available as electives. This is due to another ongoing debate in academe—how much practical experience should be included in higher education, and whether such experience should be acquired elsewhere. Case studies, however, are a popular method of study in graduate courses and therefore allow for experiential learning.

Most programs include an internship and possibly directed study of a special area of interest. This allows the student to gain experience, work in an organization that interests him or her, and build a résumé.

Despite the availability of degree and certificate programs in nonprofit management and the fact that students from these areas of study have done well, some hiring organizations still prefer candidates from traditional areas of study such as public or business administration, or a degree in the field on which the student chooses to focus and build a career, such as health care.

An overview of the type of study available—from undergraduate to doctoral programs of study—may be helpful to the person choosing to study for a career in nonprofit management and specializing in fundraising.

- *Undergraduate work is somewhat lacking.* Some introductory courses to the nonprofit sector and nonprofit management are available, and a few institutions have been innovative enough to actually offer a major or at least a program of study. Most of these would be interdisciplinary in nature. Also, summer institutes are available as well, which allow the undergraduate to concentrate on the nonprofit sector.

- *Certificate programs are available for academic credit.* Some specialize in non-profit management in general, while others focus on subspecialties such as fundraising. American Humanics, which is a national alliance of colleges, universities, and nonprofit organizations, prepares under-graduates for careers with youth and human service agencies. Certificates are also available outside of academe; these will be discussed in the following chapter.

- *Fellowships allow students to study specific issues and areas of nonprofit organizations.* Fellowships tend to attract exceptional students, who have the opportunity to specialize in a particular field. For example, at the Center on Philanthropy at Indiana University, Jane Addams Fellows spend a year in concentrated study of the sector and many go on to either work in fundraising, nonprofit management, or further graduate study.

- *Some master's degree programs allow concentrations in nonprofit management.* Frequently these are either MPA or MBA degrees. What is attractive about some master's degree programs is that they are often offered through an executive track, allowing professionals to acquire a degree without discontinuing their careers. There are additional master's de-gree programs such as the MA in philanthropic studies, offered by Indiana University.

- *Doctoral programs are few, but several allow students to focus on nonprofit management.* These may be housed in departments such as management, history, economics, or social work. There are also executive doctoral programs that allow a student to continue a career while also pursuing a degree. There will probably be doctoral programs available in the near future that focus specifically on philanthropy and the nonprofit sector; already some institutions are studying such possibilities.

Two professors from the Center for Public Service at Seton Hall University have compiled a Web site that lists all the offerings in nonprofit management education at university-based programs. This includes courses through continuing education, undergraduate programs, and graduate courses or degrees. (See "Further Information" for Web site address.)

What courses might a student expect to take if enrolling in a certificate or degree program? Following are sample descriptions of such programs.

Nonprofit Management Certificate (This program of study is offered at the School of Public and Environmental Affairs, Indiana University, Indianapolis Campus)

> *This certificate is designed to serve the needs of individuals who would like exposure to the nonprofit sector and nonprofit management issues and who do not wish or need to pursue a master's degree in nonprofit management. This certificate complements other courses of study or career experience in such areas as social work, library science, and parks and recreation. Required courses are Human Resource Management in Nonprofits, Management in the Nonprofit Sector, Financial Management for Nonprofit Organizations, and two additional graduate public affairs courses.*

Certificate in Nonprofit Management (This curriculum is offered by the Mandel Center for Nonprofit Organizations at Case Western)

> *The CNM is a nondegree professional certification for experienced practitioners. It provides knowledge in critical areas of management methodology and the operational environment of the nonprofit sector.*

Managing Institutional Advancement (This curriculum is from the University of Chicago)

> *This is a series of seminars and workshops created to help senior professionals direct the many processes that lead to increased philanthropic support. To earn a certificate, participants must complete four seminars and an institutional project.*

Master of Public Affairs (This curriculum is offered at Indiana University)

> *This master's program prepares individuals for positions of leadership in the public sector. Professional managers in the public and nonprofit arenas face complex, constantly changing issues that are difficult to resolve within the framework of a single, traditional academic discipline. This MPA program provides public and human service managers with the skills to cope with challenging human and technical issues in an era of change.*
>
> *The nonprofit management concentration is designed for persons employed in nonprofit agencies and those seeking employment in the nonprofit sector. Skills in leadership, decision making, and problem solving are learned, as well as technical expertise in areas such as fundraising, human resource management in nonprofits, legal aspects of philanthropy, and others.*

Master of Arts in Philanthropic Studies (This curriculum is offered by Indiana University)

> *This is a 36-hour credit program that includes 24 hours of course work central to the study of philanthropy and 6 hours of elective course work. Core courses include The Nonprofit and Voluntary Sector, Civil Society and Philanthropy, History of Philanthropy in the West, Human and Fi-*

nancial Resources for Philanthropy, Ethics and Values of Philanthropy, and an internship. This master's is also available as an Executive Program for students who cannot attend on a traditional residential basis.[2]

Master of Nonprofit Administration (Curriculum is offered at University of San Francisco)

The MNA is designed for managers in the INDEPENDENT SECTOR. This program applies the basic concepts, skills, and analytic tools of management to nonprofit organization leadership. The curriculum provides the student with an understanding of the issues and problems faced in nonprofit organization management. The course work analyzes the political, economic, and social environments of nonprofit organizations. The program focuses on five major areas: resource acquisition, resource management, organizational behavior and management theory, context studies of nonprofit organizational development, and quantitative analysis skills.

Master of Nonprofit Organizations (Curriculum offered at the Mandel Center for Nonprofit Organizations, Case Western)

This is a 60-credit-hour program that includes 33 hours of required core courses, 12 hours of optional "choice" courses, and 15 hours of elective courses. It also has a format to accommodate working professionals. The curriculum structure is organized within four thematic areas: nonprofit purposes, traditions and contexts; analytic thinking for nonprofit leaders; generating and managing resources; and leading nonprofit organizations.

Master of Arts, Philanthropy and Development (Offered by Saint Mary's University of Minnesota)

The MA program in Philanthropy and Development serves the development professional seeking advanced education, professional academic credentials, additional expertise, and a broad philosophical perspective. It is offered in a summer format.

▓ FURTHER READING

Mirabella, Roseanne M., and Naomi B. Wish. Nonprofit Management Education, http://pirate.shu.edu/~mirabero/kellogg.html

This web site contains information on academic programs and courses offered in nonprofit management.

Mirabella, Roseanne M., and Naomi B. Wish. "Educational Impact of Graduate Nonprofit Degree Program Needs: Perspectives of Multiple Stakeholders." *Nonprofit Management and Leadership*, vol. 9, no. 3 (Spring 1999).

An examination of how academic offerings affect the nonprofit sector, based on 10 site visits. The study addresses the goals of degree programs, what should be taught, the outcomes of academic programs, and how effectiveness is measured.

Wish, Naomi B., and Roseanne M. Mirabella. "Curriculum Variations in Nonprofit Management Graduate Programs." *Nonprofit Management and Leadership*, vol. 9, no. 1 (Fall 1998).

This is a snapshot of the current universe of programs that focus on the management of nonprofit organizations at 148 colleges and universities.

Nonprofit Volunteer Sector Quarterly (NSVQ). Thousand Oaks, CA: Sage Publications, Inc.

This is the journal of the Association for Research on Nonprofit Organizations and Voluntary Action (ARNOVA). It is an international, interdisciplinary journal that reports on research and programs related to voluntarism, citizen participation, philanthropy, and nonprofit organizations.

Young, Dennis R. "Alternative Approaches to the Education of Nonprofit Sector Leaders and Managers." *The Case International Journal of Educational Advancement,* vol. 1, no. 1 (June 2000), pp. 53–66.

▪ FURTHER INFORMATION

Center for Community Partnerships
Penn Program for Public Service
University of Pennsylvania
133 S. 36th Street, Suite 519
Philadelphia, PA 19104
Phone: 215-898-5351
Fax: 215-573-2799
Web site: www.upenn.edu/ccp

Center for Nonprofit Leadership
Regis University
3333 Regis Boulevard; Mail Stop L-16
Adult Learning Center #403
Denver, CO 80221-1099
Phone: 303-458-4302
Fax: 303-964-5538
E-mail: palezan@regis.edu
Web site: www.regis.edu/spsgrad

Center for Nonprofit Management
University of St. Thomas
Graduate School of Business
1000 La Salle Avenue
25H 525
Minneapolis, MN 55405-2001
Phone: 651-962-4292
Fax: 651-962-4810
E-mail: pswilder@stthomas.edu

Center for Public Service
Seton Hall University
400 South Orange Avenue
South Orange, NJ 07079-2691
Phone: 973-761-9510
Fax: 973-275-2463
E-mail: cps@shu.edu
Web site: http://artsci.shu.edu/cps

Center for the Study of Philanthropy
Graduate School and University Center
City University of New York
365 Fifth Avenue
New York, NY 10016-4309
Phone: 212-817-7000
Fax: 212-817-1572
E-mail: csp@gc.cuny.edu
Web site: www.gc.cuny.edu

Center for the Study of Philanthropy and Voluntarism
Terry Sanford Institute of Public Policy
Duke University
Box 90249
Durham, NC 27708-0249
Phone: 919-613-7314
Fax: 919-681-8288
E-mail: malme@pps.duke.edu
Web site: www.pubpol.duke.edu/centers/philvol

Center for the Study of Voluntary Organizations and Service
Georgetown Public Policy Institute
3240 Prospect Street, NW, LL
Washington, DC 20007-3214
Phone: 202-687-0580
Fax: 202-687-0517
E-mail: hodgkinv@gunet.georgetown.edu
Web site: www.georgetown.edu/grad/gppi/scholarship

The Center on Philanthropy at Indiana University
The Fund Raising School
550 West North Street, Suite 301
Indianapolis, IN 46202-3272
Phone: 317-274-4200
Fax: 317-684-8939
E-mail: TFRS@iupui.edu
Web site: www.philanthropy.iupui.edu

Center on Public Policy
The Union Institute
1710 Rhode Island Ave. NW, Suite 1100
Washington, DC 20036-3007
Phone: 202-496-1630
Fax: 202-496-1635
E-mail: tui.dc@tui.edu
Web site: www.tui.edu

Grand Valley State University
401 W. Fulton Street
232C DeVos Center
Grand Rapids, MI 49504
Phone: 616-336-7585
Fax: 616-336-7592
E-mail: vaniwaad@gvsu.edu
Web site: www4.gvsu.edu/philanthropy

Executive Nonprofit Leadership Program
Institute of Public Service
Seattle University
900 Broadway
Seattle, WA 98122-4340
Phone: 206-296-5440
Fax: 206-296-5402
Web site: www.mnpl.org

Haas School of Business
University of California, Berkeley
Berkeley, CA 94720-1900
Phone: 510-643-1419
Fax: 510-642-4700
E-mail: Vanloo@haas.berkely.edu
Web site: www.haas.berkeley.edu

Hauser Center for Nonprofit Organizations
Harvard University
79 J.F.K. Street
Cambridge, MA 02138
Phone: 617-496-5675
Fax: 617-495-0996
E-mail: hauser_center@harvard.edu
Web site: www.ksghauser.harvard.edu

Institute for Nonprofit Management
Hatfield School of Government
Division of Public Administration
Portland State University
P.O. Box 751
Portland, OR 97207-0751
Phone: 503-725-8217
Fax: 503-725-8250
E-mail: Feeneys@pdx.edu

Institute for Nonprofit Organization Management, CPS
University of San Francisco
2130 Fulton Street
San Francisco, CA 94117-1047
Phone: 415-422-6867
Fax: 415-422-5881
E-mail: inom@usfca.edu
Web site: www.inom.org

Lincoln Filene Center
University College of Citizenship and Public Service
Tufts University
Medford, MA 02155
Phone: 617-627-3433
Fax: 617-627-3401
Web site: www.uccps.tufts.edu

Mandel Center for Nonprofit Organizations
Case Western Reserve University
10900 Euclid Avenue
Cleveland, OH 44106-7167
Phone: 216-368-2275
Fax: 216-368-8592
E-mail: jps@po.cwru.edu
Web site: www.cwru.edu/mandelcenter

Midwest Center for Nonprofit Leadership
Cookingham Institute
University of Missouri/Kansas City
310 Bloch, 5110 Cherry
Kansas City, MO 64110-2499
Phone: 816-235-2342
Fax: 816-235-1169
E-mail: renzd@umkc.edu
Web site: www.mcnl.org

National Center on Philanthropy and Law
New York University Law School
110 West 3rd Street, 2nd Floor
New York, NY 10012
Phone: 212-998-6168
Fax: 212-995-3149
E-mail: ncpl.info@nyu.edu
Web site: www.law.nyu.edu/ncpl

Nonprofit Management Program
Robert J. Milano Graduate School
for Management and Urban Policy
72 Fifth Avenue, 4th Floor
New York, NY 10011
Phone: 212-229-5950
Fax: 212-229-8935
E-mail: mgsinfo@newschool.edu
Web Site: www.newschool.edu/milano

Nonprofit Management Studies
George Mason University, Arlington Campus
3401 N. Fairfax Drive
Mail Stop 5A7
Arlington, VA 22201-4498
Phone: 703-993-8189
Fax: 703-993-8241
E-mail: plewis1@gmu.edu
Web Site: www.gmu.edu

Not-for-Profit Management
School for Management and Technology
University of Maryland University College
3501 University Boulevard East
Adelphi, MD 20783
Phone: 301-985-7200
Fax: 301-985-4611
E-mail: gradschool@polaris.umuc.edu
Web site: www.umuc.edu

Program on Public Policy
Philanthropy and the Nonprofit Sector
Humphrey Institute of Public Affairs
301 19th Avenue South
Minneapolis, MN 55455
Phone: 612-626-0340
Fax: 612-625-3513
E-mail: wdiaz@hhh.umn.edu

I am part of the new generation of not-for-profit professionals, one of the individuals who planned his or her career path on a journey to join the ranks of the not-for-profit sector. My career focus from the beginning has been geared toward finding the best educational tools available to enable me to work and excel in this intriguing and rewarding field.

Upon the realization that I wanted to spend my professional life working in the not-for-profit sector, the first task became finding out how to best equip myself to succeed and position myself in this new market, which includes many options, from fundraising to general management.

Currently, there are numerous programs to help prepare the new generation of not-for-profit professionals, but in the early 1990s, there were not as many. My journey began with the pursuit of the higher educational programs available to individuals entering this field. The result was the achievement of a master's degree in public administration, with a concentration in nonprofit management, a master's of arts degree in philanthropic studies, and the Certification in Fundraising Management, all from Indiana University. These three programs all offer unique opportunities, skills, and perspectives that have equipped me to succeed in this field. They were not easy, but very rewarding and well worth the time. Each of these programs offers skills and perspectives unique to the program structure and goals.

Seeking higher education to prepare to enter the not-for-profit field is a new choice being made, especially by the new generation of professionals. These programs provide education in areas that have taken years to develop and professionalize. You see, without the experiences, skills, and education gained through these programs it might have taken me 15 to 20 years to have risen to the type of senior position I currently hold at age 28. I have advanced rapidly in my field largely due to the education and skills provided me through the cutting-edge advanced learning programs available to the new generation of not-for-profit professionals.

JAMIE LEVY, MPA, MA, CFRM, is executive vice president of Prevent Blindness Indiana, a 50-year-old, statewide vision health not-for-profit. His previous experience includes working as a consultant at Olive LLP and for two trade organizations. He has had articles published on the topics of fundraising and nonprofit management, and has the dual master's degrees from Indiana University, master of public administration: nonprofit management, and master of arts in philanthropic studies.

PROFESSIONALS SAY . . .

While working in the nonprofit sector immediately after college, I made a conscious decision to pursue a career in fundraising. I am interested in a variety of issues, including youth development, historic preservation, and the arts, and I felt that through fundraising I could be involved with different types of organizations throughout my career. I also realized that fundraising is a necessary skill for an executive director position, which is my ultimate career goal. Traditionally, people have "fallen into" fundraising, but in my case I made a decided effort to pursue fundraising as a career. In addition to building my skill base through work experience, I chose to complete an academic program that would round out my skill set and give me a competitive edge when seeking nonprofit positions. Through the Master of Public Affairs in Nonprofit Management at Indiana University, I was able to analyze nonprofit management issues, finances, and fundraising strategies at a level in which only top executives of an organization are engaged. The degree offered an accelerated learning curve in nonprofit management.

Joshua R. Sutton. Development Associate, Historic Landmarks Foundation of Indiana

CHAPTER 7

Training Programs and Continued Education

SIDEBAR BY DAVID TINKER

"Competence is highly prized in fundraising, and much effort is devoted to determining appropriate skills and improving them."[1] Developing special skills that are valued in the field can be done through academic programs, as described in the previous chapter, but more likely a fundraising professional will seek training programs, such as workshops, to improve the legitimacy of fundraising, and these programs are offered through a variety of venues.

> *"Continuing education in nonprofit management is pervasive, with formats, cost, and length of courses and programs varying according to location, sponsor and market."*[2]

This statement by one of the earlier books on careers in the nonprofit sector, including fundraising, effectively described the myriad of choices under the continuing education umbrella. Since that book was written, other opportunities have been added. This chapter takes a look at those opportunities.

Educational opportunities, often described as professional development, can include:

- Certificate programs
- Workshops
- Conferences

- Institutes
- In-house training
- Summer programs
- Fellowships and internships

The organizations that offer these continuing education or professional development opportunities are:

- Professional associations
- Educational institutions and "schools"
- Centers and institutes
- Affinity groups
- Technical assistance centers
- Consulting firms or individual consultants
- Continuing education programs of universities

There are many opportunities for training and education. For the sake of convenience, they can be grouped under the title of *continuing education*. At times, it is difficult for the practitioner, particularly someone new to the field, to determine which courses offer the best quality and how to judge that quality.

In contrast with formal education, as described in Chapter 6, continuing education or professional development programs offer short-term, quick, compressed, streamlined training, and they are guided by the need of employers and students, as well as the opinions and suggestions of seasoned practitioners. For the most part, they are practitioner-driven. The caveat, however, is expressed well by Bloland and Bornstein: "A preoccupation with skill development, important as it may be, combined with a neglect of theory construction and research, will be costly to the occupation."[3] To simply achieve competence without understanding the principle behind the competence, to ignore the theory on which ethical, philanthropic, successful practice is based, is erroneous. As Carbone stated in his landmark study on fundraising as a profession, "Competence is not enough."[4] A scholarly approach and a research base are vital criteria for excellence in fundraising education, and these elements should not be excluded in continuing education and training. This is, perhaps, the foremost criterion for selection of the best training possible (additional criteria will be listed later in this chapter).

The following are the most prevalent and accessible forms of continuing education or professional development. Some of these overlap in offerings and purposes. For example, some universities, in addition to degree programs, also have continuing education in the form of certificates, non-degree courses, centers, and institutes. Some associations may offer conferences as well as courses and summer institutes.

- *Major associations.* There are several associations for fundraising professionals. The most prominent are the Association of Fundraising Professionals (AFP, formerly the National Society for Fund Raising Executives), Council for Advancement and Support of Education, Association of Healthcare Philanthropy, Association of Professional Researchers for Advancement, and the National Committee on Planned Giving. These offer conferences, usually on a yearly basis, and courses, such as the AFP-sponsored First and Survey courses. Other offerings are institutes, certification programs, and training via Internet (these will be described in more detail later in this chapter).

  Continuing education offered by major associations is, generally, credible and well planned and executed. Those who present workshops and other types of offerings are usually well qualified, and for the most part their presentation skills are good. The emphasis is more often on practice, while research and theory are limited in content.

- *Schools.* The most prominent institution in this category is The Fund Raising School (TFRS), part of the Center on Philanthropy at Indiana University. It offers nine courses (in addition to customized training), covering all areas of fundraising practice. The advantage of acquiring training at TFRS is that not only is it the oldest recognized entity, established in 1974, with a curriculum based on the collective experience of its founders, faculty, and advisors, but it also draws on research and theory. Another school is The Grantsmanship Center in Los Angeles, which also offers courses in fundraising and nonprofit management throughout the country. Both schools have training programs at locations across the country, and TFRS does international work.

- *Centers and institutes located at higher education institutions.* Academic centers were discussed in the previous chapter, and a Web site that lists academic course offering in nonprofit management was also listed. Many centers offer fundraising as part of their nonprofit study, although such courses are often electives. Among the most prominent centers are the Mandel Center at Case Western, the Institute for Nonprofit Organizational Management at the University of San Francisco, and the Center on Philanthropy at Indiana University.

- *Affinity groups.* Several associations have specialized programs or are made up of similar types of nonprofits. Among these are the National Catholic Development Conference, some Women in Development groups, the Association of Lutheran Development Executives, the Christian Stewardship Association, and the American Association of Fundraising Council. The members of these associations have similarities in types of organizations or organizational missions (e.g., fundraising for religious causes). These affinity groups also hold conferences and provide training opportunities, and generally are highly credible.

- *Technical assistance and support centers.* Technical assistance centers were begun in the 1970s to assist nonprofits with a variety of services, such as nonprofit management, business skills, accounting, fundraising, volunteer management, fundraising research, and program evaluation. Most provide training programs, and some have consultation services. The Alliance for Nonprofit Management, based in Washington, D.C., is a membership association of technical assistance and support centers, and is a good place to start in seeking additional information, particularly local training, through this type of continuing education.

- *Institutes.* A number of institutes are offered by associations, such as the CASE Summer Institutes (Independent School Advancement Professionals, Communications and Marketing, and Alumni Relations), and AFP's Executive Leadership and Executive Management Institutes. These are generally held either in the summer or during a compressed time period, such as two to three days, and focus on a specific level of professionalism and tenure in the profession. AFP's ELI is offered yearly to senior professionals, who listen to experts on issues in fundraising and engage in discussion and reflection. Another type of institute is the Learning Institute, which brings together speakers and professionals through the latest technology. It is a program of the Society for Nonprofit Organizations, in collaboration with the University of Wisconsin–Extension and Television Wisconsin, Inc.

- *Consulting firms or individual consultants.* As part of their efforts to create visibility and advertise their services, consultants offer workshops or seminars. Consultants also are frequent speakers at major conferences held by associations. Since there is no set of criteria to govern consultancies, the range and caliber of offerings vary greatly.

- *Continuing education programs of universities.* An increasing number of higher education institutions are offering fundraising courses through their continuing education departments, and several have certificate programs. Some of these are New York University, the University of Chicago, Indiana University, and the University of San Francisco. Some colleges and universities combine centers, schools, and institutes in their offerings. For example, Indiana University offers:
  - The Fund Raising School courses through its Center on Philanthropy
  - The American Humanics program—a national alliance of colleges, universities, and nonprofit organizations preparing undergraduates for careers with youth and human service agencies
  - A certificate in fundraising management (through The Fund Raising School)
  - A nonprofit management certificate
  - A summer Institute on Philanthropy and Voluntary Service for undergraduates

  The distinct advantage of acquiring nondegree education and training through a university is the likelihood that research and theory are included in the overall educational offering.

- *Fellowships and internships.* Specialized fellowships are available at various academic centers, such as the Jane Addams–Andrew Carnegie Fellowship Program and the Hearst Minority Fellowship at The Center on Philanthropy at Indiana University. Internships are often arranged through academic programs but allow the student the added dimension of actual experience while enrolled in a master's degree program, for example. Internships can often lead to full-time work; at the least they give credibility to a young professional's résumé.

- *In-house training.* Large and well-established nonprofits may have training programs that they offer to their employees only, providing not just training in fundraising and nonprofit management, but also tailoring it to the specific needs of their new employees. Some of the organizations that conduct such programs are the Girl Scouts, Boys and Girls Clubs, YMCA and YWCA, Junior Achievement, and American Red Cross. This type of training is somewhat different from but can be part of on-the-job training, addressed in the next chapter.

Some of the training is expensive, but if the fundraising professional is wise in selecting among the continuing education opportunities available (see criteria suggestions below), some excellent low-cost offerings are available.

In conducting their study on fundraisers, Duronio and Tempel asked how their respondents learned to be fundraisers. The majority, 74 percent, learned on the job. The second most common method, 43 percent, was by professional development programs.

They also asked how the respondents believed would be the best way to learn about fundraising. The five top responses, in decreasing order, were professional development programs, networking, on-the-job training, reading, and mentoring. Less frequently cited were formal education, volunteering, consultants, and professional organization activities.

Generally, respondents recommended more professional development, reading, mentoring, and networking for others than they themselves had, and less on-the-job training and volunteering. Even though formal educational programs are growing rapidly, fewer than 10 percent learned fundraising this way, and even fewer than that (7.3 percent) thought this was the best way to learn. This may be because formal educational programs are quite new in the field and have not had a discernible impact at this point.[5]

How can a fundraising professional evaluate credibility and benefits of fundraising training? The following suggestions may be used as possible criteria for determining what and where the best investment in professional development can be.

1. *Conduct a personal assessment.* Determine the special areas of interest, short- and long-term professional goals, type of work that is preferred, and personal job satisfaction factors. For example, are you interested in the annual fund, proposal writing, or planned giving?

Where do you want to be in 3 years, versus 10 years? What type of organization do you like best, human service or health care? Higher education or child care? What types of working conditions are most satisfying for you? For example, do you like lots of autonomy or working in a team? Do you prefer to work alone or with volunteers?

2. *Determine the credibility of the professional development offering.* Assess the respectability of the organization offering the training. Ask your peers and mentors or teachers for suggestions.

3. *Assess your professional development needs and goals.* Do you want to study for a formal degree, or a certificate program. What do you want your professional development to accomplish for you and your work? Are you seeking improvement in your performance or seeking advancement in your career? How much time can you devote versus how much time is required by the program you select? What does your employer wish to have you accomplish through professional development? Who will pay for the training, and how are you obligated if your employer covers the costs?

4. *Put the pieces together and create a plan.* Your plan will differ from others because of the flexibility of continued education or professional development, unlike the formal structure of a higher education program. Your plan should be rationally and logically developed and be personalized.

Another excellent way to engage in continuing education is to read. Currently there are many journals and other publications on the market, and books are added on a monthly basis. Video and audiotapes are also available, as is training via the Internet and through teleconferencing. Major publishers of materials—which are, at the time of this writing, leaders in the field—are listed at the end of this chapter. Bibliographies and recommended readings are often available through the organizations or entities that offer the training. Credibility of the readings is often congruent with credibility of the training program. Also appended to this chapter is a current list of journals and newspapers or newsletters that offer excellent information for professional development.

Alternate methods of learning, such as videos, videoconferencing, and use of the Internet are often available through any of the professional development methods and organizations described above.

Finally, what about certification? Today there is a definite trend toward competency recognition in many areas, from government to professional associations. A "seal of approval" for fundraisers guarantees that persons entering a field can demonstrate an ability to perform tasks at an acceptable level, have a body of knowledge on which to base practice, and have exhibited some service to the profession. Credentialing also ensures that a profession's reputation is enhanced, and allows for some screening of those who behave in ways that discredit our profession.

The Certified Fund-Raising Executive (CFRE) Professional Certification Board offers the CFRE credential in cooperation with nine leading philanthropic organizations. It is a credential that is achieving more respect, although it isn't yet a criterion for employment. The CFRE implies that members can demonstrate a certain level of knowledge, have a certain amount of experience, and subscribe to a code of ethics and best practices. Both the Association of Healthcare Philanthropy (AHP) and the Association of Fundraising Professionals (AFP) offer advanced certification. The goals of certification are to support professional development in fundraising and provide guidelines for professional standards for employing organizations. The CFRE requires that the applicant document work experience (minimum of five years in the profession), fundraising success, service to the profession, and professional development, and pass a test.

There are proponents and opponents when it comes to certification. There are some who believe that fundraising professionals do not practice self-regulation sufficiently, or well enough, and external regulation may be necessary. This would imply licensing, which is a formal and legal process that controls preparation for and entry into a field. Licensing is not currently in place. Many hope that certification will become credible enough that licensing will not be necessary. Also, there is a trend away from licensure and toward certification; however, those who oppose certification state that it alienates those who resist change, while proponents argue that certification is not a control measure as much as it is a standard for professionalization.

Currently, the CFRE is not a significant criterion for being hired in a fundraising position. Certification doesn't translate into competent behavior; however, many claim that certification does lead to job opportunities, more professionalism, better salaries, more impressive titles, and additional perks. The best outcome of certification, however, may well be that the process of achieving certification causes a fundraiser to think seriously about what he or she knows and how this knowledge is put into practice. In this sense, certification does contribute to the professionalism of fundraisers.

▓ FURTHER READING

Advancing Philanthropy. Arlington, VA: Association of Fundraising Professionals (published quarterly).

> *This quarterly offers how-to articles and reports on successful fundraising practice.*

The Chronicle of Philanthropy. Washington, DC: The Chronicle of Philanthropy (published biweekly).

> *The latest issues in philanthropic activity from case histories and people in the profession to statistical data on major contributions are covered in this newspaper. Sections can include fundraising, giving, foundations, corporations, marketing, management, volunteering, grants, international fundraising activities, and many other areas of philanthropy. Continuing education and job opportunities are listed in the last section.*

Currents. Washington, DC: Council for Advancement and Support of Education (published monthly).

> *This is a publication of the major association for education institutions. Includes articles on fundraising, public relations, and alumni administration.*

Fundraising Management. Garden City, NY: Hoke Communications, Inc. (published monthly).

> *This monthly serial includes current topics and strategies in fundraising. Special feature articles provide helpful management and practical information for the fundraising executive. Conference reports keep readers up to date on issues and trends. Every issue includes a development section, calendar of events, club news, newsmakers, marketplace, cassettes, fundraising directory, and a classified section.*

Grantsmanship Center News. Los Angeles: Grantsmanship Center (published bimonthly).

> *This journal lists continuing education courses in fundraising, particularly proposal writing. It contains advice on writing grant proposals and articles related to foundation giving. Also lists sources for assistance and helpful advertising.*

Grassroots Fundraising Journal. Oakland, CA: Chardon Press.

> *Articles on alternative sources of funding, book reviews, and bibliographies are here. It is geared toward the low-budget organization.*

New Directions for Philanthropic Fundraising. San Francisco: Jossey-Bass (published quarterly).

> New Directions for Philanthropic Fundraising *was created to strengthen voluntary giving by addressing how the concepts of philanthropy pertain to fundraising practice. In each quarterly paperback, authors address themes related to fundraising management and technique, always keeping in mind the values of voluntarism and public benefit that characterizes philanthropic organizations. The journal is sponsored by the Indiana University Center on Philanthropy and the Association of Fundraising Professionals.*

Nonprofit Management and Leadership. San Francisco: Jossey-Bass (published quarterly).

> *Provides latest developments in theory and practice of nonprofit management; it includes articles, features, book reviews, research reports, and updates on professional conferences.*

The NonProfit Times. Skillman, NJ: The Nonprofit Times (published monthly).

> *Focus of this publication is on nonprofit management and fundraising techniques. Sections may include news/features, computer software, technology, management and finance, commentary on current issues, and other areas of interest. Job continuing education opportunities are also listed. It is free to subscribers who meet certain qualifications; check with the publisher.*

Nonprofit World. Madison, WI: Society for Nonprofit Organizations (published bimonthly).

> *This Journal publishes articles on all aspects of running an effective nonprofit organization, including fundraising, income generation, legal advice, and professional development.*

■ FURTHER INFORMATION

The Alliance for Nonprofit Management
1899 L Street NW
Suite 600
Washington, DC 20036
Phone: 202-955-8406
Fax: 202-955-8419
E-mail: Alliance@allianceonline.org
Web site: www.allianceonline.org

American Association of Fund-Raising Counsel & AAFRC Trust for Philanthropy
10293 N. Meridian Street
Suite 175
Indianapolis, IN 46290
Phone: 800-462-2372
Phone: 317-816-1613
Fax: 317-816-1633
E-mail: info@aafrc.org
Web site: www.aafrc.org

Association for Research on Nonprofit Organizations and Voluntary Action
(ARNOVA)
The Center on Philanthropy at Indiana University
550 W. North Street
Suite 301
Indianapolis, IN 46202-3162
Phone: 317-684-2120
Fax: 317-684-2128
E-mail: Exarnova@iupui.edu
Web site: www.arnova.org

Aspen Institute (Nonprofit Sector Research Fund)
One Dupont Circle, NW
Suite 700
Washington, DC 20036
Phone: 202-736-5838
Fax: 202-293-0525
E-mail: nsrf@aspeninst.org
Web site: www.aspeninst.org

Association of Fundraising Professionals (AFP)
(Formally NSFRE)
1101 King Street
Suite 700
Alexandria, VA 22314
Phone: 703-684-0410
Fax: 703-684-0540
E-mail: NSFRE@NSFRE.org
Web site: www.NSFRE.org

Association of Healthcare Philanthropy (AHP)
313 Park Avenue
Suite 400
Falls Church, VA 22046
Phone: 703-532-6243
Fax: 703-532-7170
E-mail: ahp@go-AHP.org
Web site: www.go-ahp.org

Association of Professional Researchers for Advancement (APRA)
414 Plaza Drive
Suite 209
Westmont, IL 60559-1265
Phone: 630-655-0177
Fax: 630-655-0391
E-mail: info@aprahome.org
Web site: www.aprahome.org

CFRE Professional Certification Board
1101 King St.
Suite 700
Alexandria, Virginia, 22314
Phone: 703-519-8483
Fax: 703-684-1950
E-mail: cert@nsfre.org

Council for Advancement and Support of Education (CASE)
1307 New York Ave. NW
Suite 1000
Washington, DC 20005-4701
Phone: 202-328-5900
Fax: 202-387-4973
Web site: www.case.org

Council on Foundations
1828 L Street NW
Suite 300
Washington, DC 20036
Phone: 202-466-6512
Fax: 202-785-3926
Web site: www.cof.org

Foundation Center
79 Fifth Avenue
8th Floor
New York, NY 10003
Phone: 212-620-4230
Fax: 212-691-1828
Web site: www.fdncenter.org

Guidestar Philanthropic Research, Inc.
427 Scotland Street
Williamsburg, VA 23185
Phone: 757-229-4631
Fax: 757-229-8912
E-mail: customerservice@guidestar.org
Web site: www.guidestar.org

INDEPENDENT SECTOR (IS)
1200 18th St. NW
Suite 200
Washington, DC 20036
Phone: 202-467-6100
Fax: 202-467-6101
E-mail: info@independentsector.org
Web site: www.independentsector.org

National Center for Nonprofit Boards (NCNB)
1828 L Street NW
Suite 900
Washington, DC 20036-5104
Phone: 202-452-6262
Fax: 202-452-6299
E-mail: NCNB@NCNB.org
Web site: www.ncnb.org

National Committee on Planned Giving (NCPG)
233 McCrea Street
Suite 400
Indianapolis, IN 46225
Phone: 317-269-6274
Fax: 317-269-6276
E-mail: ncpg@iupui.edu
Web site: www.ncpg.org

National Council of Nonprofit Associations (NCNA)
1900 L Street NW
Suite 605
Washington DC 20036
Phone: 202-467-6262
Fax: 202-467-6261
E-mail: NCNA@NCNA.org
Web site: www.NCNA.org

National Society of Fund Raising Executives (NSFRE)
   Effective January 1, 2001, name changed to
   Association of Fundraising Professionals (AFP)

Women's Philanthropy Institute
6314 Odana Road
Suite 1
Madison, WI 53719
Phone: 608-270-5205
Fax: 608-270-5207
E-mail: Andreak@women-philanthropy.org
Web site: www.women-philanthropy.org/aboutwpi.html

For me, as a young professional, continuing education in the nonprofit field has definitely enhanced my career. Typically fundraisers are teachers, marketing specialists, or volunteers who move into fundraising as a profession. I belong to the new generation because I chose to work in the nonprofit sector as a fundraiser while still in college. Once I decided on fundraising as a career, I sought out continuing education opportunities, such as internships and seminars, in addition to graduate school, which prepared me for my career choice.

I have interned at various nonprofit agencies in a variety of fields. For example, I interned at a national association where a fundraising program was just being established. I had many chances to present my ideas and worked closely with the fundraising professional. Although limited, my expertise was wanted and my boss listened to and implemented my ideas. This experience has provided me with the opportunity of seeing different circumstances, good and bad, in daily operations. But this type of training was not enough.

Seminars and conferences are often underutilized tools for continued education. I have attended local, regional, and international conferences, seminars, and classes. Each has offered opportunities to learn new things and to reinforce traditional ideas germane to our field. I have met new people and made good contacts through these educational opportunities.

Although I received a master's degree in public affairs with a concentration in nonprofit management, I have also enhanced my career through continuing education. Professionals such as doctors, lawyers, and teachers are required to attend classes, seminars, and conferences to keep abreast of advances in their professions. The nonprofit sector should not be an exception.

DAVID TINKER is the development director at Greater Pittsburgh Literacy Council (GPLC) and has been working in the fundraising field for more than 10 years. Prior to GPLC he worked in development at Pittsburgh Vision Services and the St. Francis Healthcare Foundation. He began his career in fundraising as an intern at Ketchum Inc., Fundraising Counsel. Tinker is a board member of the Association of Professional Researchers for Advancement (APRA). He is also on the board of the Western Pennsylvania chapter of APRA. Tinker serves as a program committee member for the Western Pennsylvania chapter of the Association of Fundraising Professionals (AFP). He has a B.A. in chemistry and English from Muskingum College, New Concord, Ohio. He holds a master of public affairs with a concentration in nonprofit management from Indiana University–Purdue University at Indianapolis.

PROFESSIONALS SAY . . .

Intelligent people wouldn't think of going on a long trip without a road map or an itinerary. A mechanic wouldn't think of attempting to work on a machine without the proper tools. That's what attempting to do fundraising without training and workshops amounts to. Fundraising is a way to realize dreams, and to be in a good position to help dreams come true. I have been involved in a capital campaign to build a facility for people who need services that I once needed, and through training I received in workshops and the accumulation of experience I have helped others as well as myself reach our goals. It's most gratifying to be able to give back to a cause through expertise in fundraising.

Jim Hession, Administrator, Progress House Inc., Indianapolis, Indiana

CHAPTER 8

On-the-Job Training and Mentoring

SIDEBAR BY TONJA CONOUR

"To do good is noble. To help others do good is also noble—and much, much easier."—attributed to Mark Twain

The attitude of collegiality among fundraising professionals, for the most part, is conducive not only to producing professionals of caliber but also to providing alternative forms of professional development.

Throughout most of the history of formalized fundraising, on-the-job training and mentoring were *the* means for acquiring fundraising knowledge and skills. Although options have expanded considerably, they are still significant methods of professional development, either singly or as part of an overall plan for acquiring skills and experience—and mentoring and on-the-job training aren't only for entry-level personnel. Experienced professionals can enhance their career development through these avenues as well. This chapter explores the roles that on-the-job training and mentoring can play in fundraising education.

ON-THE-JOB TRAINING

On-the-job training is a time-honored way of learning. Sometimes it is simply a matter of being in the right place at the right time, but more often the fundraiser must take the initiative. On-the-job training, of course, occurs regularly. Often, it is accompanied by formal training such as conferences or workshops, but sometimes it is the primary or only way a professional will acquire knowledge and expertise. As noted in a previous chapter, the majority of fundraising professionals, 74 percent, learned on the job. The second most common method, 43 percent, was by professional development programs.[1]

There are several reasons why on-the-job training is still prevalent and preferred. Some people learn best by experience, observation, and experimentation. Some work in organizations that can't afford to send personnel to training, even to conferences. Some simply don't see the necessity of any other type of learning.

If learning on the job is either necessary or preferred, the entry-level person should pick the position carefully and match it to identified career goals. For example, proposal writing is a good entry-level area and may lead to corporate and foundation relations positions, but will generally not prepare a person to manage and organize people and projects.

Junior professionals should figure out what eventual goal is desirable—what they want to ultimately achieve, such as major gifts, planned giving, or management or leadership positions. As fundraising professionals climb the career ladder, each step demands more in competence, knowledge, and skills. Annual fund programs, for example, are good entry-level positions because many aspects of this program translate well to more serious responsibility in fundraising, or in jobs that are leadership roles but that still include fundraising. While on the job, the novice can learn organizational ability, management of projects according to a timeline, good writing skills, reporting, and working with committees.

Greenfield has defined the general timetable for a fundraiser's professional career in the following way:

Years in Fundraising	Career Progression
0–8 years	Entry-level assignments Mastery of the methods Specialty concentration
5–10 years	Manager of fund development programs Specialty assignments and competency
8–15 years	Executive for resource development
10–plus years	Senior management executive Institutional leadership[2]

Career progression means that the entry-level professional or the novice may begin with a mastery of the basic techniques and competencies, then may specialize and expand in responsibility, continue to increase comprehension of knowledge, and finally exercise leadership in planning, designing, motivating, and sharing expertise. This may occur within one organization or among several in the progression up the career ladder, or it may occur within one type of organization such as education or health care.

The following are some suggestions on how to implement a personal on-the-job training effort.

- *Take personal responsibility.* Although many organizations assume the role of providing for on-the-job training, the professional should not take this for granted but should appropriately initiate such an effort. This calls for some personal study on the profession, its opportunities, its pitfalls, and the sources of information.

- *When taking a job, inquire how much professional guidance you will get.* On-the-job training is often available, but some organizations make it a low priority and have high expectations of the new employee's expertise when hired.

- *Plan, and update your plan.* Determine what professional goals you have and share these with your boss whenever possible. In general, organizational leaders appreciate employees who wish to learn, and such leaders are usually willing to provide feedback and opportunities. On rare occasions profession development and ambition are discouraged or become a threat to personnel already in place. These are signs of a dysfunctional organization and may be accompanied by other problems that are a threat to the organization and its mission. A situation of this nature may be difficult to discern, but an entry-level person can ask questions that will at least give clues as to the health of an organization and opportunities for excellence in work and professional development (see Chapter 21 on how to avoid a no-win job situation).

- *Find a mentor, or at least an advisor.* This topic will be discussed in more detail later in this chapter.

- *Ask questions.* The best way to learn is to ask questions, but a professional should do so selectively and should identify the right persons from whom to seek information. Most professionals like to share information, but on occasion knowledge is equated with power and collegiality ceases to exist.

- *Volunteer for committees and jobs others may not want.* Becoming involved without being asked or coerced is a good way to develop collegiality and for a person's abilities to be noticed. Besides, it is helpful to the organization in the achievement of goals, and is therefore appreciated. Sometimes the best learning takes place when a person learns by doing something that others have avoided, because then there's room for experimentation and information sharing.

- *Read.* If your organization doesn't subscribe to the major publications, use your own initiative to find them in a good library or on the Web. In the last decade, resources by way of journals, newspapers, newsletters, and similar print material have increasingly become available. Now there are free resources available on the Web as well, and Web pages sometimes contain the latest and best professional knowledge.

- *Learn from others who do fundraising.* Call people who do your kind of work and ask to have lunch or meet. People who are committed to their work and their organizations generally like to talk about what they do and know. Take advantage of this natural phenomenon; both parties will benefit.

- *Request to shadow a professional whom you admire, and ask the right questions.* Get permission from your organization to spend a day every now and then with a senior professional in your area of interest at another organization. Observe, take notes, ask questions.

- *Expand your geographic range.* Do not limit your learning to your city or region; call others across the country and ask questions. Through professional associations' membership lists, you can find people who work at a level and at organizations that you admire. Make contact by phone or e-mail and learn from these professionals.

- *Belong to a professional association and learn from your colleagues.* If your hiring organization won't pay for this, find some way to fund it yourself. Association memberships aren't inexpensive but usually are worth the investment. If your organization has a small budget, perhaps cost-sharing is possible, with you and your employer each paying half of a membership fee. Meeting with professionals who share the same challenges and concerns as you is not only reassuring and invigorating, but provides for a great learning opportunity.

- *Make your qualifications known appropriately, so that you will be called when opportunities for short-term service or position openings become available.* Since most jobs are usually filled in-house, be collegial, not just with your immediate peers but with superiors as well. This does not mean an arrogant flaunting of credentials but a matter-of-fact demonstration of achievements and abilities.

- *Do not get stuck in a discipline, unless that is your plan.* Even if a professional has set his or her sights on staying in annual giving and becoming the best in that area, cross-learning and training will strengthen capabilities and expertise. In most cases, the professional careerist will want to experience many types of positions while aiming at an ultimate, high-level position of responsibility.

What should you look for in putting together your in-house learning plan? Ask these questions.

- What are the precedents for on-the-job training?
- Is there a collegiality and openness in the organization?
- What exists in-house, and what can be acquired inexpensively in the community or professional associations?
- Who in the organization is willing to help you? Is it your immediate boss or a peer?
- What kind of commitment is there to professional development, or is the focus on work and more work?

FINDING MENTORS

Mentoring is an important part of professional development, whether on-the-job training is involved or more formal education is available. Mentoring is a major key to success under any circumstances, but particularly if learning experiences are limited for a novice or entry-level professional. At the ideal, a mentor will be available for advice, will help a deserving professional by paving the way to advancement or acquisition of knowledge, and will be that person's advocate. At the least, a mentor can be someone who listens, is willing to share experiences, boosts the confidence level of the person being mentored, and passes on information about the profession. At any level, fundraising professionals can learn from others who show an interest in them, who will help in learning the ropes and provide some knowledge of the community and its donors, and who will be the key in making friends among professionals. Wise professionals will seek out two or three close mentors and therefore benefit from a variety of connections, available advice, and viewpoints.

For some people it is natural to hook up with a mentor. Some mentorship relationships come by chance, almost by serendipity. For most, it is not that easy. Here are some suggestions on ways to find mentors.

- Join AFP chapters and other professional associations that have mentoring programs.
- Get acquainted with professionals who give workshops, write for publications, or teach. These people may take an interest in you, or you may ask them for help.
- Identify and seek out your own mentor, with a plan in hand. Determine what you need and want and ask the prospective mentor if he or she is willing to help you. By identifying your needs and what you would desire from a mentor, you make it possible for that person to respond favorably.
- Get acquainted with people in your field, or type of organization, such as health care or the arts. Within such affiliations you can find a mentor who is willing to take you under the wing.

Most people are willing, if not eager, to share their background and experiences, and to provide information on best practices. There usually aren't proprietary or "turf" secrets in the nonprofit sector, although sharing of information may stop short of actual donor information. A mentor can be a positive influence on a fledgling professional, and such a relationship can turn into a lifelong friendship. Mentoring reminds you that you don't have to do it alone.

Who might be your mentors? They could come from the ranks of teachers and trainers; senior professionals, who have successful years of experience; senior colleagues; consultants; and people outside the field who can provide counsel and give objective viewpoints.

The ideal professional development plan, of course, involves education, training opportunities, on-the-job training, and mentoring, but if such a complete package isn't possible, the entry-level professional can still utilize the most inexpensive and accessible methods of learning—mentoring and on-the-job training.

Sharon arrives at work ready to hit the ground running in her new job as director of development at a prestigious nonprofit organization. After arranging her desk, leafing through a dozen files, and learning the phone system, she reviews the organization's fundraising plan for the upcoming year and reality hits her. The plan calls for private donations to double within the next year!

Taking a deep breath and reflecting on her previous five years as a development assistant for a grassroots nonprofit agency, Sharon wonders how she is going to reach these new challenges that initially attracted her to the position. She thinks to herself, "I'm well educated, I've been to all the latest seminars, and I recently earned a certificate in fundraising management." However, despite of her education, Sharon feels like she might be in over her head.

In the midst of a self-motivational pep talk to rebuild her confidence, the administrative assistant enters the office and asks Sharon if she needs help with anything. Sharon pauses, smiles meekly, and answers, "Yes, please bring me a mentor!"

A mentor is a coach, a confidence builder, a wise leader, a trusted colleague, and someone who empowers others to succeed. Passion and competence are a winning combination for fundraising professionals, but often the extra boost to one's career comes from a valued mentoring relationship. Sharon can learn the ropes of her new position the hard way by going at it alone, or she can rely on the guidance of an experienced mentor to help her make informed decisions on which tools to utilize in blazing a new trail to success.

With the help of a seasoned mentor and positive on-the-job learning experiences, Sharon will be empowered to reach her organization's fundraising goals and climb higher on the ladder of success . . . possibly even sooner than she thinks.

TONJA CONOUR MPA, is a native of Indianapolis, Indiana, who now resides in Overland Park, Kansas. While earning her master's in public affairs with an emphasis in nonprofit management from the Indiana University Center on Philanthropy, Tonja founded and directed The Mentor Program at Indiana University–Purdue University of Indianapolis (IUPUI). She received the "Experience Excellence Award" from IUPUI, an award granted to the top 5 employees of IUPUI's 8,000+ staff members. In her honor, the university established an annual "Conour Mentor Award" granted each year to the most outstanding mentor at IUPUI. Currently, Tonja serves as the director of program and services for American Humanics, Inc., a national alliance of colleges, universities, and nonprofit organizations preparing undergraduates for careers with youth and human service agencies. During her tenure at American Humanics, the national alliance has grown from 16 to 75 campus-based American Humanics Programs. American Humanics is the leader in the national movement of undergraduate nonprofit management education for future nonprofit professionals.

PROFESSIONALS SAY . . .

Consider yourself lucky to find a mentor. Chances are you may not recognize a mentor as such at first. But later you will see their gifts of persistence and vision. Mentors weave words and actions with people and programs. They strive for something more, something better. Whether your mentor takes you by the hand to show you "how" or you observe from the sidelines, you can't help but see the passion spill out. Gather it and pass it on.

Elizabeth A. Elkas, Director of Development at the Indiana University School of Medicine, Office of Gift Development, Indianapolis, Indiana

Having a mentor is essential. So much of successful fundraising is intuitive. One can learn lots from listening and watching others with proven success in asking and receiving.

Jane W. Schlegel, MSW, Director of Community Programs and Development, International Center of Indianapolis, Indiana

I encourage all individuals to spend time working or volunteering for a variety of nonprofit organizations in order to discover the best fit for themselves. Large organizations offer opportunities for specialization and a rich

environment for learning from others. Small organizations provide opportunities to be involved in every aspect of the fundraising process.

Brad Kruse, Organizational Development Specialist, Initiative Foundation, Little Falls, Minnesota

The most unlikely people can be good at fundraising, with proper on-the-job training and good mentoring. I, a black woman, born and raised in the 40s in Mississippi with a love for people, an excitement for life, and an eagerness to learn, became a fundraiser by default. While volunteering for a national nonprofit, I saw the power of people helping others with no thought of compensation. This was, and still is, amazing to me. Only in America. Ozzie Keller, an older white gentleman in Wisconsin, taught me informally, most of what I know about how to build relationships with people of very diverse backgrounds. That really was the defining period in my career.

Kathryn Bowen, Director of Development, Voice of Calvary Ministries, Jackson, Mississippi

A good mentor is your career's best personal resource. Opportunities such as academic programs, workshops, conferences, and Internet learning give structured access to information and help you keep current. But a good mentor will help you evaluate what you read, hear, learn, and experience as well as assist you to weave it together and maximize your personal and professional potential. If you do not have a mentor, identify and recruit one whose personality and experience is a good fit for you. And remember, "give forward" to the next generation of professionals by mentoring someone following after you!

Roberta A. Healey, MBA, CFRE, Principal, Farr Healey Consulting LLC

CHAPTER 9

Suggestions for Career Changers

SIDEBAR BY RANDY BLACKMON

Although the numbers of young people seeking a career in fundraising are growing significantly, an equal number of mid-career professionals also find fundraising to be a viable and desirable career option. This chapter focuses on the professional who wishes to change careers or professions, and discusses the issues, concerns, and possibilities in such a career move.

Job mobility and turnover are prevalent in the nonprofit sector as well as the business world. There are many reasons for changing jobs, and even changing careers. Some people are dissatisfied with their jobs, others find that what they are doing only partially fulfills life's needs, such as the need to make a difference or see tangible results. Some must make changes in their careers because of downsizing, mergers, or changes in operations at their places of employment. Others can't or don't wish to keep up with the demands of a job, such as technological changes. A significant segment of the U.S. population finds career paths interrupted or vastly diverted. This means that they not only have to find ways to translate skills and experience to new areas of work, but they also have to add to their knowledge and expertise.

It is not uncommon to find someone from the other two sectors, government and business, wanting to work in the nonprofit sector. Some reasons are based on myth and therefore not valid. For example, during downsizing by corporations, some personnel believe they can use their abilities on a temporary basis to help nonprofits, which supposedly are "soft" on management skills and financial accountability, and therefore could use the help of professionals from the corporate sector. Although there are many business concepts and principles that should be applied to organizations of both sectors, a condescending attitude hinting at superiority does not gain friends in the nonprofit sector. Corporate employees who have been downsized or find themselves without a job for whatever reason often don't understand the significant differences between the management of a business and a nonprofit. Some of these differences are related to income. The bottom line is not the focal point for a nonprofit, which exists to carry out a mission. The nonprofit may make a profit, but those funds are used to improve the organization, not its personnel or board. Also, the nonprofit is served by a volunteer board whose members do not receive payment for their services.

Another erroneous idea that executives from other sectors may hold is that fundraising is a snap or a set of techniques or rules. They may not realize that it is a thoughtful process that involves mastering principles and managing resources, and is a demanding profession.

There are more legitimate reasons for wanting to find employment in the nonprofit sector:

- The nonprofit sector is about people and meeting their needs and wants. It is satisfying and meaningful to work in such an atmosphere.

- The nonprofit sector is equally demanding in terms of professionalism and accountability, and a person's skills can be transferred from an existing job in government or business to a nonprofit that represents a worthwhile cause and is of interest to the job-seeker.

- The nonprofit sector includes a great variety of organizations and causes, and professionals can find a suitable match for their skills and interests. For example, someone who has worked in marketing for a corporation can elect to work in a human service or arts organization and not only use acquired expertise but also be in a setting that is compatible with personal interests.

- The nonprofit sector should be financially accountable, but the focus and mission are the mission and cause, not financial profit. There is much opportunity for fulfillment, for making a difference in the lives of people.

- The challenges facing the nonprofit sector are great, and increasing consistently. These provide not just professional challenges but intellectual challenges as well.

- There are ample opportunities for leadership and for career advancement within the nonprofit sector.

What are some of the ways that persons from other careers in business or government could enter the nonprofit sector and find employment in fundraising? Also, how would persons employed in the nonprofit sector make the transition to fundraising?

- Seek opportunities to gain experience through activities such as volunteering, serving on boards and committees, interning.
- Make a case for your credentials and experience, and match them to the demands of the job you desire. For example, if you have communications or public relations experience, seek a position that capitalizes on these abilities while you acquire the other essential knowledge and expertise needed for the fundraising position.
- Network with people who do what you want to do, and make appointments with the right people to pick their brains, share ideas, and ask questions. Most people are willing to share information if asked appropriately. Also, most good jobs, especially the ones that a mid-career professional may want, aren't necessarily advertised but often referred by other professionals.
- Build a résumé based on qualifications. In making a career change to fundraising, begin a résumé by listing qualifications such as managing, communicating, working with volunteers, or editing. You can then tailor your résumé so that qualifications fit what is needed for the job you are seeking.
- Attend events such as monthly meetings of the local AFP chapter and become acquainted with persons in the profession. Build confidence in your abilities by becoming involved and by working with future colleagues and peers.

Any change in a person's lifetime requires certain steps that carry the dream to reality. According to experts in change theory, the following are general guidelines to follow. First, describe to yourself why change is desired and needed, and outline the specific changes you wish to make. This means identifying a goal—such as a fundraising position of certain responsibility and rank—and learning all you can about it. As you develop a plan, ask for reactions and advice, both from people who work in fundraising and others who can provide objective viewpoints and advice. While doing this, seek ideas on how to make the change as smoothly as possible. Be sure you are committed to the change. If it is a drastic change, visualize what it means to yourself, your family, and your future, and verify your commitment. Develop a plan, and in doing so, find out how to achieve a goal in finding a job in fundraising.

For example, Fred had been working in middle management at a large corporation. Then, as downsizing became more common and he could see what was coming, he decided to opt out with a year's pay that allowed him to seek career counseling and that also paid for retraining. He enrolled in workshops offered by a university and while studying for a certificate in nonprofit management, decided to focus on fundraising. While taking a directed readings course, he became acquainted with a professor who was well acquainted with nonprofit organizations in the community. Fred shared his volunteering efforts with her and sought her advice on how to focus his volunteering and internship activities so that they might lead to a career in fundraising. He wasn't excited about some entry-level jobs, which would not have tapped into related expertise he had already acquired in his career.

Through these educational and experiential activities, Fred and his advisor began to see several possibilities for his future. He could establish a consultancy that focused on his unique expertise in financial management; this possible consulting experience would have a niche in the community not readily filled by others. Another option was to establish himself as an advisor to personnel in companies who were in charge of corporate giving. A third possibility was to parlay his experience into a mid-level position in fundraising. Through this examination of possibilities, Fred realized he really did want to be part of a fundraising program, and he shared this vision with his academic advisor. Because she frequently was asked to refer people to job openings, and was called by organizations seeking to fill positions, the advisor could not only give Fred a strong reference when the right position opened up, but could also advise him on how to approach this opportunity.

This is just one example of how professionals from other careers and sectors can, over a planned period of time, move into a career in fundraising.

There are some realities, however, of making a change in career and profession. Most are manageable, but should be addressed so circumstances and situations don't unduly discourage professionals from managing effective change in their careers and work.

First, a career change may mean that finding a job takes longer than for the person who has prepared for a career in fundraising. It takes time to seek the right match between identified personal and professional characteristics and the possible job.

Second, it may be necessary to take an entry-level job, at least for a while, until enough credentials and credibility are accumulated. This is not necessarily detrimental, because such experience, while perhaps short term, will enhance the professional's capabilities and lead to greater responsibility and rank.

Third, some professional development will no doubt be necessary, such as enrolling in workshops that teach about fundraising. Although it is true that personnel are hired because of a wide variety of characteristics, most employers do want some evidence of training or experience.

Fourth, employers sometimes actually seek professionals from other areas because of previous negative experiences with professional fundraisers. Such opportunities are a boon to the high achiever, although they are also quite rare. This means that the career seeker should be alert to what is happening in the fundraising profession in his or her community, and also should have a network of persons who can inform him or her of opportunities.

Some people thrive on change and seek it. Others dread it but are willing to face change because of personal goals and dissatisfaction with the status quo. Eliminating and managing personal resistance to change makes it possible for persons seeking new professional challenges to approach a different career with a plan and with vision.

We can look around us and see many refugees from change—people who struggle against change or lack the courage to move with possibilities and challenges. Managing change creates the opportunity for *breakthrough* rather than *breakdown*. Managing change causes us to stop treating it like an enemy and helps us see that change is our greatest ally.

FURTHER READING

DiMarco, Cara. *Career Transitions*. Scottsdale, AZ: Gorsuch Scarisbrick, 1997.

> *This brief book guides a person moving ahead on a personal journey, and helps meet basic survival skills, explore resources, values, and priorities. Good as a guide for self-assessment and career exploration.*

Hayes, Kit Harrington. *Managing Career Transitions.* Scottsdale, AZ: Gorsuch Scarisbrick, 1996.

Written to address career concerns and unique circumstances of adults who change careers, this book provides information, skills, and support.

SIDEBAR   RANDY BLACKMON

The good news is that in today's world of work, career/job changes are not viewed as a negative in and of themselves. In fact, in many cases they are viewed as a positive, and are even expected. (The question may now be, "Why did you stay in the same job for five years?") So, the playing field may be different these days, but that does not always make the personal decision to pursue a career change an easy one. I found that a thoughtful, reflective "pause" in life helped me make a smart decision when I decided to leave the for-profit sector and join an organization in the nonprofit sector. With the pace and responsibilities of life today, the biggest challenge may be to take the time to ask some tough questions and then figure out the answers.

I would recommend that you ask yourself the following questions when considering a career change:

How do you view "working" in your life? Is it a way to make the most money possible? Is it a way to contribute to the world (if yes, what impact would you like to make)? Is it a way for you to grow as a person (if yes, in what way)? If the answer is a combination of the above, then spend some time thinking about the relative value of each and what is most important to you. Also consider what you are missing in your current career that has contributed to the decision to pursue a change.

After you have answered the above questions, then start talking with professionals in the career(s) in which you have an interest. Your goal is to determine if there seems to be a match between your values and expectations and the opportunities to meet those in a chosen career or field.

RANDY BLACKMON MPA, is director for Structure Initiatives for the Alzheimer's Association national headquarters, located in Chicago. The primary focus of the team he leads is a nationwide realignment of the chapter network. Prior to his work at the Alzheimer's Association, Randy was director of the Strengthening the Nonprofit Sector project at the Center on Philanthropy at Indiana University. This project's focus was to test different models of organizational self-assessment with various levels of support products and services and to measure the impact on organization effectiveness. Randy has been a department director for Marriott Hotels, executive director of an affiliate of the American Heart Association, and a campaign director for a United Way. He has served on local, regional, and national boards and advisory councils.

PROFESSIONALS SAY . . .

Having worked in the "for-profit" sector in both hotel and real estate management, I found myself questioning how to make a successful career change into the not-for-profit arena. I discovered the best suggestion is to simply volunteer! This is the best way for you to learn more about an organization and for them to learn more about you. You'll discover first-hand the dynamics of working within the not-for-profit sector among both staff and volunteers, with each offering their unique perspective. You will also have the opportunity to work hands-on with a particular cause and community issue. There are so many important causes and worthy organizations. Strive to find the one you are truly passionate about. It will make all the difference in your efforts as a volunteer, as an advocate.

Susan Foellinger, Director of Development, Prevail, Inc., Noblesville, Indiana

My background in sales taught me how to listen to what people want and tell a compelling story about what I have to offer. I have found that it is often easier to convince people to donate to a worthy cause than it is to persuade them to make a major purchase.

Judi Anderson, CFRE, Development Director, Santa Barbara Zoological Gardens

CHAPTER 10

Successful Career Case Studies

SIDEBAR BY MARK A. DENNIS, JR.

In an article by Guy Kawasaki, former director of software product management for Apple Computer Inc., there are some valuable "life lessons" drawn from truly remarkable people. One is, "Do it because you love it and you'll do it better." Many of the fundraising professionals who can be classified as "successful," including those whose stories are summarized in this chapter, worked as fundraisers because they loved their work and always strived to do their best.[1]

Success is defined in many ways, sometimes by status and power, sometimes by recognition, and sometimes by a legacy. For the sake of this chapter and this book, success in fundraising is defined as reaching goals and making a difference in the lives of people and institutions. It is in this spirit that the following stories are recounted. Fortunately for the profession of fundraising, a vast number of individuals could have been selected for featuring excellence in achievement. Those who are included in this chapter serve as examples of many who have either sought fundraising as a career or have made the transition from another profession. The stories are inspirational and factual, and their intent is to help the career seeker learn from professionals who exemplify what is good, exciting, and meaningful in fundraising as a career. For each vignette, the following questions will be considered.

- How did you get into fundraising, and why?
- What are the highlights of your career?

- What do you think are your greatest achievements?
- What advice would you give to persons entering the profession?

Each of these questions draws on some aspect or chapter of this book, and therefore this chapter is valuable as a real-life example of what works. Although each person introduced in this chapter is a seasoned professional, each has also remained up to date in professional practice and information. They represent the best combination of what has been accomplished with what is changing in the profession.

PAT BJORHOVDE

Pat Bjorhovde's path to being a fundraising professional was a circuitous route. She majored in music in college and spent approximately seven years teaching in public schools. This career did not satisfy her, however. After marrying and having a child, she rejoined the work force and was employed by a consulting firm for two years. Her job involved evaluating use of government grants by public schools. At the same time she volunteered and served on boards.

Then her husband's career took her to Canada, where she continued to be active in music and board service. The music director for the Edmonton Symphony Choir, of which she was a member, was also the director of performing arts for Alberta Culture, an organization similar to state arts councils in the United States. When the position of music consultant became vacant, the director felt that Pat qualified because of her volunteer and board experience. She administered grants while at the same time she received her first formal training in fundraising. When she served as interim managing director of ProCoro Canada, a newly formed professional choir, she managed her first fundraising campaign. From then on, she was hooked on development. "I feel as though my career found me!" she says.

For more than 20 years Pat has worked in fundraising, sometimes as development director and at other times as an executive in a management position with a strong focus on fundraising. Some of the highlights of her career were to develop and manage the Tucson Symphony Orchestra's deficit elimination campaign, establish new programs and raise money for the first European tour of a professional modern dance company in Pittsburgh, Pennsylvania, and raise more than $8 million for an arts program at the University of Arizona. "I am proud of the fact that the College of Fine Arts has emerged as a real leader on the campus and in the community. I know that my work was significant in bringing about that change. But my greatest joy has been in working with the many hundreds of individuals who care deeply about the arts and whose passion and generosity ensure that the arts will continue as a vital force for the future."

Any description of Pat's career would be incomplete without mentioning her involvement with the Association of Fundraising Professionals. She has been active locally and nationally since 1984, and received her CFRE in 1987. "AFP is very important to me," Pat says, "as my association with this organization has given me the opportunity to learn from remarkable colleagues around the country, to serve my profession in a meaningful way, to be a mentor to younger development professionals, and to help shape the future of our profession."

When asked to list her greatest achievements, she stated that being recognized by her peers for her achievements in fundraising when she received the Outstanding Fundraising Executive of the Year by the South Arizona Chapter of NSFRE was the honor she most cherished. It indicated that she was recognized not just for being a good fundraiser but also for her leadership and commitment to philanthropy.

Pat's advice to those entering the profession involves several steps. "Volunteer to get as much diverse experience as possible. Find a mentor, find someone you connect with on a personal level, who is a respected professional in fundraising, and spend as much time talking about not only the particular how-tos of fundraising but also the philosophy of philanthropy and what it means to our community and society. Keep an open mind to opportunities in many areas of the nonprofits. Another bit of advice is that of being passionate about the job of being a development professional."

FRANK BENTZ

Frank Bentz made the transition to fundraising from owning his own business for seven years to accepting a position in the admissions and scholarship offices at Western Michigan University. "They came to me and asked if I had thought about getting into development, as they were looking for someone to take over all development," Frank explains. He spoke to a friend in the alumni department about his confusion. "Why would they want me in development?" he wondered. He thought that it had something to do with campus planning. His friend, at the time the alumni director for Western Michigan and later a chairman of NSFRE, retorted, "No, dummy, this is fundraising!" Frank took the job and since that time has had, as he puts it, "the great fortune to be in this profession for over 32 years."

After Western Michigan, Frank went to a fundraising institute and was advised to look at other potential opportunities. He then went to the University of Minnesota, which became a great experience. When he joined as director of development, the university had been raising about $2 million annually. At the close of the first year and a half, Frank and his staff raised more than $10 million. He then moved to another educational institution, Franklin College in Indiana, and helped raise $10 million for the celebration of its 150th anniversary. After this he formed his own national company, Bentz, Whaley Flessner, which is still active in Minneapolis, Minnesota. During this consulting partnership came what he considers the highlight of his career, "the biggest thrill of my life."

As Frank relates it, "One firm with dedicated volunteers raised $150 million for the restoration of the Statue of Liberty and Ellis Island Campaign. As I sat on the banks of the East River at the great celebration that followed the restoration, in the light of the magnificent fireworks, I thought back to being that little country boy and coming all the way to that night and having the experience of my lifetime."

When asked about his achievements, Frank mentioned his burning desire to pass along values and to mentor people who enter the field and partnering with dedicated and involved volunteers and professional fundraisers. "I love working with people and love to ask for money if it is for the right cause, and doing something for other people."

His advice to those entering the profession is, "Love people and listen to them. Believe in the cause and the product." Frank recently retired after serving for 10 years at St. Vincent's Hospital in Indiana. When he joined the institution, they had raised $6.5 million. When he retired, the foundation had raised $70 million. "While I was there I had the wonderful experience of receiving a donation from a woman who had sent in $2.00 after losing her husband to cancer in the St. Vincent Hospice program. I framed those two dollars and kept them on the wall, because every gift is important, no matter what the size of the gift."

Frank continues to serve his profession as a part-time consultant and mentor to others.

WENDY BOYLE

Wendy Boyle took time to start a family, then returned to the work force. She responded to an ad for a development position at the Indianapolis Museum of Art. "I knew nothing about development, but I loved the museum, so I applied. I began at the bottom of the ladder, writing grant proposals and providing general support. Over the five-year period that I was there, I was promoted twice, eventually heading all of development and membership. I loved the many facets of development, and I still do."

While at the Indianapolis Museum of Art, Wendy was asked to head the department on an interim basis and to serve on the museum's management team. That opportunity solidified her increasing commitment to fundraising and philanthropy. After a few months in that capacity, she learned from the departing development director of the Indianapolis Symphony Orchestra that she was one of three persons he had proposed to fill his position. "And so it was that I was off to another wonderful position that fit so well with my personal interests and my professional career path."

After a few years, she realized that to advance in development often meant job-hopping. That's when she considered consulting as her next step. "Yet another rewarding experience was in store when I joined the national fundraising consulting firm of Ketchum, Inc. I began as a resident campaign director, traveling and living and working all over the country and coming home only one weekend a month. I was promoted two or three times, and by the time I left nine years later, I was president of the firm's Midwest region. The firm suffered some serious declines, and I was among many who lost their positions just before the firm was sold." She then joined the American College of Sports Medicine as senior vice president for Corporate Relations and Development, where the primary thrust of the program involved developing substantial partnerships and sponsorship packages with national corporations. After two and a half years, she discovered that she missed consulting, and so she established her own firm, Boyle & Associates.

Wendy has been in fundraising for 25 years. She was among the first professionals to earn the CFRE designation, and she served as president of the

Indiana Chapter of NSFRE. She continues her involvement in the profession by presenting workshops at conferences. "In each position I've held there has been some special accomplishment. As a consultant, I am gratified to have my clients' confidence as I help them achieve goals that have lasting value to their constituents. My work has led me to many wonderful experiences and many lasting friendships."

Wendy has this advice to give to those entering fundraising as a profession. "Development is so much more diversified, and so much more professional than it was when I stumbled into it. So, I would encourage a newcomer to savor the many opportunities to learn more: join and participate in a professional membership society such as AFP, AHP, or CASE; read professional periodicals and Internet resources; talk with peers; find a mentor. And, no matter whether you choose to be a specialist or generalist in fundraising, enjoy the rewarding work of linking generous donors to your worthy cause."

HERBERT JONES

Herbert Jones did not plan to be in fundraising. He was an organizer for a very large farm organization in Iowa and sold insurance, as well. He served in the army during the Korean War, and was sent to Germany as a public information noncommissioned officer. He returned to his former employer after his tour of duty. Then the college he attended established a development officer, which was a new concept at the time. He was invited to interview, was hired, and began his career in fundraising.

After 46 years in fundraising he retired, but he still does consulting work. He had served higher educational institutions for 35 years, worked for a national symphony orchestra, and been a full-time consultant. In considering the highlights of his career, he remembers three that were particularly memorable. "I was at a private college in Michigan when we received a Ford Foundation Challenge Grant. I wrote the proposal and we did a 10-year financial plan and kicked off the campaign. This was a major breakthrough in fundraising for the institution and I was part of it. It was a terrific experience." The other two highlights were being part of the merger of two educational institutions and a capital campaign for a major symphony orchestra.

His first piece of advice to a fundraising professional is, "Know the organization you serve very well. It's not enough to be an employee; it's got to be a passion. Study, understand, and embrace the AFP code of ethics. Remember, few people got up this morning to give away money. Be absolutely honest and do exactly what was agreed. Show your humanity, civility, and grace in your relationships with other people." Herbert also counsels professionals to be prepared for disappointment. "It's not necessarily a personal failure." His final advice is, "Always be on time! If you're late, you have to apologize, and you never want to start a conversation with an apology."

TRISH JACKSON

When Trish Jackson received her undergraduate degree in 1982, she knew she wanted to be in fundraising. She had been an active student at Scripps College in Claremont, California, and during her senior year was invited to serve on the search committee for a new vice president for advancement. The candidate who was selected invited Trish back a year later as the assistant director of annual giving, where she became responsible for starting a parents' program and a paid-student caller program for Scripps. "I have never regretted my entry into the development field. I made a fairly standard trajectory through the profession, feeling quite fortunate to be at the right place at the right time on several occasions during my professional life."

Why did Trish enter the profession? "Because as an undergraduate I realized it was something I could get very excited about that I could feel passionate about advancing a cause. Then, I was also mentored by many who pointed out what a wonderful field it would be for women in the next decade or so. I would also note that I grew up knowing the importance of philanthropy and voluntarism, and this had an effect on my chosen lifepath."

Trish has been in the profession for more than 19 years. After Scripps College she joined Claremont McKenna College, where she was coordinator of campaign and related activities. "This was a fabulous generalist position in which I had the opportunity to gain an understanding of many different facets of development." She then went on to become CMC's director of corporate relations and also did much major gifts work, because these two areas were natural partners at CMC in that many of the college's alumni were successful corporate leaders. "There were three of us in the development office who were about the same age, and had been hired around the same time. The vice president would switch our jobs around as he saw any of us become bored or not challenged by our current job."

In 1988, Trish moved east to become the director of major gifts at Mount Holyoke, where she was responsible for coordinating a regional major gifts program and supervising four major gifts officers as well as the planned giving officer. In 1991, she became the director of development at Wheaton College in Norton, Massachusetts, where she was responsible for a comprehensive campaign, and the conversion to a new software package. In 1998, Trish joined the Council for Advancement and Support of Education (CASE) as vice president for education, overseeing all conferences and educational program development opportunities.

When asked what she considers her greatest achievement, Trish said, "Having had the chance to work for people who have taught me much, and for organizations to which I have deep and abiding commitments. This is why I believe that I have had the privilege to succeed in this field in real ways. I am tremendously blessed to be surrounded, embraced, and upheld by both the institutions I have served and the many mentors with whom I've worked." In particular, Trish relishes the success of the campaign for Wheaton College, where a $65 million campaign was initiated. Five years later, the Wheaton family had raised $90 million. This was accomplished through hard work throughout the campaign, and the confidence that every bit of effort made a difference.

Trish advises, "If you don't love it, don't do it! It is a profession that requires passion. It is a tremendously fulfilling calling in a real sense. You can learn everything else; you can never learn the passion."

ART FRANTZREB

Art Frantzreb was trained as a business executive but entered the fundraising field as the team member with the least experience in a capital campaign for Cornell University. His job was to research prospects. At the time there was no fundraising office. He then moved to Rutgers, the State University of New Jersey, and was given the position as the first resource development officer. Following this experience he was retained by George Brakeley, Jr., to create an East Coast firm for capital philanthropic purposes. From there, he established his own firm in 1961, where he worked with almost 500 clients before closing his firm in 1979.

As a senior member in the roster of outstanding fundraising executives, Art has had a major role in pioneering new dimensions in the management of nonprofit board, chief executive, and staff responsibilities. His comment on a career that is replete with honors, published writings, board service, and successful consulting is, "I viewed that the act of philanthropy is a humanitarian ministry. The word *philanthropy* comes from the Greek language meaning 'love for mankind.' Therefore, all team members must be or become specialists in the art of achieving humane, spiritual, cultural, and secure benefits for society." Art is the author of a book that is a blueprint for what nonprofit organizations' boards should and should not do, titled *Not On This Board You Don't* (Chicago, IL: Bonus Books, Inc., February 1997).

The selection of professionals included in this chapter is just a tiny slice of life that represents achievements and success by many in the profession, particularly during the 20th century, when fundraising took root as an organized activity in the United States. Building on this basis, a new generation of career seekers will establish careers in the twenty-first century that will remind us of what the beloved American poet, Henry Wadsworth Longfellow, wrote:

> "Lives of great (people) all remind us
> We can make our lives sublime.
> And, departing, leave behind us
> Footprints on the sands of time."[2]

SIDEBAR   MARK A. DENNIS, JR.

Effective fundraising provides mutual benefits and satisfaction for everyone involved: charitable organizations receive funds to carry out important, worthwhile work and donors have the satisfaction of expressing their life values through philanthropy. The most important qualification for becoming an effective fundraiser is the ability to form authentic relationships with people based on mutual respect, integrity, and a sincere desire to help them achieve their philanthropic goals.

Professional organizations, including the Association of Fundraising Professionals and The Fund Raising School at Indiana University, have outlined educational requirements and best practices that form the basis of effective fundraising; however, the ultimate foundation of effective philanthropy is derived from the ability to build genuine relationships and to nurture the capacities of both donors and organizations.

Key trends in philanthropy make this a critical qualification in this new century. Successful fundraisers will be those who have the ability to build confidence in and nurture relationships with individuals and other stakeholders, building capacity through a systematic process of strengthening the organization via the identification, cultivation, and involvement of individuals. These individuals later become advocates empowered to lead, recruit, and solicit others through effective relationship building.

The idea of capacity building calls many of us to new ways of interacting with staff, board members, and increasingly diverse groups of donors. Indeed, this model of nurturing philanthropy calls for us to truly be leaders, not simply managers. We must examine best practices in fundraising through a different lens that is focused on involving and inspiring people, in addition to empowering them to involve and inspire others.

Equipped with best practices, we must conscientiously use our expertise to inspire confidence in our donors, volunteers, and staff. Helping our organizations understand the importance of communicating mission-driven programs and initiatives, visionary leadership (staff and volunteer), a compelling case for support, excellent stewardship of gifts, value-added benefits for all stakeholders, and credibility, integrity, confidentiality, and honesty are critical to building solid relationships and expanding our philanthropic capacities.

Ultimately, nurturing relationships is about building trust. We certainly must be equipped with best practices, academic training, and technical expertise; however, our most important qualifications come from deep within: We must be trustworthy people who genuinely respect and trust others. There are no short-cuts. We must be willing to risk trusting others to help us build our organizations, to deliver the services that fulfill our mission, and to garner the capacity and support we need to accomplish our philanthropic vision.

MARK ANDREW DENNIS, JR. M. Div., M. Mus., is president of The Alford Group Inc. He has more than 30 years of service to the nonprofit sector and has been active with the Association of Fundraising Professionals (formerly NSFRE). As a trainer, he has conducted seminars and workshops at professional associations and universities, and currently is a senior adjunct faculty member of the University of Chicago. His educational background is varied, including a master of music degree from Bowling Green State University and a master of divinity from Howard University.

PROFESSIONALS SAY . . .

The role of function of a professional fundraiser is to create, inspire, and facilitate philanthropic behavior, philanthropy being the expression of love (phileo) and care for all human kind (anthropos). If we take money from people who really do not wish to give, we are practicing some degree of extortion. If we take money from people on the basis of inaccurate representation, we are practicing some degree of fraud. If we take money from people for reasons and causes they really do not understand, we are practicing some degree of "con." If we take money from people for the psychological, social, and economic benefits that accrue to them as a result of their giving, we are practicing some degree of business for return on investment. There may be a little of the above in a gift transaction; however, we are at our professional best and also achieve at the highest possible level when we can inspire and facilitate authentic charitable motivation. You can be a professional Agent of Philanthropy as a fundraiser or just another person whose job it is to collect money for something.

Harvey DeVries, Managing Partner, Retired, Currie, Ferner, DeVries Minneapolis Consulting Group

PART FOUR

Issues and Aspects of a Fundraising Job

ccording to writer Kevin McCarthy, there are four questions that a person planning a career should ask.[1]

- Why am I here?
- Where am I going?
- How will I get there?
- What will I choose to do and not to do en route?

Although these are basic questions and are often recommended by career counselors, they do merit some thought by a person contemplating a career in fundraising. The first question implies a commitment to the concept of service, of being a steward of funds, of benefiting a cause, of understanding and accepting fundraising as vital to the nonprofit sector and its organizations. The second question involves setting goals, including long-term ones in career advancement. The third question induces a career seeker to ponder a career path, including education, professional memberships, collegial relationships, training, and other activities that promote career development. The final question emphasizes values, a consideration of ethical principles, an acceptance of the role of stewardship in fundraising, a sense of belonging, and commitment to the profession.

This section of the book includes the multidimensional considerations in seeking a job, understanding the opportunities, and working with the constraints as well as possibilities the field and specific jobs entail. By now, the context in which fundraising takes place has been considered. Preparation steps have been outlined, and the importance of fundraising for the non-profit sector—ergo, the value of the fundraising professional—has been established. In this section some practical aspects of finding and keeping a job will be considered.

First is an overview of what the professional can expect to be paid for the various positions discussed in Part Two. Included in Chapter 11 are suggestions on how to ask for the salary that is appropriate.

Chapter 12 discusses the logical progression in career advancement, how to qualify for promotion, and how to balance personal and professional goals with the goals of the institution.

The profession of fundraising provides a myriad of opportunities for minorities. Nonprofit organizations seek diversity in hiring, especially as attention is increasingly placed on cross-cultural fundraising in the United States. Chapter 13 provides information on minorities in the field through interviews with professionals representing various ethnic groups. Minorities raise money across cultures. They must not only know the philanthropic attitudes and habits of their own population groups but understand mainstream fundraising practices as well. Included in this chapter are the voices of professionals from the Hispanic, African American, Native American, and Asian American ethnic groups. At the end of the chapter, a list of references includes research studies and volumes dealing with philanthropy and fundraising among minorities.

It is highly important for a professional to learn to communicate with the boss, to understand how to motivate an organizational leader who is reluctant to raise funds, to provide the right kind and amount of support for institutional development, and at the same time meet the fundraising goals. The concept of *responsibility without authority* is addressed in Chapter 14 and suggestions are provided on how to be a respected professional in the larger setting, while at the same time giving appropriate respect to the leadership of the organization.

Fundraising success depends on a team effort that involves the board, other volunteers, leaders of the organization, colleagues, and staff. Relationships and communication with team members is vital. Chapter 15 looks at the fundraising team and the role of the fundraising professional as the manager of the process. Also included will be board relationships and how to work with committees, as well as ideas on what to do if access to board members and volunteers by the fundraising professional is limited.

A significant number of nonprofit organizations function on low budgets and therefore cannot afford a full-time fundraiser. A professional who must carry out fundraising without benefit of a staff, or who has other responsibilities in addition to fundraising, experiences unique challenges. Suggestions for setting priorities, handling difficult situations, finding time for the necessary tasks, and determining realistic goals are included in Chapter 16.

As the concept of civil society and nongovernmental organizations' (NGOs') role in developing such a society has spread globally, fundraising has also received much international attention. Chapter 17 provides an overview of opportunities for working outside of the United States, what the differences are in working in other cultures and countries, and the importance of an international outlook during the twenty-first century. That is to say, the fundraising professional is part of a global community as emphases on fundraising, philanthropy, and NGOs increase in importance. The readings appended to this chapter include major references concerning international aspects of fundraising.

Finally, burnout and stressful situations are not uncommon in the profession. Chapter 18 offers ideas on how to bring balance to a professional life, how to handle difficult situations and people, and when to seek help. Particularly significant is a listing of the symptoms of burnout.

Revisiting McCarthy's four questions is perhaps useful prior to reading Part Four:

• Why am I here?
• Where am I going?
• How will I get there?
• What will I choose to do and not to do en route?

Understanding the possibilities as well as liabilities of fundraising as a career is important for conducting a job search and working productively and successfully once the job has been acquired. This section, therefore, serves as a bridge between the understanding of the context and preparation for a career (Parts One to Three) and the actual work of a fundraiser in seeking a position and being successful in a fundraising career (Parts Five and Six).

CHAPTER 11

Salaries and Wages

SIDEBAR BY JAMES M. GREENFIELD

Charles Stewart Mott wrote, "When people are serving, life is no longer meaningless." Leo Tolstoy said, "The sole meaning of life is to serve humanity." And Robert Louis Stevenson composed these words, "Don't judge each day by the harvest you reap but by the seeds you plant."[1]

In fundraising, service is what gives a professional life its meaning, but while service should be, and in most cases is, the most important motivator for a career in fundraising, the realistic person also understands that money earned is important for our livelihood.

Salaries and wages in the nonprofit sector have generally been lower than for the for-profit and government sector; however, any generalizations about nonprofit salaries are difficult to make because of variables such as:

- Geography
- Type and size of institution
- Importance of fundraising in an institution
- Gender
- Type of role or position in fundraising
- Level of expertise
- Inflation and the economy

According to a salary survey conducted by the National Society of Fund Raising Executives (renamed Association of Fundraising Professionals, AFP), in 1999 the median salary for a fundraising professional was between $40,000 and $50,000 a year. Fewer than 5 percent of those who responded made less than $25,000, and approximately 18 percent made more than $75,000. Approximately 9 percent made more than $90,000 a year.[2]

In 2000, AFP's Professional Advancement Division undertook the first detailed compensation and benefits survey, and this will be conducted annually. The stratified sample was 2,026 U.S. members. The average salary was $62,032, with a median of $54,000. CFREs have a higher rate of compensation than the average respondents. Most respondents reported that they have good benefits programs such as retirement, health insurance, professional development, and disability insurance. Contracts, however, are not common; fewer than 20 percent said they have an employment contract.[3]

The *NonProfit Times* (NPT) did a survey in December 2000, and responses from 340 organizations were tabulated. The national averages for eight positions were:

President/chief executive	$96,715
Chief financial officer	$62,361
Program director	$56,862
Planned giving officer	$59,939
Development director	$59,220
Major gifts officer	$60,945
Chief of direct marketing	$52,758
Director of volunteers	$35,285

The NPT determined that size of organization does matter, and region also figures into the salary picture. Also, only 33.1 percent of respondents in this study received contracts.

Discussion persists as to what level of compensation is appropriate for someone who is primarily responsible for raising money. Some argue that salaries comparable to the for-profit sector, or at least narrowing the gap, are important in order to attract the best employees. Others believe that not-for-profit employees should (and do) work because of commitment to the mission, and the sector and salaries are not a major concern. There is also the dichotomy of nonprofits being urged to be more businesslike in their management practices, while criticism has surfaced that this is the very reason why the sector is experiencing many problems.

In general, there is agreement that low salaries simply do not attract and retain qualified workers and that progress must be made. Without a doubt, most fundraising professionals believe in their work and the organizations for which they work, but the reality of salary and wage needs remains an issue not easily resolved.

As acknowledged, generalizations are difficult to make without consideration of many factors that affect salaries and wages.

- *Geography affects pay.* There are regional differences in salaries and living expenses, such as the West Coast versus the Southeast. Major metropolitan areas offer a larger salary when compared to small towns or rural areas.

- *The type and size of institution affects pay.* Usually higher education and health care offer the higher salaries, while small human service and environmental organizations tend to offer the lowest.

- *Importance of fundraising in an institution is another determinant in salary and wages.* If fundraising is valued at the organizational level, and leadership of the organization is committed to the practice, the salary is likely to be higher.

- *Women often draw a lower salary than men, but the difference appears to be due to the amount of fundraising experience.* The average salary for women in the 1995 AFP survey was $41,207, while men received an average of $52,917. Women fundraising professionals reported salaries between $25,000 and $50,000, and men's salaries were between $40,000 and $75,000. By the 1999 survey, the highest percentage of males earned in the $60,000 to $75,000 range, while the female range stayed the same; however, the 1999 survey indicated that when incomes of males and females with similar years of experience are compared, such as 20 or more, there was little difference in income. Also, according to Anne Preston,[4] women who change jobs from the for-profit to the not-for-profit sector have a wage loss of only 0 to 5 percent, while men may take a loss as high as 47 percent. Women are well-represented in the nonprofit sector, although some say they are overrepresented in the low-paying jobs. In the AFP survey of 2000, the data showed the same relationship between age, experience, and salary level as noted previously, and the disparity between gender salaries is also the same.

- *The type of role or position in fundraising also defines salary.* Those who specialize in planned giving, major gifts, or building endowments are likely to receive higher salaries than personnel who work in special events or gift receipting. Naturally, senior development officers, such as vice presidents for advancement (often in higher education), receive the highest salaries, and sometimes this amount may be more than the chief executive officer's salary. Also, persons who manage complex programs, particularly in a leadership role, receive higher salaries; however, a 1992 AFP member survey indicated that entry-level positions in fundraising pay relatively well when compared to the business sector. A wider discrepancy exists at the higher levels of fundraising responsibility.

- *Level of expertise determines salary level in many cases.* Some fundraisers, however, choose to stay in a particular niche and thus forgo possible higher salaries. Years of employment also affect salaries. Often, entry-level personnel and junior professionals must seek positions at other institutions in order to move up the career ladder and receive higher pay. Senior executives are more likely to stay at the same institution and in the same type of work.

- *Inflation and the economy are two additional factors in the compensation picture.* At times nonprofit salaries do not, or cannot, keep pace with inflation, and at the same time they are affected by downturns in economy.

- *Benefits also vary according to the same criteria.* Most organizations pay for professional organization dues and travel expenses, although health and dental insurance may not be covered in small organizations. Other optional benefits are disability insurance and retirement programs. Kelly maintains that "fundraisers generally enjoy excellent fringe benefits. Among the benefits included in their compensation—often fully funded by employers—are health insurance, major medical, dental and prescription plans, eye coverage, disability insurance, tuition reimbursement, professional dues, club memberships, and car and mileage allowances."[5]

- *Race is not a factor.* No difference seems to exist between salaries of minorities and Whites, according to research compiled by Kelly.[6]

Fundraising professionals receive a salary or a fee and do not work for a commission. Although the concept of commission or percentage payment continues to be debated, most organizations and professionals agree that such payment is not appropriate for a nonprofit organization. Donors may lose confidence in how their funds are used. Questions will arise as to who or what the fundraising professional is serving—whether it is private gain or the organization's mission and cause—and the difference between for-profit and not-for-profit institutions becomes blurred. The Code of Ethical Principles and Standards of Professional Practice, issued by AFP and amended in January 2000, clearly states in its Standard No. 16 that "members shall not accept compensation that is based on a percentage of charitable contributions; nor shall they accept finder's fees." Bonuses that are congruent with the organization's practices, and are not provided just for dollars raised, are allowed, but they should not be based on a percentage of charitable contributions raised.

How should you address the compensation issue when being considered for a position in fundraising?

1. *Let the organization bring up the subject of salary.* If the question of salary is raised too early, try to postpone the discussion until you have had a chance to fully present your qualifications.

2. *Be sure to do your homework and understand what equivalent types of positions offer for a person of your experience and expertise.* What titles correlate with what responsibilities, and therefore receive what ranges of salary? Remember that the market decides how much you should be compensated. Professional organizations will also provide some general figures to serve as guidelines.

3. *Have a good idea of what you're worth and what you're willing to accept.* Be sure to base this on a defensible position. You have already discussed, during the interview process, your achievements and your credentials. You have done your homework and know what similar positions pay for a person of your caliber in your geographic region and type of organization. Remember that a large salary may go along with an unhealthy dependency on the fundraiser to work wonders!

4. *Don't hide your salary history.* If an explanation is warranted, provide one, such as, "I worked for XYZ organization for a lower salary because I saw the opportunity for growth," or "I had a special commitment to the organization, but now it's time to move on." Don't leave a low salary issue open to questions about your worth or allow hints to surface that perhaps your caliber of work wasn't up to par. Some professionals have also found a high salary history to be a bit of a drawback. They may want to work for a certain cause to which they

have a strong commitment, but a previous high salary might seem to disqualify them. Also, a high salary is accompanied by high expectations of what the professional should be able to do, and sometimes those expectations may be unrealistic. Nevertheless, being open and honest about salary history is important, although appropriate explanations may be warranted.

5. *If necessary, negotiate.* There may be good reasons why the salary being offered is lower than you expected. These reasons may also hint at problems in the organization; however, it is equally likely that the organization is trying to get the most for the money. In this case, if you give the image of being a "bargain," your value will also be equally decreased.

6. *Remember to get the full picture of what your salary involves.* This could include base salary, benefits, retirement plans, insurance, medical and dental coverage, vacations and holidays, memberships, travel allowances, and other items.

7. *If you are asked what salary range you expect, give a range based on your research.* Indicate whether this is total compensation or base salary. Also, substantiate your request with reasons why you believe you are worth the amount you are stating.

8. *Don't give the impression that you are going to quibble over money.* Try to assess how much to focus on financial issues. You are, no doubt, more concerned over what you can do with the organization than you are over a bonus or vacation policy. Avoid giving the wrong idea to the interviewer and therefore the organization. Also, don't feel pressured to accept the salary on the spot. It is perfectly all right to ask for time to think, or to evaluate the offer.

If you stay at a certain organization and in the same job for some time, you will no doubt need to request a raise. Some organizations give raises based on performance; others have annual across-the-board increases. In many cases you will have to ask for a raise. Begin by talking with your boss about your work, particularly in asking how you can improve what you are doing for the organization, and if you are measuring up to expectations (if a periodic review doesn't take care of this automatically). Add to your responsibilities voluntarily and beyond what your job description defines, and record these achievements.

Then plan your case and presentation, and practice your presentation, either by taping it or having a willing friend listen. Be confident. Don't ask for an unsubstantiated or unreasoned raise. Have your facts in place, including comparisons among other organizations and the salaries that are paid for the equivalent of your position.

Negotiation may be part of the process. You may have to anticipate any objections or hard questions, particularly if the budget is tight, as it often is at nonprofit organizations. You must prove your worth and define why a raise is justified. If you are turned down, ask if you can discuss this at a later date, and request guidance on how to measure up to expectations so that you can make a case in the future. Don't threaten to quit; your boss and organization might find this the easiest way to deal with your request for a raise and agree to your departure.

Although job satisfaction often does come in association with a cause that we care about, be realistic about compensation for the work you are and will be doing.

The 1999 AFP member survey found that the more funds raised, the higher the respondent's income, and vice versa. The 1995 survey summarized the characteristics of those who received the highest salaries among fundraisers. These included meeting or exceeding fundraising goals for the previous five years, working in health care or education, working long hours (51 hours or more per week), obtaining the CFRE, staying in the profession for 10 or more years, staying with one employer and not switching jobs frequently, working with four or more colleagues on the staff, and having at least a college education. Although these qualities or characteristics are not immediately possible to attain by the novice or entry-level person, they do provide guidelines for what influences the best compensation in the field.

Overall, according to the 1999 survey, most respondents expressed satisfaction with their salary and benefits package. Almost half (46 percent) were somewhat satisfied and 36 percent were very satisfied. This, coupled with the fact that almost all respondents stated they had positive feelings about their careers in fundraising, indicates that salaries are competitive and generally indicate a respected status in the nonprofit sector.

Annual Professional Income by Type of Organization

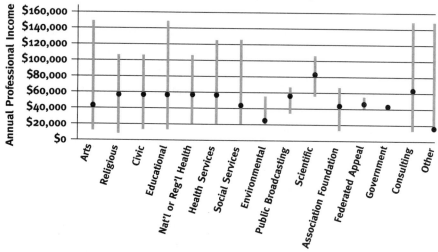

Type of Organization
(Each line shows the range from high to low reported income. The dot represents the median.)

Caution: Because of small numbers in some categories, the data in the following three tables should be taken as illustrative rather than representative.

Annual Professional Income by Type of Organization (Percentages), 1999

	Arts	Religious	Civic	Educational	National or Reg'l Health	Health Services	Social Services	Environmental	Public Broadcasting	Scientific	Association Foundation	Federated Appeal	Government	Consulting	Other	None (unemployed)
$12,000 or less	0.0	3.6	16.7	0.9	0.0	0.0	1.1	0.0	0.0	0.0	10.0	0.0	0.0	2.9	0.0	33.3
$12,001–$18,000	3.1	7.1	0.0	0.0	0.0	0.0	0.0	0.0	0.0	0.0	0.0	0.0	0.0	0.0	0.0	0.0
$18,001–$25,000	3.1	7.1	16.7	2.6	3.8	1.3	2.2	16.7	0.0	0.0	0.0	0.0	0.0	0.0	4.0	0.0
$25,001–$33,000	9.4	7.1	0.0	11.1	7.7	9.0	12.2	50.0	0.0	0.0	10.0	0.0	0.0	5.9	12.0	33.3
$33,001–$40,000	28.1	14.3	0.0	12.8	7.7	16.7	21.1	16.7	25.0	0.0	20.0	20.0	0.0	0.0	20.0	0.0
$40,001–50,000	25.0	10.7	16.7	15.4	23.1	14.1	26.7	0.0	25.0	0.0	10.0	40.0	100.0	11.8	16.0	0.0
$50,001–$60,000	9.4	17.9	33.3	17.9	23.1	19.2	11.1	16.7	0.0	20.0	20.0	20.0	0.0	14.7	28.0	0.0
$60,001–$75,000	9.4	10.7	0.0	18.8	7.7	15.4	12.2	0.0	50.0	20.0	20.0	0.0	0.0	29.4	4.0	0.0
$75,001–$90,000	9.4	17.9	0.0	9.4	15.4	3.8	11.1	0.0	0.0	20.0	0.0	20.0	0.0	8.8	4.0	0.0
$90,001–$115,000	0.0	3.6	16.7	7.7	7.7	12.8	0.0	0.0	0.0	40.0	0.0	0.0	0.0	17.6	4.0	0.0
$115,001–$140,000	0.0	0.0	0.0	0.9	0.0	3.8	1.1	0.0	0.0	0.0	0.0	0.0	0.0	0.0	0.0	0.0
Over $140,000	3.1	0.0	0.0	0.9	0.0	0.0	0.0	0.0	0.0	0.0	0.0	0.0	0.0	5.9	8.0	0.0
No Answer	0.0	0.0	0.0	1.7	3.8	3.8	1.1	0.0	0.0	0.0	10.0	0.0	0.0	2.9	0.0	33.3
Total	100.0	100.0	100.0	100.0	100.0	100.0	100.0	100.0	100.0	100.0	100.0	100.0	100.0	100.0	100.0	100.0
Number of Cases	32	28	6	117	26	78	90	6	4	5	10	5	2	34	25	3
Median Category	$40K–$50K	$50K–$60K	$50K–$60K	$50K–$60K	$50K–$60K	$50K–$60K	$40K–$50K	$25K–$35K	$50K–$60K	$75K–$90K	$40K–$50K	$40K–$50K	$40K–$50K	$60K–$75K	$40K–$50K	$12K–$18K

Annual Professional Income by Position and Type of Organization (Percentages), 1999

Type of Organization	Chief Development			Associate Development Director			Program Director		
	Range	Median	# Cases	Range	Median	# Cases	Range	Median	# Cases
Arts, Culture or Humanities	$18K–$140K+	$40K–$50K	18	$12K–$75K	$33K–$40K	3	$25K–$75K	$33K–40K	6
Religious or Religion-Related	$12K–$115K	$50K–$60K	18	$18K–$60K	$25K–$33K	3	$33K–$90K	$50K–$60K	2
Civic and Public Affairs	$12K–$115K	$25K–$33K	4	N/A	N/A	0	N/A	N/A	0
Education	$18K–$140K+	$50K–$60K	65	$18K–$140K	$40K–$50K	13	$25K–$115K	$40K–$50K	20
National or Regional Health	$25K–$90K	$40K–$50K	7	$33K–$75K	$50K–$60K	4	$50K–$60K	$50K–$60K	3
Health Services	$25K–$140K+	$60K–$75K	42	$18K–$60K	$40K–$50K	10	$33K–$75K	$50K–$60K	10
Social Services	$18K–$140K	$40K–$50K	57	$25K–$90K	$40K–$50K	6	$25K–$60K	$40K–$50K	8
Environmental	$25K–$60K	$33K–$40K	3	$25K–$33K	$25K–$33K	1	$25K–$33K	$25K–$33K	1
Public Broadcasting	$40K–$50K	$40K–$50K	1	N/A	N/A	0	$33K–$75K	$60K–$75K	3
Scientific or Research	$90K–$115K	$90K–$115K	1	N/A	N/A	0	$90K–$115K	$90K–$115K	1
Association Foundation	$12K–$75K	$40K–50K	4	$40K–$50K	$40K–$50K	1	N/A	N/A	0
Federated Appeals	$40K–$90K	$60K–$75K	2	N/A	N/A	0	$40K–$60K	$50K–$60K	2
Government	$40K–$50K	$40K–$50K	1	N/A	N/A	0	N/A	N/A	0

Median Annual Professional Income by Type of Organization, 1981–1999

	1981	1985	1988	1992	1995[1]	1999
Arts, Culture or Humanities	$31,000	$32,270	$35,590	$47,027	N/C	$40K–$50K
Religious or Religion-Related	$26,500	$34,400	$37,778	N/C	$40,000	$50K–$60K
Civic and Public Affairs	N/C	N/C	N/C	N/C	N/C	$50K–$60K
Education	$31,000	$33,000	$41,073	$45,245	$50,535	$50K–$60K
National or Regional Health	N/C	$32,680	$35,590	$47,027	$39,104	$50K–$60K
Health Services*	$37,159	$43,200	$45,543	$54,196	$62,294	$50K–$60K
National Social Service**	$28,000	$31,260	$35,129	$42,190	$44,984	$40K–$50K
Regional/Local Service**	$26,650	$29,260	$30,049	$38,077	$36,371	**
Youth Organization	N/C	$32,172	$35,848	$42,115	$39,899	N/C
Environmental***	N/C	***	$51,681	$43,576	$44,984	$25K–$33K
Retirement Community	N/C	$30,661	$33,020	$44,367	$41,233	N/C
Conservation & Wildlife	N/C	$33,000	$25,000	$35,800	$33,000	N/C
Public Broadcasting	N/C	N/C	N/C	N/C	N/C	$50K–$60K
Scientific or Research	N/C	N/C	N/C	N/C	N/C	$75K–$90K
Association Foundation	N/C	N/C	N/C	N/C	N/C	$40K–$50K
Federated Appeals	N/C	N/C	N/C	N/C	N/C	$40K–$50K
Government	N/C	N/C	N/C	N/C	N/C	$40K–$50K
Consulting Firm, Partnership	$38,570	$50,000	N/C	N/C	N/C	$60K–$75K
Large Consulting Firm	N/C	N/C	$64,202	N/C	$48,348	N/C
Small Consulting Firm	N/C	N/C	$47,170	N/C	$50,000	N/C
Independent Consultant	$38,000	$44,375	$42,100	N/C	$47,593	N/C
Other	$34,666	$33,954	N/C	N/C	N/C	$40K–$50K
None (Unemployed)	N/C	N/C	N/C	N/C	N/C	$12K–$18K

[1]   Data for 1995 are not representative. By design, the 1995 survey over-sampled ethnic minority members.

*   Labeled "Hospital/Medical Center" prior to 1999.

**   1999 figure includes national, regional, and local social service organizations.

***   Considered part of Conservation/Wildlife in 1985. Includes Conservation/Wildlife for 1999.

N/C   Data not collected or reported.

▓ FURTHER READING

Bolles, Richard Nelson. *What Color Is Your Parachute?* Berkeley, CA: Ten Speed Press, revised annually.

The most comprehensive and well-known volume on conducting a career search. This book is updated yearly and includes all information relevant to finding a job.

Kelly, Kathleen S. *Effective Fund-Raising Management.* Mahwah, NJ: Lawrence Erlbaum Associates, Publishers, 1998.

This book explores the critical area of fundraising management. Fundraising management can be the key to success or the door to demise. An organization that does not understand and effectively manage their fundraising programs will soon be suffering.

Langer, Steven. *Compensation in Nonprofit Organizations.* 11th ed. Crete, IL: Abbott, Langer & Associates, June, 1996.

This is a study of salaries, allowing for perspectives when being offered a job.

Lauber, Daniel. *Non-Profits' Job Finder.* River Forest, IL: Planning/Communications, 1992.

A valuable resource for understanding the range of opportunities available for employment in the nonprofit sector. It includes suggestions for the job-seeker in matching skills and interests with the right organization.

Information from the Association of Fundraising Professionals (formerly the National Society of Fund Raising Executives).

National Society of Fund Raising Executives. *Membership Survey Profile.* Alexandria, VA: NSFRE, 1996.

National Society of Fund Raising Executives. *1999 Profile of NSFRE Members.* Alexandria, VA: NSFRE, 1999.

National Society of Fund Raising Executives. *Code of Ethical Principles and Standards of Professional Practice.* Alexandria, VA: NSFRE, 2000.

Web sites that contain salary information:

Association for Healthcare Philanthropy (www.go-ahp.org)
Action Without Borders (www.idealist.org)
Abbott, Langer & Associates, Inc. (www.abbott-langer.com)
Bureau of Labor Statistics (www.bls.gov)
Council on Foundations (www.cof.org)
The NonProfit Times (www.nptimes.com)
The Chronicle of Philanthropy (www.philanthropy.com)

Careers in fundraising offer full- or part-time employment in nonprofit organizations, or may be full- or part-time engagement as a consultant. Each will have a separate salary and wage schedule, depending on factors such as organization size, fundraising history, annual budget, fundraising goals, and more. Salaries and wages are negotiable, depending on the employer, level of responsibility, and position, and will be guided by institutional policy.

Organizations hiring full- or part-time staff also will provide a defined schedule of benefits beginning with health and dental coverage, life insurance, disability insurance, retirement programs, vacation, and sick leave. More senior executive positions also may offer supplemental programs for retirement, memberships, a vehicle, travel allowance, and much more. Bonus plans, based on overall institutional as well as departmental and individual goals, are permitted at many organizations and are limited to a percentage of current salary.

Nonprofit employers who use a written contract will set forth detailed provisions on performance expectations, as well as salary and benefit plans. Others observe employment agreements as with other employees in standard salary and benefit plans. Annual performance reviews are conducted against specific objectives leading to salary increases with a 0–4 percent or 0–5 percent merit pool.

Individuals who choose to be consultants are employed in consulting firms or are independent contractors. These for-profit corporations may offer greater flexibility in salary and wage policies, including performance bonus plans based on business volume and company profits. The benefits package will vary with the employer.

For those new to the profession, salary expectations will be competitive with other entry fields. The employee must demonstrate competence and results in order to earn higher compensation. Experience with managing many areas of fundraising simultaneously also will be required for promotion. Qualifications for higher-level positions include multiple solicitation and support program management experience, where staff and budget as well as volunteer management skills are required.

Senior executives have overall responsibility for entire programs that also may include knowledge of and experience with accounting, board recruitment and management, budgets, human resources, investment management, performance analysis, and more for all fundraising activities. In addition, a firm knowledge of the organization's industry is required. Collateral duties such as planning, marketing, advertising and public relations, government and community relations, and more may be part of senior executive positions.

JAMES M. GREENFIELD ACFRE, FAHP, is now senior associate vice president of The Alford Group Inc., a national full-service fundraising consulting firm. Previously, he was for 14 years the Senior Vice President, Resource Development, and Executive Director, Hoag Memorial Hospital Presbyterian and Hoag Hospital Foundation, in Newport Beach, California. Jim has been a fundraising executive in higher education and healthcare since 1962 and has been an active member of both AFP and AHP at the national and local levels for 30 years. A frequent speaker at conferences and workshops, he has written or edited six books and more than 35 articles on fundraising management. In 1993, he was awarded the Harold J. (Si) Seymour Award by AHP as the outstanding hospital fundraising professional, and in 2000, was honored by AFP as their outstanding fundraising executive.

PROFESSIONALS SAY . . .

The future of fundraising is bright! This is the only profession that I hear people say, I would do my job without pay. I am sure it is because people are often tied to the mission emotionally that they market. Oprah Winfrey recently wrote, "The real joy is in direct proportion to how connected you are to living your truth." I believe that fundraising professionals live their joy everyday in giving themselves to contribute to a higher purpose through service. That's why so many people in this profession have to be forced into retirement.

Dwayne Ashley, President, Thurgood Marshall Scholarship Fund, Inc., New York, New York

CHAPTER 12

Promotion and Career Advancement

SIDEBAR BY J. RUSSELL RAKER, III

Oliver Wendell Holmes wrote, "I find the great thing in this world is not so much where we stand, as in what direction we are moving: To reach the port of heaven, we must sail sometimes with the wind and sometimes against it—but we must sail, and not drift, nor lie at anchor."[1]

This is an appropriate metaphor describing advancement or promotion within the profession of fundraising. There are ample opportunities, there are many challenges, and a plan is required to move ahead on a career path.

Fundraising has been growing, along with the number of nonprofit organizations. As competition has increased along with nonprofit sector growth, more and more fundraising professionals are needed, and more and more demands are made of these professionals. Also, there is more need for specialists who have built on general experience. These include capital campaign management, major gift solicitation, fundraising administration, planned giving, and marketing for fundraising. In short, as a *Chronicle of Philanthropy* article stated, "Despite the tumultuous nature of the field—or perhaps because of it—the job market for fundraisers is booming. The potential rewards of a fund-raising career are a job seeker's dream: good salaries and benefits and plenty of opportunities for advancement."[2]

Another article in *The Chronicle of Philanthropy* stated, "As more and more charities seek large donations from individuals, the demand for senior fundraisers has exceeded the supply."[3] Senior fundraisers with good track records often don't have to look for a job but are sought after by organizations and executive search firms. In fact, many veteran development officers who command high salaries and hold highly desirable positions are now being invited to move up to the CEO's job in some organizations. Fundraising has become so critical that this kind of career advancement has become another option.

There is a shortage of qualified fundraising professionals who have credible achievements and have stayed at an organization for a reasonable length of time—at least the length of time required to bring in major gifts. Consequently, there is ample opportunity to move up the professional ladder. "Charity executives say they are dismayed by the lack of experience and motivation among many of the candidates they are forced to consider when no one else applies for high-level fund-raising openings."[4]

"Moving up" may mean several things. There might be advancement from entry-level positions, such as researcher or records keeper to positions of greater responsibility, status, and pay, such as director of development. There could be promotion within a specific area such as health care, the arts, or international nonprofit work. Career advancement could also mean a move from a small, limited-staff organization to a larger, multi-employee institution. In other words, professional advancement is definitely possible in a number of ways for the person wanting to move up the career ladder.

In planning for promotion, or for advancing in the profession, the first thing to do is ask yourself questions such as these:

- Where do you want to work? If in a different type of organization, do you want to stay in your current geographic location, or are you mobile? If moving to a new city or state aren't possible options, what opportunities will you find in your current environment?
- Have you tracked your achievements, and can you prove them? Do you have, or are you planning to get, your CFRE?
- What makes you attractive to the organization you want to work for or the position you desire to achieve?
- Have you mastered the status of "generalist." What special qualifications have you acquired?
- Can you identify your ideal career position, and do you know why you want this promotion?

- What is your motivation for seeking advancement in your career? Are your motivations a good match for what the position you desire needs from its next employee?

The best way to manage career advancement is to outline a plan that can be adapted to a changing environment and need. The plan should not, however, detract from your current focus and efforts to produce well for your organization. Often career development goes hand in hand with a person's excellent job record at an organization. That is to say, professional advancement can occur while a person is carrying out current responsibilities—it is a part of the attempt to improve and meet professional goals in the best way possible.

Some of the ways to manage career advancement are:

- Inventory your skills and achievements, and add to them each year. Keep track of what you need to learn and have mastered, and how this achievement helped you reach your goals.

- Acquire a reputation for being an expert at something that fits into your eventual career goal. This may mean increased proficiency in some aspect of fundraising, or a related skill such as writing or computer expertise.

- Volunteer for projects that give you contact with trustees and other persons who can influence your promotion or next career step. This allows you to learn and develop an appropriate network while you contribute to some organizational effort.

- Take courses in nonprofit management or fundraising, or some specialty area such as fundraising. Keep up with cutting-edge information and best practices, and implement your knowledge.

- Become acquainted with people who can influence your promotion. A good place for this networking is in a professional association.

- Don't exaggerate your claims of competence when networking, interviewing, or putting together your résumé. Be realistic about your achievements, but also line them up right so they fit your ultimate career goal.

- Be prepared to take risks in order to achieve the promotion. These risks, however, should be calculated and be likely to succeed. For example, don't promise to bring in a major gift as the annual fund lead gift unless the prospect is ready to give, but do volunteer to cultivate the prospect with the understanding that you will be the one to solicit that person for a kick-off gift.

• Determine that you not only can duplicate your best efforts but can also exceed them.

• Hang on to your energy, and "mind the store." Keep your performance level in your current responsibilities high, and don't shirk any duties while looking ahead for the promotion.

• Remain focused while you take on new activities and roles. You can't afford changes that divert you from your current work responsibilities and goals, but you can accept new responsibilities that build on your expertise.

As you plan ahead for career advancement, remember to not let your attention digress on the fundamental question—"Why are you in fundraising?" If your honest answer includes more money and status, that's not all bad, but the ultimate focus should be on serving the mission of the organization and its clients. "Leaders of executive-search firms say that more and more nonprofit leaders are telling them that they have had enough of fundraisers whose focus seems to be on the next high-paying job rather than on developing a depth of experience at any one organization."[5] Don't cycle through jobs too quickly. You may actually be missing opportunities for advancement right within your own organization. In fact, some organizations are developing their own in-house strategies to help entry- and mid-level fundraisers move into senior positions, so they can avoid the need to continually hire fundraising personnel. Some of the strategies in training, mentoring, and appropriate salaries increase incentives.

The person who will advance in a career is not the one who is afraid to do too much. It is the one who will not let him or herself do too little. It is the professional who wants to give the best that is possible, and perform well, even if immediate rewards aren't apparent or even tangible. Career advancement is a natural desire in most people, and it doesn't happen without personal planning and effort.

When I began work in the fundraising profession almost 40 years ago, it became obvious that there was a critical need for trained professionals. What was needed were individuals who could respond to the fundraising, leadership, and capacity-building needs in the ever-proliferating world of nonprofit organizations. We needed individuals with natural talents for relating to, guiding, and motivating professional colleagues, staff, and volunteers. We needed individuals who had a God-given talent to write the spoken word. We needed individuals who had the ability to explain the values, vision, and mission of the institutions they represented. We needed individuals who were eager and willing, through education and on-job experiential learning, to acquire the basic skills and techniques necessary.

Today, the needs have not changed. In our "climb to professional competency," they have only expanded. Jim Greenfield points this out in his book *Fundraising: Evaluating and Managing the Fund Development Process.*[6]

Our expanded needs require that we look for those willing to undertake improved training and certification of basic and advanced knowledge. I believe we need those who embody the ethics of fundraising and who are willing to serve as good stewards of the funds entrusted to us. I believe we need those who understand and use the fundamentals of nonprofit management and leadership. I believe we need those who do not hesitate to use technology to facilitate today's tasks of fundraising and managing the process of resource development.

Professional advancement within the nonprofit organization can be rapid and challenging for those having all of the combined skills. In addition, in smaller organizations or one-person shops, advancement requires a willingness of going outside of the organization to move up in the profession. Most importantly, it requires that one remain open to new ideas, learn from colleagues, and work well with staff.

Advancing successfully in our profession is challenging but rewarding for those willing to expand their skills and competencies.

J. RUSSELL RAKER, III Ph.D., ACFRE, is president and CEO of Tall Pines Network & Associates, Redlands, California, and also serves as administrative director of advancement for Loma Linda University and Medical Centers in California. In addition, he is associate vice president of The Alford Group, Skokie, Illinois. Prior to this position, he served as president and COO of the Family Foundation of North America; president and COO of the Morton Plant

Mease Foundation; vice president for community affairs and institutional advancement of Kettering Medical Center Corporation; executive director of the Kettering Medical Center Foundation; and president and CEO of the Nebraska Independent College Foundation. He has also worked in higher education, been active in NSFRE, both at the local and national levels, and twice received the Professional Fundraiser of the Year award.

PROFESSIONALS SAY . . .

The skills and qualities the aspiring fundraising professional needs to cultivate are many. At the most basic level, a fundraiser needs to have a love for people and a burning desire to be a part of a very special process that challenges and assists people and organizations in bringing out the very best of what they are and represent and makes it possible for big and exciting dreams to be realized for the betterment of others. The professional fundraiser needs to have a good balance between a healthy sense of ego and self-worth on the one hand and an appropriate measure of humility and commitment to serving others on the other hand. Being full of oneself may allow for the one-time-only, "flash-in-the-pan" gift to happen, but sustained fundraising that moves donors forward over the years toward ultimate gifts of significant size requires the fundraising professional to have an authentic and ongoing focus on the donors being served. In the final analysis it is not a matter of me reaching my goals and looking good in front of the board or my supervisor, but it is a matter of the donors achieving their goals and dreams for the charity that is near and dear to their hearts.

Rev. Gary L. Pohl, Executive Director, Lutheran Foundation of Texas, Austin, Texas

CHAPTER 13

Diversity in the Profession

SIDEBAR BY CLIFFORD V. JOHNSON

Marilyn Fischer wrote, "To treat persons alike regardless of gender, sexual orientation, degree of disability, and ethnic background is NOT to treat them as an individual, but to ignore factors crucial in understanding who they are."[1]

We are living in a time when communities of the world are becoming more alike. Economies are more interdependent. Lifestyles, values, and aspirations are more similar. People are turning inward to discover their own values, and looking outward to ways of sharing values. Ironically, this is happening, in part, because within communities, populations are becoming more diverse. While there is a search for common ground, however, each culture also has the need to assert a unique heritage. The challenge is to honor our heritage in such a way that we do not dishonor others. As Emmett Carson puts it, "Creating a nation in which all citizens are treated equitably and have uniform access to opportunities based on their skills and talents continues to be America's unrealized dream." He says that significant disparities based on race and gender continue to exist, and he points out that some of this disparity occurs in employment and wages.[2] This chapter looks at how the fundraising profession is addressing this disparity issue and, more broadly, the issues of diversity.

For sometime, the nonprofit sector and its institutions have been seeking diversity in hiring, especially as attention is increasingly focused on cross-cultural fundraising. According to a *Chronicle of Philanthropy* article, "As non-profit organizations scramble to hire more fundraisers and reach out to new constituencies, they are turning increasingly to members of minority groups."[3] The AFP (formerly NSFRE) survey conducted in 1996 noted that only 17 percent[4] of the membership consisted of minorities, which was, however, an increase from 1.8 percent a decade earlier. The article also noted,

> As communities across the United States become more ethnically diverse, many nonprofit organizations have seen a growing need to cultivate support among minority groups. Some organizations have been actively recruiting fundraisers with diverse backgrounds, to help them gain access to donors in minority communities.[5]

Duronio and Tempel wrote, "Unlike the major changes in the growth of the field and the shift in the gender of fundraisers in the last decade, there has been no significant change in the ethnic background of fundraisers, at least among fundraisers who join professional organizations. Fundraisers in professional organizations continue to be predominantly white."[6]

Defining diversity often means discussing differences. Most professions and professional groups see diversity-related issues as opportunities, although in some cases diversity is not a priority. There is sincere commitment in many quarters, and at least lip-service in others, to become inclusive of people representing different groups. Despite good intentions, most find that achievement of diversity continually takes on new dimensions and one size does not fit all.

Several questions would appear to be highly relevant to the fundraising professional, and therefore to the causes we represent. The first is, How do we define diversity? Certainly it includes race and ethnicity, but it can also include level of education, gender, age, and religious beliefs. The second question is, How do we achieve diversity? We can't hold people accountable for what they think, although we can urge them to be accountable for their actions. The third critical question is, How well do we understand ourselves and our attitudes, beliefs, and actions regarding diversity? We need to acknowledge that differences exist and not try to live as if we are all the same. At the same time, we need to acknowledge that many shared qualities exist, and that we can be different and still end up in the same place, wanting to accomplish the same goals.

There are several points to note about diversity as it relates to current nonprofit operations and plans for the twenty-first century:

- Demographics point toward an increasingly multicultural work force, and therefore, a multicultural donor pool.
- Minorities and women will account for a large portion of the labor force growth.
- A multicultural workplace creates a multitude of opportunities and issues; such a workplace results in different organizational cultures that might cause tensions or prove to be highly beneficial.
- Developing a vision of diversity and managing the reality of diversity does not happen overnight.

Organizations reap great rewards and benefits as they meet the needs of multicultural, multifaceted, and multitalented staff, clients, and constituents. We shouldn't fear diversity. We should fear what happens without diversity. This is the concern of many leading professionals in the nonprofit sector.

As has been noted, in the United States, the majority of fundraising professionals are white, yet increasingly they wish to or must relate to fundraising markets that reflect strong cultural differences. Consequently, the issue of diversity takes on an additional dimension. We need to have diversity among professionals, with representation from all minorities, but at the same time we need to understand the differences among various potential donor groups. Unless we understand these differences and know how to approach potential donors from various cultural backgrounds, we risk offending the donor or not acquiring the gift. Minorities raise funds not only among their own constituents but also across cultures. They must not only know the philanthropic attitudes and habits of their population groups but understand mainstream fundraising practices as well.

The matter of diversity in fundraising could be summed up with this quote: "Indeed, we are connected, interchanged, exchanged, and most importantly, denationalized. But even with all of this, we are not the same."[7]

Minorities often are generous philanthropists, but in ways not recognized by the nonprofit world and the Internal Revenue Service. Much ethnic philanthropy is informal and not recorded in tax returns and Gallup polls.

The U.S. traditional models and expectations of charitable giving were developed by white men, but these may not reflect philanthropy in other cultures because minorities don't give for the same reasons white men do. Support to community and church is usually direct and informal, and some distrust of traditional nonprofits exists. This does not, however, diminish the value of philanthropy among minorities, much of which is unrecognized. Convergence of wealth accumulation, education, career growth, and increased earning capacity allow many individuals of minority groups to become philanthropists in their own right.

FUNDRAISING AND HISPANICS

Differences also exist among minority groups. It may be expedient to label population groups as Hispanics or Latinos (preferred terms vary according to area of the country and country of origin), or Asian Americans, but generalizations are often not warranted. Hispanics or Latinos in the United States come from more than 20 countries. They vary greatly in levels of affluence and education. While for many Hispanics Spanish is a first language, some persons with Hispanic names do not even speak Spanish.

Among Hispanic population groups, philanthropy often is not well understood. Giving consists largely of one-to-one donations to relatives or gifts to church. The idea of organized philanthropy is relatively new, although Hispanics give generously in informal ways and through noninstitutional means.

Ricardo Rodriguez, an independent consultant who has been in fundraising for 17 years, states, "There are not many Hispanics in the field of development. There is a great potential to involve Hispanics, but I think there are structural limitations. We don't often find traditional organizations bring on Hispanics to raise money. There is a conception that if you are Hispanic you're not part of the mainstream as a chief fundraiser. There is a perception that people will not give you money if you're not part of the mainstream."[8]

Ricardo got involved in fundraising because someone invited him to learn how to raise funds. He was working with an organization that had a capital campaign underway but no development officer to lead the campaign. Ricardo took on the challenge, never expecting that it would become a full-time career.

Adam Martinez, who is currently with the University of St. Thomas in Houston, Texas, believes that the number of Hispanics in fundraising is low, even considering how many may be engaged in the activity without membership in professional associations where their numbers would be counted. He believes, however, "The potential for Hispanics in fundraising is becoming increasing large, especially as more and more Hispanic professionals achieve corporate and entrepreneurial positions. Out of the changing population will come new needs for the Hispanic community. And as the communities grow, so will their needs, and therefore, so will the need for professional fundraisers."

Adam has been fundraising for approximately eight years. During this time he developed a bilingual stewardship program for the Diocese of Galveston, Texas, and also worked on a capital campaign. He is pursuing doctoral studies in higher education with an emphasis in philanthropy and is active in AFP.

Ricardo and Adam are representative of Hispanic professionals in fundraising and have advice to share with aspiring professionals from Hispanic populations. Adam describes what makes fundraising among Hispanics unique and successful: "I think the biggest difference is the cultural recognition of values unique to the community." Ricardo offers this advice to Hispanics entering the profession: "I think it's challenging, both from a professional as well as personal perspective, but it's hard work. You are challenged by society's perspective of how they see you in the field of philanthropy. You get typecast, and in that case you work only with your ethnic group. There is the premise that I, as a Hispanic, can fundraise only within my organization, but I can do it just as well for another organization, not necessarily Hispanic. Fundraising is not an ethnic thing!"

FUNDRAISING AND AFRICAN AMERICANS

"Black fundraisers and other professionals, years after first taking positions at predominantly white charities, are still a scarce commodity in philanthropic circles." This comment by France K. Moseley at a National Conference on Black Philanthropy illustrates both the need for African American fundraisers and the vast opportunities available.[9]

African Americans' views on philanthropy, while sharing many white values, at times differ from the mainstream. They often do not view what they do to help others as philanthropy; they tend to help more informally and within families and neighborhoods, and philanthropy, in their view, is something done within a formal organization. The church continues to be the primary institution through which African Americans engage in helping others, and they are reluctant to make donations to general funds and charities, preferring to focus on specific causes and individuals. African Americans are often skeptical about how mainstream charitable organizations use their money.

As Aristide Collins, associate vice president for development at California State University, Long Beach, explains, "In the African American community we have been doing fundraising longer than anyone realizes. It began in the black churches with people not only giving their contributions, but supporting educational organizations and community-based groups. The black church was the focal point of organization for social purposes and had been for hundreds of years. People give to people. I don't think the black community is different than any other because people give to causes that they believe in."

Just a couple of years ago, Aristide was hired as the first black fundraiser at George Washington University. When he moved back to California State University, there were only three black chief development officers, including him. At age 32, Aristide is the youngest chief development officer in the CSU system.

"I believe people don't know about career potential in fundraising and that is why the numbers aren't as large as they probably could be. The potential is great for a broader representation. It's going to be necessary for all sorts of organizations to recruit from diverse pools of talent as individuals in minority communities achieve greater education and wealth."

Having moved through the profession to the point that he can mentor others, Aristide recommends that potential fundraisers reach out to mentors quickly, ask lots of questions, become active members of the community in which they work, and take every opportunity to attend workshops and training programs. Aristide received his own start as a student representative on a search committee for a new chancellor for the California State University system and as student body president. He was encouraged to get into fundraising by mentors who felt he had the aptitude and characteristics conducive to success in the field.

Charles Stephens, managing partner for the Atlanta office of Staley Robeson Ryan St. Lawrence, is a well-known name to many in the fundraising profession because he was the first African American to serve as chair of the National Society of Fundraising Professionals. "It was fascinating and rewarding, but also very draining at times," Charles says, "because there were many who did not think I should have been there, and who tried to make me understand I shouldn't be." Many others thought this was a breakthrough for diversity in the profession, however, and his tenure was a profitable one for the society and for the profession.

Charles believes that African Americans are significantly underrepresented in fundraising and that the potential for careers in the field is great for African Americans. "Nonprofits are a mainstay of the African American community, starting with the church. And that has always been the case from the earliest history of African Americans. There still is a tremendous appreciation for philanthropic organizations for African American communities."

In the African American community, according to Charles, there are fewer resources and the approach to giving and asking has been less organized as in some other communities; however, as with all other cultures in the United States, African Americans must seek funding from all sources while also tapping into their own ethnic group. African Americans understand and appreciate giving, although that has been guided by a familial attitude—someone will see a problem and make a gift on the spot, usually, but not necessarily, to a family member.

Charles attended Morehouse College in Atlanta, majoring in psychology, and his first professional opportunity was to become a probation officer. That plan did not work out because he had participated in the 1960s sit-ins; however, one of the people on the committee that reviewed his candidacy was general secretary of the YMCA, and he offered Charles a job as a fundraiser.

"I had no idea what a fundraiser was. I told him that if he would invest the time in me to find out what fundraising was all about, I would do it. I am happy that things happened that way because it gave me the opportunity to pursue a career that is absolutely marvelous and rewarding and offers success. I'm still at it, and look forward to doing it for another few years."

After the YMCA position, Charles worked for the United Negro College Fund and then at Clark College and Atlanta University (which later merged). He was also at the Center on Philanthropy at Indiana University, which provided different challenges in fundraising. "Trying to fashion an approach," he says, "to raising money for an organization that was twice removed from direct service was difficult. We weren't feeding any hungry people or providing clothes. We provided training and research that would increase the understanding and appreciation of philanthropy and fundraising."

Charles has this advice for the person thinking of fundraising as a career. "Be sure you are the kind of person for whom credit is not important. If you're someone who expects to be patted on the back, then this isn't for you." He also suggests enrolling in an overview course very early in the career search, because this will provide an understanding of the principles and techniques of fundraising.

FUNDRAISING AND ASIAN AMERICANS

There are nearly 10 million people in the United States who are designated as Asian Americans, and they represent more than 30 to 40 distinct ethnic groups. Some immigrated to the United States in the early 1700s, while others are newcomers. Generalizing across so many cultures—Filipino, Chinese, Japanese, Vietnamese and others—is difficult, but a few philanthropic values exist across Asian cultures. Family is important, particularly the elderly. Hard work, education, respect, and honor are traditional and significant values. Extended family and ethnic members of the community are more important than organized charity. Sending money to needy relatives and friends at home is also important.

Differences among Asian American communities emerge quickly after the generalities have been considered. For example, Chinese are often reluctant to raise money for charitable causes because of a need to "save face" and be successful. Filipinos make gifts to reciprocate instances when they feel indebted. Japanese tend to give to their own community groups, therefore helping maintain ethnic identity. Koreans prefer to take care of families and neighbors before making donations to churches, schools, and other nonprofits. Chinese have the tradition of stressing group needs and values over those of the individual. They would be willing to give to mainstream groups if their family association has endorsed the idea. Filipinos have strong family ties; they do not look to charitable organizations and services when facing hard times. Among Asian Americans, giving is often thought of as sharing, not charity.

When asked about Asian Americans in fundraising, JoAnn Yoshimoto, director of major and capital gifts for Campfire Boys and Girls in Washington state, replied, "I don't have a grasp on how the representation from my ethnic group looks. There are a few professionals from my ethnic group in Seattle, but I don't see it as proportionate to the demographics of the community. What worries me is that several of these Asian American development officers are considering leaving the field. Regarding potential, as organizations fully incorporate the concept of diversity, my feeling is that a broader funding base will follow for every organization. Funding bases will really begin to diversify. And as such, it makes perfect sense that our profession should look more and more like our donor base and our community. We would be wise to develop a profession that mirrors that diversity."

JoAnn entered the nonprofit world because of a strong commitment to the values of the nonprofit sector. "When I finished college, I went to Planned Parenthood for a job, and the only opening at the time was in fundraising. I took it, not knowing quite what I was getting into. During the 1970s, no one went to college to become a fundraiser. There was quite a bit of turnover at the time in the field, and that created the opening I was offered to fill. I kind of got into by default, but I stayed in it because I found it was a good fit." Her advice to persons from Asian American population groups is, "I would just say that anyone entering the profession must truly love a challenge in life. Fund development is not for the timid. It is an extremely dynamic field, and a newcomer must be willing to be adaptable and incorporate change at a more rapid pace than the rest of the work force." JoAnn points out, as do others from minority populations, that Asian American fundraisers do not just raise money from their ethnic groups, nor do they serve just Asian American organizations.

Sanae Tokumura of Hawaii is a third-generation Japanese American. According to her, the number of Asian Americans in fundraising is very small. "When I earned my ACFRE, I was the only Japanese or Asian in my group," she says, but she also believes the potential is great. "Fundraisers almost never work in a single ethnic group, and I use the same strategies, professionalism, and behaviors as colleagues who are not Japanese Americans. It is not the color of the skin, it's the professionalism that counts."

For 20 years Sanae has worked in fundraising. Her first job was with a hospital, helping create a foundation. She began her own business in 1983. Some highlights of her career have been working with a stalled campaign to bring it to a successful completion, and serving on the board of NSFRE in Hawaii. She considers one of her greatest successes to be her work with the stalled Japanese Cultural Center of Hawaii capital campaign. "I shifted the focus of the rather ethnocentric campaign to one that included involvement with the greater cultural environment of Hawaii. The campaign's 'sharing' personality not only completed the $5 million goal, but also more than tripled that original campaign goal by the time I left the organization three years later."

Her advice to those who enter the field is to begin with a small organization. "You learn so much more by having to do it all, versus being a small part of a big organization." She also advocates taking courses in fundraising and joining the Association of Fundraising Professionals. "Never get the attitude that you know everything. There's always more to learn. Evaluate your progress under great scrutiny. Stay humble."

FUNDRAISING AND INDIAN AMERICANS

Sanjay Choudhrie, who is currently employed by the San Francisco Theological Seminary in San Anselmo, California, believes that the Indian American community has much potential for fundraising because there is a lot of new wealth, but at the same time he knows of few professionals in his ethnic group. He says, "In the United States, I know of no one from India in fundraising. The only other person I have seen was at the last NSFRE conference I attended, so I would say there are relatively few. The Indian immigrant is very highly educated, and I feel there are many people who could be potential fundraisers. They have some insight into the commitment of people with wealth."

When asked how fundraising might be different among Indian Americans, Sanjay replied, "I don't raise funds from just my cultural group. Fundraising is a process where one adapts oneself to the culture, values, and commitments of the donor, and one would not ask for funds for projects that are not valued by that donor's culture. There is a spirit of philanthropy among Indian Americans."

FUNDRAISING AND NATIVE AMERICANS

One of the most common misperceptions in philanthropy is a saying that is actually pejorative—Indian Giver. The common interpretation is not correct. Among Native Americans, giving is a spiritual act that honors both giver and receiver, and the focus is on the exchange and mutual respect, not the money that changes hands. There is a renewed interest in tribal customs, languages, and self-sufficiency, and philanthropy is one foundation of the Native American culture.

Debra Harry, who is the executive director of the Indigenous Peoples Council on Biocolonialism, states that there are a good number of Native Americans who are effectively raising money. "However, the potential is vast, since the number of people in the profession represent only a tiny portion of all Native American communities throughout the country and the hundreds of current and potential new projects needed to make real changes in their quality in life."

According to Debra, Native Americans are not like other minority groups in significant ways. Native American communities exist within a distinct framework of federal law that has resulted from numerous federal legislation and court cases that govern tribal relations with the United States. Tribes essentially exist as nations within a nation, and they maintain unique governmental jurisdictions and powers over their lands and peoples. This creates a need to understand the unique cultural, legal, and political context of community development in Native American communities. Since federal Indian law is usually outside of the average American's education, understanding issues and community change in Native American communities requires some additional effort. Donors who participate in Native American causes are usually rewarded with opportunities to participate in unique vibrant communities and cultures making positive change.

Her advice to those consider fundraising as a profession is important for people from all ethnic groups. She says, "While expertise as a fundraiser is essential and necessary to the well being of an organization, I think it is important to remember that the process of fundraising is intrinsically linked to positive social benefit and change. So one's professional stance as a fundraiser is always linked to an ethical requirement to ensure one's actions contribute to the social good. Its quite an honorable profession, and one in which we must always walk the high road. That means we need to honor both the communities we serve and those who contribute funds and resources to help make the changes possible. This requires our special attention to ensure honesty, respect, accountability, and stewardship is reflected in every aspect of our work. It is extremely rewarding to be a part of positive community change derived from the efforts of special people who are driven by compassion, vision, and commitment. This is usually what nonprofit organizations are all about."

SUMMARY

The questions regarding diversity that were listed early in this chapter merit reconsideration. How do we define diversity? While it is, without a doubt, related to race and ethnicity, there are also other forms of diversity that we should treat with respect. These can include gender, age, religious belief, economic status, and other differentiating factors. While understanding diversity in any form can be both an opportunity and a challenge, most important is the question, how well do we understand ourselves and our attitudes, beliefs, and actions regarding diversity? Differences exist, while population groups also share commonalities in wanting to reach goals that are universal. The nonprofit sector is capable of bringing unity and the sharing of goals while acknowledging differences. The fundraising professional plays a significant role in this, and the opportunities for significant employment are numerous.

"Diversification is desirable not only because it is the right thing to do, but because doing so will increase the effectiveness of fundraising and charitable organizations." Kelly quotes Sanford Cloud, Jr., president and CEO of the National Conference of Christians and Jews, "If the fund-raising profession hopes to interact effectively with the evolving diversity of philanthropy, the profession itself is going to have to work harder to diversify its ranks."[10]

■ FURTHER READING

Campoamor, Diana, William A. Diaz, and Henry A. J. Ramos, eds. *Nuevos Senderos: Reflections on Hispanics and Philanthropy*. Houston: Arte Publico Press, 1999.

These essays provide historical studies, sociological surveys, and analyses of policies and practices in the philanthropic sector.

Hall-Russell, Cheryl, and Robert H. Kasberg. *African American Traditions of Giving and Serving*. Indiana University Center on Philanthropy, 1997.

This book details the common patterns of the philanthropic tradition that permeated the laughter and tears of 180 reflective conversations with African Americans in the Midwest.

Hamilton, Charles H., Warren F. Ilchman, eds. *Cultures of Giving*. No. 7 (Spring 1995), and No. 8 (Summer 1995). San Francisco: Jossey-Bass.

These two issues of New Directions for Philanthropic Fundraising *discuss how region, religion, heritage, gender, wealth, and values influence philanthropy.*

Rogers, Pier, ed., *Philanthropy in Communities of Color: Traditions and Challenges*. ARNOVA Occasional Paper Series, Vol. 1, No. 1 (ARVONA, 2001).

Scanlan, Joanne, ed. *Cultures of Caring: Philanthropy in Diverse American Communities*. Washington, DC: Council on Foundations,1999.

This report examines potential ways to expand the use of institutional philanthropy in four population groups: African Americans, Asian Americans, Latinos, and Native Americans.

Smith, Bradford, Sylvia Shue, Jennifer Lisa Vest, and Joseph Villarreal. *Philanthropy in Communities of Color*. Indiana University Press, 1999.

This book describes the specific practices and customs of giving money, goods, and services within communities of color.

Wagner, Lilya, and Allan Figueroa Deck, eds. *Hispanic Philanthropy: Exploring the Factors That Influence Giving and Asking*. San Francisco: Jossey-Bass, 1999.

A collection of articles on the characteristics of Hispanic philanthropy, as well as the educational, religious, and cultural influences on giving and fundraising. A good survey of what shapes Hispanic philanthropy.

Well, Ronald Austin. *The Honor of Giving: Philanthropy in Native America*. Indiana University Center on Philanthropy, 1998.

This report explores the ways, means, and meanings of philanthropic giving, receiving, obligation, reciprocity, exchange, and community across more than a dozen indigenous cultures native to North America.

SIDEBAR   CLIFFORD V. JOHNSON

In recent years many nonprofit sector organizations have acknowledged that it makes good business sense to diversify the membership of their staff and board. Some have asked me if this is a professionally insulting situation to the person being hired.

In a profession that depends on cultivating relationships, there is nothing fundamentally unethical in taking advantage of a staff or board member's personal or professional attributes to help convince a prospective donor to give. We "diverse" fundraisers know the score when we are hired. The problem I have with this situation does not relate to what will be expected of me. I am savvy enough to know that. My complaint is with the manager who fails to grasp the full implications of what, as a minority, I bring to the table.

Thought of as only a means to reap more financial benefits for the organization from other minorities diminishes my professional self-image. I think I can safely say that we professionals from minority racial, ethnic, or religious backgrounds want also to be appreciated for the cross-cultural communications skills we have gathered, moving day-to-day across diverse communities in this multicultural society.

By encouraging the "diverse" staff member to share this knowledge with other staff members, managers can diffuse a potentially awkward situation and gain his or her respect. After all, we minorities have had to study the subtleties of cross-cultural communication, and how to negotiate the hidden obstacles that often lurk just below the flowing surface of seemingly familiar social intercourse. These are transposable process skills.

Be alert, managers!

CLIFFORD V. JOHNSON CFRE, is currently the director of development at Southeastern University in Washington, DC. He has spent 17 years in development in the following positions: chief development officer for AFP, director of development at the Amistad Research Center on the campus of Tulane University, executive director of the Afro-American Pavillion at the 1984 Louisiana World Exposition, and vice president for Development at Dillard University. He has served on local and national AFP boards and committees, including the Education Advisory Council, the AFP Foundation Board, the 2000 AFP International Conference Host Committee, and the Diversity Task Force. In 1992 the AFP Louisiana, Greater New Orleans Chapter honored him with the Outstanding Fund Raising Executive Award.

PROFESSIONALS SAY . . .

The biggest changes I've seen over the past 29 years in this profession have dealt with who my peers were and how long they stayed at what they were doing. Although it was my good fortune to be mentored by people who enjoyed their work, loved their institutions, and stayed in one position for lengthy periods of time, I'm pleased to say, there is diversity in what we do. My colleagues are no longer all male and caucasian. Sometimes I wonder why it took so long for our profession to understand the importance of diversity and the strength it engenders.

Richard M. Markoff, Ph.D., President, Star Alliance for Drug-Free Youth, Inc.

I was overwhelmed by the number of African American fundraisers who gathered for the first conference on black philanthropy in Philadelphia. Over 500 plus African Americans descended on the city and they were excited about their career choices and eager to share their experiences. They were also honest about the challenges they face, especially in corporate America. Racism was still a big factor and in some cases hindered their ability to raise funds. Participants who were responsible for major gifts had to be more resourceful in their approaches to funders because they were not often invited to golf or have lunch at the club.

Cheryl Hall-Russell, Executive Director, Indianapolis Coalition for Neighborhood Development

The greatest need in the foreseeable future is for more qualified Latinos in the development profession (Latinas will likely get established sooner through female networks already in place). Announce your development vacancies in newsletters read by professionals, such as lawyers, MBAs, and military officers. Senior advancement leaders who want to diversify their development staffs should aggressively work their informal word-of-mouth networks. Be clear. State, "we are looking for candidates who enjoy persuading people, and who have succeeded in project conceptualization, writing, and management. By the way, underrepresented males are especially welcome to apply." This is not discrimination; it's working smart, given the demographics of the development field today.

Chuck Rodriguez, Ph.D., Assistant Vice President for University Relations, University of Texas Health Science Center at San Antonio

With the changing demographics in our nation, it is imperative that fundraisers learn to understand the cultures of communities of color and respect those differences in their solicitation strategies.

Darryl L. Griffin, Assistant Director of Corporate & Foundation Relations, Meharry Medical College

Recent findings about the philanthropic motivations and giving patterns of women, younger donors, and communities of color indicate that the future of fundraising is in relationship building. Although these groups have long been philanthropic, their contributions have tended to be overlooked by development professionals who are on the lookout for individuals who control great wealth. Now that many women, people of color, and young adults control more wealth, we are finding that they are not motivated by fundraising methods designed to reach traditional major donors. These "new donors" bring a fresh approach to their giving, and their new approach will transform the development profession as well as the nonprofit organizations it supports.

Andrea R. Kaminski, Executive Director, Women's Philanthropy Institute, Madison, Wisconsin

There are tremendous opportunities for African Americans and other minorities in the profession. We must be better represented as practitioners, researchers, and consultants. American philanthropy will not reach its fullest potential until the rich philanthropic traditions of communities of color are respected and valued, and not viewed solely as untapped markets.

Tyrone Freeman, Director of Development, Reach for Youth, Inc.

If we are going to keep the profession strong and vibrant, the current generation of professionals must help to usher a new generation of diverse professionals in to pass the torch too. As America's cultural diversity has

changed, the fundraising profession must embrace the changes to maintain a stable flow of professionals to assume future leadership roles.

Dwayne Ashley, President, Thurgood Marshall Scholarship Fund, Inc., New York, New York

In today's discourse, the terms diversity and multiculturalism are commonly heard, but we might ask how much we really understand their importance to our society and their relevance to the philanthropic process. That process, of which fundraising is a key part, is ultimately one of exchange, where each party gives and each party receives. In Native America, "Indian Country," for example, even though there will be differences in practice among tribes, traditions of giving are central to the culture. The "potlatch" and the "giveaway" are but two among many ways in which balance and harmony are restored to the community, where individuals are honored, and social relations are developed and nurtured. In my view, there is a lesson here for everyone who is connected with philanthropy in general and with the fundraising profession in particular. Hank Russo's precept that fundraising is "helping people experience the joy of giving" can be extended even further. From the Native perspective, philanthropy means "the honor of giving." It means respecting and honoring the donor, and respecting and honoring the recipient. Since in life all things are connected, and, as the Lakota prayer puts it, "we are all related," the gift provides or restores balance for both participants and works to create harmony in the world.

Ronald Austin Wells, author of *The Honor of Giving: Philanthropy in Native America* (1998)

CHAPTER 14

Working with a Boss

SIDEBAR BY F. DUKE HADDAD

$\mathbf{I}$n a volume called Cutting Edge Leadership 2000,[1] the editors collected information from leadership scholars and practitioners. In one section, David Chrislip analyzes and proposes new leadership that is characterized by the following:

- Inclusivity
- Management of a constructive learning engagement
- Information provided for good decisions
- Building of coherence in the group
- Negotiation for agreement that leads to action

This new type of leadership, he says, is not as easy or romantic as past notions of leadership. He proposes different concepts of leadership and the behaviors and practices that make them work. This includes:

- Getting people to the table and keeping them there
- Subsuming one's personal desire for a specific outcome or solution and focusing on the larger good
- Ensuring the participation of others
- Helping others solve problems without having to know or provide the answers
- Acknowledging and celebrating the successes of others without taking credit
- Leading as a peer rather than supervisor

This type of leadership is what many fundraising professionals must practice and exhibit. Often, the fundraiser has the responsibility but not the authority to get things done. Real leadership is not a matter of authority, but a collection of attributes that set you apart from others. Colleagues acknowledge leaders by listening and valuing their ideas and suggestions, and by turning to them for advice. Additional attributes of a leader include having a reputation for hard work and integrity, being prepared with information, and soliciting input from colleagues.

The entry-level professional in fundraising may have several challenges in working with a boss. First, however, it is important to define what lines of authority there might be in a fundraising program or office.

If the organization is small, there may not even be a formal development office, and the person in charge of fundraising may also be assigned other duties, such as program development, administrative assistance, office management, or public relations. In such cases professionals are often left alone to handle fundraising, and it is up to them to inform and motivate the leadership of the organization, including the board. In these cases, the fundraiser truly becomes the manager of the process; however, unless the goals, functions, and tasks of fundraising are fully explained by the professional, preferably by a fundraising plan that includes a gift range chart, expectations from others in the organization may be unrealistic, and the fundraiser is left alone to take the blame if funds don't come in to support the organization. Therefore it is important for the person in the small organization to inform, gather a team, involve others in appropriate ways, and ensure that fundraising is an organizational effort, not just the duty of the fundraiser.

If fundraising is the responsibility of the executive director, then the director must rely on board and organizational support for fundraising efforts. This type of professional may have the authority to carry out a fundraising program, but must still motivate others because the task is too great for one person.

In a large development office the entry-level person may have a supervisor for the particular area of fundraising, or may report to the director or vice president directly. The chief development officer, in turn, must interact with the executive director or president of the organization, and manage the fundraising process from the middle.

When an organization has a foundation[2] allied with it, the foundation is usually led by a chief development officer who is in charge of the rest of the foundation staff, but accountability to the organization's head is still necessary.

Reporting lines, ranks, and strata of management may be complex, and the line of command often resembles this diagram.

Entry-level personnel (gift receipting, prospect research, data management, etc.) report to → assistant or associate director of development, who reports to → the director of development, who may report to → a vice president for development.

Specialty areas such as major gifts, planned giving, and foundation and corporation programs may also report to either a director of development, a vice president, or a foundation head.

LEADING FROM THE MIDDLE

Although chain of command may vary considerably, the idea of the fundraising professional being a leader at his or her level of responsibility is universal. Some like to define this as "leading from the middle." At any rate, the concept of leadership without authority is true in many cases. The fundraising professional should become proficient in practicing leadership in many ways.

Managing from the middle is not new. Leading is. Fundraising professionals are uniquely placed so that they can accomplish a great deal. They work in service to others' goals and purposes, but free themselves from the idea that the only power that is significant is positional power.

Fundraisers often have more expertise than authority. They may not have the final say, but they have important influence. We share the challenge of working with people and processes that move the organization toward its primary mission. Most of us do this from the middle, not the top, of "corporate" pyramids. We are support or service professionals. This role is important in determining the organization's strategic direction and is essential for getting results; it may be difficult, challenging, and rewarding.

SERVANT LEADERSHIP

In 1970, retired AT&T executive Robert Greenleaf coined the term *servant leadership* and launched a quiet revolution in the way in which we view and practice leadership. When he retired in 1964 at the age of 60, he began his second career, setting up the Center for Applied Ethics. At the end of the tumultuous sixties he wrote *The Servant as Leader,* and since that time more than a quarter of a million copies of his essay have been sold. Here are some of the highlights of his idea of what servant leaders are.[3]

- Servant leaders take people and their work very seriously. Valuing people is essential, Greenleaf maintained.

- They listen and take direction from the troops. Servant leaders know they do not have all the answers so they also ask questions and work to build consensus. Although it takes time because everyone's view is solicited, when everyone is on board, great things can happen.

- Servant leaders heal; they have an openness and a willingness to share in mistakes and pain.

- Servant leaders are self-effacing. They do not draw much attention, do not glorify leadership, but focus instead on the greater good of the group.

- Finally, servant leaders are stewards, careful with what has been entrusted to them.

Successful fundraising professionals embody each of the characteristics defined by Greenleaf when they carry out the responsibilities assigned to them. Fundraising managers provide leadership by listening to donors, volunteers, colleagues, and bosses. They use empathy in understanding how volunteers may feel about fundraising. They bring healing when necessary through communication, and create awareness of the organization and its mission, which is a vital foundation for successful fundraising. Fundraisers persuade others to become champions of the cause, they have foresight in planning for the financial support of the organization, and they not only practice good stewardship but also foster those attitudes and practices in an organization. Their commitment to the organization and its constituents is exemplary and therefore aids in building community.

Accomplishing all this means that fundraising professionals not only function as managers of the process, as responsible professionals who carry out the tasks assigned to them, but as leaders who help their bosses reach the overall goals of the organization.

TYPES OF DECISION MAKERS

In addition to understanding leadership traits, we must also understand how to communicate with our superiors, our defined leaders, to gain support for our fundraising programs. We must think about "leading up." Based on the concepts of Dewey and organizational management specialists, Mary Lippitt identified six types of leadership, or behaviors of bosses.[4]

- Inventor
- Catalyst
- Developer
- Performer
- Protector
- Challenger

Type of Decision-Making Leader/Boss	Question They Ask to Determine Priorities	Priorities for Each Type of Leader/Boss	How to Provide Support for Each Type of Boss
Inventor	What is the latest thinking? What is possible?	Developing new ideas, products, and services.	Remain current in your knowledge of fundraising, know what works now and what the trends in fundraising are.
Catalyst	What can help us compete? What do our clients and donors want?	Gaining market share and acquiring donors.	Provide information about donors, be involved in determining their needs and desires, be part of a team that promotes excellence in the organization.
Developer	How can we improve or clarify roles and responsibilities? What systems can leverage our resources and talents?	Building infrastructure and creating systems and processes for high performance.	Have a fundraising plan that is congruent with the organizational plan, ensure that goals are met, report to the boss regularly on progress.

(continued)

Type of Decision-Making Leader/ Boss	Question They Ask to Determine Priorities	Priorities for Each Type of Leader/ Boss	How to Provide Support for Each Type of Boss
Performer	How can we do it better? How can we become more efficient?	Improving processes and procedures for effective use of resources.	Know your fundraising budget and costs, show how efficiency and effectiveness help build a better fundraising program and therefore a better organization.
Protector	How can we develop talent? How can we develop a supportive environment?	Developing a committed work force, building capabilities, supporting culture, identity, values.	Understand that a nurturing relationship works both ways—up and down. Be loyal to the boss, understand and support the corporate climate, maintain and promote values of the organization.
Challenger	What opportunities are there? How can we prepare for the future?	Identifying strategic options and positioning the organization for the future.	Look ahead at how the organization can not only have financial stability now but work to promote sustainability.

Each type of boss has distinct priorities and ways of functioning. As fundraising professionals we need to know how to provide the right information, motivation, and recommendations for each decision-making type.

Max De Pree, a noted writer on leadership, wrote in *Leading Without Power: Finding Hope in Serving Community,*

> People working in not-for-profit groups grapple with the full complexity of today's society and have become indispensable to our national sense of identity. They allow no room in their work for the deceptive simplic-

ity of a single bottom line. To me, they're clearly leading us to reach the potential our culture so urgently needs to be realized. They are demonstrating a quality of leadership and service arising from their understanding of and commitment to a common good. . . ."[5]

De Pree's statement underscores, once again, the vital significance of providing leadership in the procurement of funds for running nonprofit organizations—for carrying out the causes that make up the fabric of our society. He talks about leaving a legacy. We may not be recognized for the legacies we leave at the institutions we serve, but nevertheless, our role in their success is a legacy. More often than not, buildings would not be built, programs would not be run, people would not find fulfillment of needs and solutions to problems if we did not play not only a managerial role but a leadership role as well in listening, motivating, providing information, encouraging, and being an example to those whom we serve—which includes our bosses.

■ FURTHER READING

Bellman, Geoffrey M. *Getting Things Done When You Are Not in Charge: How to Succeed from a Support Position.* San Francisco: Berrett-Koehler Publishers, 1992.

This book provides excellent insights on how to exert leadership, motivate and support others, accomplish goals—and do it not from top leadership positions but because leadership characteristics are practiced. Excellent source for staff members on how to reach personal and professional goals while achieving organizational goals and supporting designated leadership of an organization.

Bramson, Robert. *Coping with Difficult Bosses.* New York: Simon and Schuster, 1992.

Through this book, an employee can learn how to deal successfully with supervisors who pose a challenge.

Chrislip, David D., and Carl E. Larson. "Skills for a New Kind of Leadership." *Collaborative Leadership—How Citizens and Civic Leaders Make a Difference.* San Francisco: Jossey-Bass, 1994.

Drawing on extensive research that includes six in-depth case studies and 46 additional studies of successful community collaborations, the authors show how leaders who are most effective address public issues and therefore have credibility to bring together people.

De Pree, Max. *Leading Without Power: Finding Hope in Serving Community.* San Francisco: Jossey-Bass, 1997.

From the best-selling author of Leadership Is An Art *and* Leadership Jazz *comes this compelling work that discusses the purpose of nonprofit organizations. De Pree shows today's leaders how to lead without power and transform causes and organizations.*

Gardner, John W. *On Leadership.* New York: The Free Press, 1990.

The development of more and better leaders is the objective of this book by a renowned writer on the topic of leadership. This is not a how-to book, but a thoughtful perspective on how ordinary citizens can acquire the traits of leadership and transform their communities.

Greenleaf, Robert K. *Servant Leadership: A Journey Into the Nature of Legitimate Power and Greatness.* New York: Paulist Press, 1977.

Written by the renowned author who coined the term servant leader. *An explanation of his theories on how successful leaders function with attitudes and behaviors of service. A landmark text that should be read by all who strive to acquire leadership qualities.*

Haas, Howard, and Bob Tamarkin. *The Leader Within: An Empowering Path of Self-Discovery.* New York: Harper Business, 1992.

This is a guide to becoming a leader, based on 150 interviews with leaders in business. It provides realistic guidelines for developing leadership skills through problem solving, role modeling, and networking.

Kellerman, Barbara, and Larraine R. Matusak, Eds. *Cutting Edge Leadership 2000.* University of Maryland: The James MacGregor Burns Academy of Leadership, 2000.

A collection of essays that discuss the current stage of leadership research, with recommendations for future directions. A compilation by authors who are recognized as experts in the field of leadership development.

Leader to Leader, A Publication of the Drucker Foundation and Jossey-Bass Publishers, 350 Sansome St., San Francisco, CA 94104-1342.

This journal contains features on all aspects of leadership, published by one of the best foundations focusing on leadership.

The Leader of the Future, The Drucker Foundation, Eds. Frances Hesselbein, Marshall Goldsmith, Richard Beckhard. San Francisco: Jossey-Bass, 1996.

A collection of essays on special perspectives on leadership, such as how leaders emerge, how roles are defined, how leaders motivate, and how the leader of this millennium will create a culture based on principles.

Maxwell, John C. *The 21 Indispensable Qualities of a Leader: Becoming the Person Others Will Want to Follow.* Nashville: Thomas Nelson, 1999.

Maxwell maintains that understanding leadership and actually leading are two different activities. He provides the laws of leadership and discusses how leaders are effective because of who they are on the inside. Character qualities activate and empower leadership ability.

Maxwell, John C. *The 21 Irrefutable Laws of Leadership.* Nashville: Thomas Nelson, 1998.

A study of leadership successes and mistakes, using examples of persons known for their achievements and leadership.

"Bosses" in a fundraising context have an impossible job. They must create grand game plans, implement strategic plans, educate internal plus external constituencies on the value of their fundraising program, plus identify organizational priority needs for philanthropy. Somehow, they need to motivate and direct a staff that is hopefully on the same page as the boss.

Daily sand shifting leads the boss into a variety of productive and nonproductive fundraising and administrative tasks. Many individuals cannot balance their responsibilities and play to their perceived strengths.

Fundraising professionals who seek to work effectively with a boss must understand the boss's strengths and weaknesses, likes and dislikes, and personal styles of management. Subordinates need to think in terms of counterbalancing. This means you must evaluate yourself and seek to understand your abilities. Constantly question how your strengths can play to your boss's weaknesses. Most importantly, you must focus your energies on developing a comprehensive fundraising program. There is no substitute for your total immersion in the fundraising process.

Through a consistent high level of performance, you will gain the confidence of your boss over time. Provide "best of class" models. Help the boss stay financially focused while providing suggestions to keep the administrative machine running smoothly. Seek and succeed in obtaining and performing additional responsibilities outside of your job description. Volunteer and assume tasks you know the boss doesn't like to handle. Obtain the management philosophy of your boss and seek to motivate him or her through your interpretation of this philosophy.

The ultimate goal for you is to make your boss look good while seeking the praise and confidence of your boss's boss for your performance. If this is secured in a positive, nonthreatening way, the confidence in you by your superior will soar, and you will be on your way to becoming a boss, too!

Who said the food chain theory is dead?!

F . DUKE HADDAD , ED.D., CFRE, is vice president of development for St. Vincent Hospitals and Health Services, and executive director for the St. Vincent Foundation in Indianapolis. He has 25 years of experience in development for health care and higher education, and has authored numerous articles for professional publications.

PROFESSIONALS SAY . . .

Like any bosses, Abraham Lincoln and Robert E. Lee each had field commanders who resisted headquarters' strategies. History records that both leaders had great difficulty finding and motivating leaders to cooperate fully with established plans. The same opposition can exist in a development department. With so many varying approaches to fundraising, with differing interests among personnel and excessive demands on staff time, priorities of leadership and staff can grow in different directions. Most fundraisers' job descriptions include multiple functions. Therefore, functions must be prioritized, with resources allocated accordingly in order to focus team members' primary work on common goals. Staff should identify their true top three priorities. Coordinating top priorities and focusing on the leader's and each staff member's top three priorities moves the team in a common direction. Secondary functions will receive appropriate attention when energy, resources, and accountability are focused on integrated top priorities.

Wesley Rediger, Partner, Rediger Taylor Group LLC, Upland, Indiana

As a staffer, I believe my job is to (1) add value to our mission, and (2) make my boss look good to our funders and board. Learn to anticipate the questions, assumptions, and needs of your supervisor. "No negative surprises" for my boss is my watchword and screen for filtering everything.

Gregory Long, Director, Outreach and Partner Relations, Quest International, Newark, Ohio

15

Working with a Team

SIDEBAR BY J. PATRICK RYAN

"The Desert Survival Situation" is an exercise in synergistic decision making in which a situation is described and the "life" or "death" of each participant depends on how well the group shares knowledge so that the team can make decisions that lead to survival of the individual.[1] The creators of this exercise state that effective human action in dealing with problems depends on two key factors—the resources, both human and material, and the process, which is how the resources are utilized. If either of these factors is missing, the chance of success, or "survival," in terms of the exercise, is nil. "But if people work together utilizing their resources rationally and humanely (process), they can produce results beyond the mere sum of their individual outputs."[2] Teamwork is a generally accepted condition for success in business. Almost without exception, successful people stress the importance of teamwork.

Teamwork is equally essential in the fundraising setting. It is possible that one person can be successful while doing it alone, but it is unlikely. The team can accomplish more and do better. There has to be organizational commitment to the principles and philosophy of fundraising. Various people bring not just valuable perspectives but also expertise to the fundraising process. Relationships with donors, clients, and other constituents are enhanced when the right person is in touch with the right prospect. Fundraising should become an institutional mentality, with each employee or volunteer contributing to the process with his or her unique talent or expertise.

For example, when a case statement is prepared by an organization's staff, input is required from the person in charge of finances, the program personnel, support staff, and the leadership. Each contributes to the preparation of this essential document. Therefore, it serves as the basis on which fundraising is planned and implemented. If the case statement were prepared by the fundraiser alone, few others would understand it, much less be able to support and use it in expressing the case to prospects, donors, and other essential audiences.

A fundraising effort is most successful when everyone—the board, the staff, and the volunteers—plays a significant role, participates in appropriate ways, and balances fundraising with other assignments and roles. In fact, most employees believe that their jobs are more gratifying if they participate in the "big picture," are informed, and are involved in suitable tasks. A mistake that organizational leaders make is to assume that volunteers should be spared from doing fundraising, that board members already give their time so they should not have to raise fund besides (much less give), that staff are overworked anyway, and that the executive director is too busy, so it comes down to the fundraiser being charged with fundraising—and only the fundraiser, working alone.

The entire team—staff, board, volunteers, and leaders—brings information, talent, and insight to the fundraising effort. Each may have contacts that are important for the organization, ideas on how to position the organization and create awareness, training to provide support in specialized areas such as technology or finances, and human relations skills appropriate for certain constituent groups. Most importantly, each individual working for or associated with the organization becomes an advocate and an ambassador for the organization and its cause.

Key members of a team, and those who enable institution-wide acceptance of and participation in fundraising, are the CEO (president or executive director), the chief development officer, the chief financial officer, the chair of the board's development committee, and the board chair. These team members should set up strategy for organization-wide involvement, helping employees and volunteers see how their participation in fitting roles and tasks promotes a successful fundraising program.

Entry-level or even mid-career professionals may not be in a position to put into effect the teamwork mentality and processes, but they can understand how they can fit into a team, and what unique qualities may enhance teamwork. Professionals must understand how their style of thinking and functioning fits into the team.

An article in *Training & Development,* a journal for corporate and non-profit trainers, stated that "everyone . . . has different styles or approaches to generating solutions and bringing about change."[3] As an example, the article cited four styles used by the Wilson Learning Corporation, a worldwide training firm.

First, the *modifiers* are stimulated by facts and make decisions based on them. They like moving ahead in a deliberate and planned manner, and they add stability to the team. They are thorough in their work and information acquisition. Modifiers believe there are standard ways of solving problems and that there is one best answer.

The *explorers* thrive on the unknown and the unpredictable. They like to question, play with ideas, approach problems from new angles. They contribute to the team by questioning basic assumptions and models. They are comfortable with uncertainty and have good insights because they are not hampered by preconceived ideas or plans. Explorers often believe there has to be a new way of solving problems, and they are open-minded to the range of possibilities. They want many perspectives and insights, and want to have the chance to consider them.

Visioners focus, predictably, on ideal results, and they provide teams with long-term direction. They can imagine and create, and have good insights into situations others might find dense or unsolvable. Visioners sometimes leave others behind because they are focused on future goals, but they also can imagine the best possible outcome for everyone because they are idealists.

Facts stimulate the *experimenters,* who generate new ideas by combining established processes. They are excellent at helping everyone reach a workable unit, to reach solutions with consensus. Experimenters can get lost in the details and forget the goal, but they are also committed to making things work. They combine the most practical ideas of many people.

This model is just one, simple way of looking at differences among people. Many other possibilities exist, of course, for determining how you may fit into a team, how you can promote teamwork, and how you function best. Some of these are the Dimensions of Behavior (DISC) and the Myers–Briggs Type Indicator.

The important point to remember is that a combination of expertise, talents, thinking and working styles, and knowledge promotes teamwork. Therefore, teamwork, in turn, leads toward the best outcomes in fundraising. Teamwork implies that the viewpoints and experience of key people are considered and implemented. Teamwork ensures that there is commitment by many who work for the organization, and fundraising isn't just the domain and vision of one person. Finally, teamwork makes certain that fundraising isn't directed just from the top down and imposed on the rest of the organization's employees; people from all levels of rank and professionalism are involved.

Whether the fundraising professional is the chief development officer, development director, planned giving officer, prospect researcher, or someone in another position, teamwork begins with that person. A compilation of ideas on how to become a good team player is listed here.

- Maintain a positive mental attitude. Shun negative words and deeds. Don't criticize, condemn, or complain needlessly.

- Understand and accept your preferred style of work, which may be as a loner, but acquire those characteristics that make you effective when working with others as well.

- Be generous. Share knowledge, time, effort. Help others with what you know and can do in a selfless way.

- Focus on benefits of teamwork, and take action that leads to outcomes. Be able to explain to your colleagues how what each brings to the collective effort enhances the success of the organization.

- Listen! Most people can easily talk about themselves and their work. It takes a good team member to listen to others, to ask questions, to avoid interrupting someone else.

- Talk, look, and act enthusiastic. Of course, you must first believe in the cause and in your role in fundraising, but an enthusiastic approach motivates others and builds team spirit.

- Don't worry unnecessarily; take positive action instead. Conventional wisdom states that 90 percent of what we worry about never comes to pass. We expend a lot of unnecessary energy in worrying when we could be working toward a solution.

- Look for the best in people, in situations, in problems. Be realistic, of course, when negative issues must be resolved, but even then look for the positive side on which solutions can be built.

It is true, of course, that the novice or entry-level professional may not be able to implement or even motivate a team mentality in an organization; however, every employee can try to become a team player by following these suggestions. It does go against the natural tendencies of some personality types, but in the long run, the individual and the organization win if such an effort is made.

Some problems may surface in trying to achieve a team mentality:

- *Inaccessibility to senior management or the board by employees not at the senior level.* This provides little opportunity for working together with superiors and volunteers. When this occurs, the fundraising professionals should attempt to have the best relationship with their own boss and should develop at least a two-person team. Fundraising professionals should try to motivate the boss to interact with other team members for common good.

- *Friction among potential team members, or "turf" issues.* Sometimes lack of communication is a simple culprit in situations where a team mentality and effectiveness can't be achieved. The fundraiser can try to understand the others' viewpoints, and—while not subsuming his or her personality and professionalism—can help others see the value in cooperation, in discussion, and in reaching consensus.

- *Personality differences.* Differences in personalities are often a problem when teams are formed. It is the differences that cause a team to be vibrant, exciting, and productive because various viewpoints and solutions are expressed, but it is also those differences that can cause conflict. An organization would be well advised to hold a workshop on personality and thinking styles and make a concerted effort to capitalize on differences.

- *Lack of clearly defined roles.* Poorly outlined roles, and thus the responsibilities that go with those roles, can cause teams to fragment and fall apart. The fundraiser can try to remedy this situation by asking for clarification of assignments and by keeping colleagues informed about the work. Developing a strategic plan that includes assignments can be helpful; the fundraising professional can recommend that this be accomplished.

- *Poor morale.* When personnel are not made to feel significant in the organization, are not recognized for their achievements and contributions to the common good, feel like they are being taken for granted, and in general work in an atmosphere of distrust and discontent, a team mentality is almost impossible to achieve. At this point the professional acknowledges that some situations just don't work out successfully!

Working as a team in fundraising may not be the easiest; however, not only is it an effective survival technique, but it also promotes the greatest success in fundraising—the ultimate goal of every professional working on behalf of the organization he or she is serving.

▓ FURTHER READING

Kroeger, Otto, and Janet M. Thuesen. *Type Talk.* New York: Dell Publishing, 1988.

> *The authors show how to determine your personality type, using a scientifically validated method based on the work of C. G. Jung. This book offers insight into why others behave the way they do, and why you are the person you are—on the job and in all aspects of life.*

Kroeger, Otto, and Janet M. Thuesen. *Type Talk at Work: How the 16 Personality Types Determine Your Success on the Job.* New York: Dell Publishing, 1993.

> *The authors take Typewatching to the workplace and reveal how managers, executives, and workers can use the technique to better handle both personal and personnel matters.*

Tieger, Paul D., and Barbara Barron-Tieger. *Do What You Are: Discover the Perfect Career for You Through the Secrets of Personality Type.* Boston: Little, Brown and Company, 1995.

> *This book introduces the Myers-Briggs personality type and shows you how to discover your own. It uses exercises and specific job search strategies to help you determine the best fit. It lists occupations that are compatible with your type and provides career advice as well as highlights of the strengths and pitfalls of each personality type.*

The best institutional development programs benefit from a close working relationship between the chief development officer, the president/CEO, and key trustees. It is the chief development officer giving real energy to these relationships that forges this successful team: identifying issues, organizing meetings, initiating actions, and following up. Here are six key activities affecting fundraising in which the chief development officer can team with the president and trustees to produce maximum results.

Recruiting, Working With, and Inspiring Trustees

Trustees want to serve your nonprofit organization and have a good experience while doing it. They appreciate quality staff assistance. Development officers who are actively involved in recruiting trustees and in working closely with the president/CEO can, in return, expect high-level trustee involvement in fundraising.

Strategic and Long-term Planning

Good planning usually ends with a case for fundraising; when it also starts with the chief development officer's participation, the strategic plan benefits from the talent and focus you bring and the institutional relationships that are built during the planning process.

Approving and Overseeing the Institutional Advancement Program

Trustees and presidents/CEOs work best in helping carry out the fundraising program when they've helped shape it. Frequent communication helps keep them focused on their roles: program oversight and, ideally, helping with key cultivations and solicitations.

Developing Relationships with Key Friends

Most key constituents want to have a direct relationship with the CEO and key trustees. You can help your leaders focus attention heavily in this area: creating forums for interaction with major prospects, providing meaningful advance briefings, and providing effective follow-up support.

(continued)

Recruiting Key Volunteer Leaders

Identifying the right candidates for important institutional development tasks should be a joint decision. You will often be depended on to help shape and define the job, to identify the optimum recruitment strategy, and to be part of the team that recruits such volunteer leaders.

Asking Key Prospects for Support

Rarely do we have the opportunity to include the president/CEO, a key trustee, *and* the chief development officer in a solicitation team, although often it is two of the three. But for all top solicitations, all three should work together to develop the right strategy and prepare the presentation.

J. PATRICK RYAN is president and CEO of Staley/Robeson/Ryan/St. Lawrence, Inc., one of the leading fundraising consulting firms in the United States. During his career, Pat has planned and supervised successful capital campaigns, institutional development, and expansion and fundraising programs for numerous universities, schools, hospitals, social service, and civic and community organizations throughout North America. He is also actively involved in international fundraising activities. His recent international consulting activities include work with the legion of Good Will, South America's leading nonprofit, and major capital campaigns in Greece, Rome, and Argentina. He has chaired the World Fundraising Council and is past chair of the American Association of Fund-Raising Counsel (AAFRC). He has been active in the Association of Fundraising Professionals (AFP) and is past chair of the AFP Foundation for Philanthropy. He is a frequent speaker at professional conferences both in the United States and international and has written a number of articles and publications on fundraising.

PROFESSIONALS SAY . . .

No person in the fundraising field becomes a success without the support of others, without the support of the team. When we forget this and begin to attribute success solely to our own efforts, we are on the road to failure. All of us have our moments of success, but behind every accomplishment— every winning basket—there is someone who "passed us the ball." To ignore this basic fact by refusing to give graceful credit to those who have helped us in our fundraising efforts is to invite a sudden and drastic reversal of our fortunes. We must never neglect to give credit where credit is due—not arrogantly or patronizingly—but humbly and in simple grati-tude. I love Thurgood Marshall's quote: "None of us has gotten where we are solely by pulling ourselves up from our own bootstraps. We got there because somebody . . . bent down and helped us."

Bob Mueller, Director of Development, Alliance of Community Hospices and Palliative Care Services, Louisville, Kentucky

When working in a team of committed, intelligent, and energetic people, it is important that all recognize that each member can contribute a por-tion of the solution to any challenge. Some contribute more at times than others, but the importance of each voice on the team should not be underes-timated. Building an effective and supportable consensus is completely dependent on this consideration.

Daniel D. Sayger, MPA

"Build it and they will come. Involve them and they won't have to come; they're already there." I'll always remember when I heard this play on words from the movie Field of Dreams. *It truly summarizes one of the most important aspects of a successful fundraising job—working with teams. From building an internal organization of people with com-plementary skills who shape and enthusiastically work toward a common goal, to working with donors based on a true partnership—one based on meaningful communication, joint decision-making, mutual fulfillment of needs and the lifelong perpetuation of values, working effectively as a team means reaching maximum potential and yes, making dreams reality.*

Bettyann O'Neill, Vice President for Institutional Advancement, Berry College, Mount Berry, Georgia

In fundraising, it takes a team to raise one gift. You need a bus to carry all the people who deserve recognition and credit for a successful solicitation. From the receptionist who answers the phone, to the development officer who stewards the donor and asks for the gift, to the writer who pens a com-pelling proposal, to the volunteer who supports the institution's cause, to the gift administrator who processes the gift, they all play a critical role in clos-ing the gift. Being a team player is key to becoming a successful fundraiser.

Phillip K. Hardwick, Vice President, Indiana University Foundation-Indianapolis

CHAPTER 16

Working in a One-Person Shop

SIDEBAR BY D. MARK HELMUS

The total number of 501(c)(3) organizations in the United States is 734,000.[1] Of these, almost 98,000 have budgets of $100,000 and below. This means that many of the smaller organizations have limited fundraising staff and often no full-time person in the position. Sometimes fundraising is part of the array of responsibilities given to an employee. It could be that the executive director combines fundraising with administrative duties, or staff members must raise money for their programs as well as participate in securing financial resources for the entire organization. The challenges of wearing many hats can be exciting but also stressful and difficult, and fundraising sometimes doesn't get the attention it needs or deserves. Even when a small organization has one or more than one full-time professional raising funds, the demands made by others, such as bosses or board members, can be daunting.

Working in a small shop that has limited staff who devote time to fundraising can also be an opportunity for acquiring a wide range of skills and developing expertise quickly. Members of a larger development team, which could include anywhere from 5 to 100 or more persons, may be better paid and have more predictable assignments and work hours, but they also may have limited exposure to the full range of fundraising tasks. The fundraiser who works alone or has few colleagues must develop a wide scope of expertise, learn to co-opt others who aren't skilled in fundraising, hone traits and abilities for working in complex situations, and be well organized. If successful in such a set of circumstances, the fundraising professional will be better prepared for greater responsibility in larger organizations, if that is the career goal, or be eligible for promotions in smaller organizations. For those who like variety and constant challenges, working in a small shop is excellent experience and preparation for career progression. Those who want to refine a highly defined set of skills, such as proposal writing, would do better in larger organizations.

As has been noted in previous chapters, fundraising ability is highly useful for a variety of positions, either when moving up the ladder of increased responsibility in the field, or when changing roles and assuming other positions that may require fundraising skills. Novice fundraisers should decide how they learn best, what brings most satisfaction in a work experience, and what career goals they have.

Some of the questions a person looking at a position in a small organization might ask are:

1. What type of achiever am I? Do I want to move quickly in my career development, or does a comfort zone appeal to me?

2. What kind of environment do I need in order to excel in my work, and what situation is most conducive to my learning? Do I like to be independent, or do I need others to energize me?

3. What am I willing to give up? A small shop may provide less security and make greater demands on my time and expertise.

4. Do I want to develop one or a few skills to the optimum, or do I want to be a generalist?

5. Do I want to think for myself, or do I like to do "group think?" Is working alone my preference?

6. What is my working pace? Does my type of personality perform well under stress, or do I need more reflection time than some others?

7. Do I like to focus on a single task or responsibility, or do I like to juggle multiple tasks?

8. Is being a leader important to me, and if so, can I assume that role best in a small organization or a large one? Although both types of organizations can provide leadership opportunities, they will differ in style and quality. An astute professional will research to find out which organizations are most suitable for his or her career goals.

9. Do I handle decision making with ease, or does this cause me undue stress? Am I eager to weigh options and see solutions, or do I want others to help me in making decisions?

10. Am I flexible and do I react to change favorably?

The person choosing to work in a small organization must obviously find it a compatible environment or fundraising success is jeopardized. If a one-person shop seems to be the workplace of choice, the answers to the above questions might be:

1. I prefer to acquire expertise as quickly as possible and therefore am willing to risk not having a comfort zone in which to grow professionally.

2. While colleagues and others do energize me, I prefer to work independently for the most part.

3. I like a working environment that makes great demands on my time and expertise.

4. Because I have a variety of interests, I want to be a generalist first, then hone my skills in one specific area of fundraising.

5. I prefer to think for myself first, then test my ideas on others.

6. I work fast and quickly, and enjoy a fast pace.

7. Juggling multiple assignments brings me much satisfaction.

8. I believe I can exert more leadership in a small organization because I am needed and listened to.

9. Making decisions is not something I fear; rather, I welcome each opportunity.

10. I like change, sometimes even for its own sake.

Once an entry-level fundraising professional has elected to work in a small organization, and has addressed the relevant issues that indicate whether this is a compatible environment, the next question is, How can I be successful in this type of organization, given the lack of resources, time, personnel, and perhaps even institutional or external support for fundraising? Some essential steps to take are listed as follows. The list is not exhaustive but indicates seven areas that should at least be considered:

1. *Being well organized is essential for success in a small organization.* Multiple tasks may become confusing. A plan for fundraising should be in place, because this will help in defining what must be accomplished and when.

2. *Dependence on a team approach, which includes others in the organization, is important.* Sharing information, providing input into plans and strategies, providing encouragement, participating in appropriate ways, and being fundraising conscious are significant ways that all organizational employees can promote success.

3. *Volunteers are important to the process.* They can provide planning and implementation expertise, be advocates for the cause, serve on the development committee, provide perspectives, and aid in all steps of the fundraising process. Managing volunteers should be an important part of a professional's role in a small organization.

4. *Learning how to prioritize can be the key element in success.* What prospects are the best ones for us to develop and solicit? Where is the greatest return for our effort? How should my time best be used? Who can be motivated and mobilized for what component of our fundraising program? What strategies are best for our use? These and other questions will help the professional maintain a focus and not be overwhelmed by the myriad of demands in running a fundraising program.

5. *Outsourcing some tasks may be feasible or even essential.* Can someone help with prospect research? Whom can we engage to write a proposal? Is there an affordable expert who can create our Web page and also maintain it?

6. *Defining goals and verifying that they are reachable is perhaps the most important step.* Creating a gift range chart, which helps you and your team understand whether there are sufficient prospects as well as financial and human resources available for raising a defined amount of money, is one excellent activity. Good planning will ensure that the goal is realistic.

7. *Person doing fundraising for a small shop must learn to be a leader, regardless of rank in the organization.* He or she must be able to motivate other members of the fundraising team and lead by example.

Along with the opportunities for learning and for achieving measurable goals come a range of possible problems. These may derail a budding professional, resulting in unmet goals and disappointing experiences. Some potential problem areas to watch for and anticipate may be:

- Fundraising professionals may suffer under the *Tinkerbell syndrome,* meaning that others expect them to perform something akin to a miracle. Fundraisers may discover that there are great expectations for their performance, that they are supposed to know everything about fundraising, and—because everyone else is busy, too—that they must function alone in the role of fundraiser. Every professional, but especially the entry-level, should remember that fundraising is best accomplished when it is a team effort, and collegial support and engagement is vital.

- Burnout is a definite possibility, particularly if fundraisers are left to do the job alone, with no input or support from others in the organization or volunteers. Time becomes tight, tasks are daunting, results are discouraging, and small achievements go unrecognized. All these and other situations cause burnout. Professionals will need to be constantly vigilant and anticipate situations that can be overwhelming. Sometimes, admittedly, nothing can prevent burnout, but most situations are workable if the professional has at least some sense of how to handle the difficulties.

- Loneliness or a sense of aloneness can become endemic and even paralyze a fundraiser. It is true that at times people in a small organization are too busy with the multiple tasks they have to perform, but at the least fundraising professionals should try to develop a team mentality and elicit support for their responsibilities, while also providing support for the efforts of colleagues.

- Sometimes fundraising professionals and their teams have bitten off more than they can chew. Vision and goals exceeded reality. Expectations were unreasonable. This may be a self-imposed situation. The professional and the team may have to step back, survey the problem, and regroup.

There is an old saying that originated with people from the mountainous region of southern Appalachia. "Rough weather makes good timber." On the tops of the mountains, trees stand unprotected from the wind and are subjected to constant stress. Often these trees become strong and sturdy and produce the finest timber.

The lesson in this illustration is that the professional in the small organization may be faced with difficulties and tough times. Sturdiness of spirit is essential when accepting the challenges of succeeding in fundraising for a small, often one-person, shop. Our ability to handle problems is, at least to some degree, a learned process. Our day-by-day actions build our expertise to manage difficult situations, and we develop the skills necessary for greater responsibility.

The person working in a small organization may do well to remember this example from many years ago. In the early 1800s, Rebecca Lukens and her husband took over a small, water-driven iron mill that made nails. They had big plans to build their small business in rural Pennsylvania, but before they could achieve their goals, Rebecca's husband died, leaving her at the age of 31 with four young children and a fifth on the way. Most people expected her to sell the mill and become a full-time mother and housewife. But she had made a promise to her husband, and despite of several financial difficulties, she took over the management of the ironworks herself. She made up her mind that the dream was achievable, and said, "If it is to be, it is up to me."

Rebecca Lukens carried through with expansion plans, enlarged the mills and product line, and included plate iron. She provided the iron hull and boiler plates for the Navy's first iron ship in 1825. Many of the Mississippi riverboats came to rely on Lukens's ironwork for their boilers.

For 30 years she managed the business, motivating employees to work toward visionary goals, promoting her company, achieving success even in a depression, and finally moving her team forward to become one of the nation's major ironworks. The company eventually became a Fortune 500 company.

The person choosing to work in a small organization may do well to follow Rebecca Lukens's example. In challenges lie opportunities to achieve and grow. The small shop professional's motto can be, "If it is to be, it is up to me."

◾ FURTHER READING

Grassroots Fundraising Journal. Oakland, CA: Chardon Press.

> *Articles on alternative sources of funding, book reviews, and bibliographies. Geared toward the low-budget organization.*

Klein, Kimberly. *Fundraising for Social Change.* 4th ed. Inverness, CA: Chardon Press, 2001.

Written specifically for low-budget (less than $500,000) organizations, this book offers practical information on various strategies used by successful small organizations. It discusses mail and phone fundraising, campaigns, special events, and overall management. It includes sample letters, record-keeping forms, checklists, and project evaluation forms.

SIDEBAR   D. MARK HELMUS

Many development professionals feel as though there is too much to do and too little time in which to do it. This feeling is even greater in small shops, where the development director is often responsible for direct mail, the phonathon, planned giving, major gifts, board and volunteer training, gift entry, annual reports, database management, marketing, and public relations, amid other administrative responsibilities.

Because of the breadth of these demands, fundraisers have a tendency to focus on completing activities that shorten to-do lists, decrease piles, and appear to be "productive." In short, they make us feel better because we're doing *something*.

Unfortunately, the things that often don't get prioritized in small shops are the development basics—identification, cultivation, and solicitation of donors.

Why don't we make these seemingly obvious activities our top priorities?

Because donors usually don't call or write to ask why they haven't been solicited. Yet projects from boards, bosses, and colleagues continue with amazing regularity, and communication (e-mail, letters, phone calls, etc.) is seemingly continuous and often comes with misplaced urgency.

So why do fundraisers *really* tend to put off the very things they are hired to do?

Primarily because these activities are long-term, provide little immediate feedback, and often *create* more work and follow-up. Another common factor is a lack of patience to work the plan (rather, we and our supervisors and boards often want quick solutions—special events, shotgun grant-request proposals, and so on.).

It is our responsibility, however, to constantly battle these challenges. Perhaps the best form of stewardship we can provide is not *just* raising immediate dollars. Rather, it may also be helping to shift our organization's focus to the core business of development—building and maintaining relationships that will maximize our fundraising potential, and in the process and final analysis, further our organization's mission.

(continued)

D. MARK HELMUS is director of development and major gifts at Franklin College in Indiana. Prior to joining the college he did fundraising for the Milton and Rose D. Friedman Foundation and the Ruth Lilly Health Education Center, both in Indianapolis. He also worked as a consultant for Ruotolo Associates Inc. and was vice president for alumni development for the Delta Tau Delta Educational Foundation. He has a master's in college student personnel management from the University of Tennessee–Knoxville and a B.S. in psychology from Ohio University. He is active in the Indiana chapter of the Association of Fundraising Professionals.

PROFESSIONALS SAY . . .

One of the most rewarding aspects in my fundraising career has been mentoring a young university graduate. This young woman joined the Fine Arts Society at WICR-FM in a new position, Education Coordinator. As the Director of Development in a one-person shop, I was desperate for assistance, and our broadcasting budget was unable to add a new staff member. My needs were unusual since I needed someone with knowledge of music along with excellent writing skills. Through our affiliation with the University of Indianapolis, I obtained a real jewel: a talented young woman with a double major in both music and English. My objectives were to hire her as an intern, mentor her writing skills as the main contributor for our new music education Internet project, and guide her through the grant-writing process. By the end of her internship, I knew that she would be a valuable addition to our staff. The next step was to obtain a grant to hire her full time. She has blossomed into an exceptionally talented young professional who now heads our new after-school music education program. Her grant-writing skills have enabled our organization to expand its mission from broadcasting classical music to music education in the Fine Arts Society Music Academy, an after-school music education program for disadvantaged children. Finding talented young people and nurturing their skills in the fundraising field will stand as one of my most rewarding accomplishments as a fundraising professional.

Betty Darbro, Director of Corporate Development, Fine Arts Society of Indianapolis

It is imperative that nonprofit organizations understand that revenue be received from a variety of sources. Successfully moving an organization from dependence on one source of revenue to a diversity of funding sources requires a solid fund development plan that has been embraced by organizational leaders on the Board of Directors as well as inside the organization. Doing this as the only person in the development department can seem overwhelming, but is not impossible. When a good plan has been developed and carried out, it is very rewarding to see the organization grow and prosper because of the good work that has been accomplished by the fund development area.

Beth A. Karnes, President, Indiana Mental Health Memorial Foundation, Inc.

It might well be that the most demanding position any professional fundraiser could have today is working in a one-person shop, and that is exactly where many fundraisers find themselves, especially early in a budding fundraising career. The responsibilities are many and the delegation opportunities are often less than one would like to see. There are only so many hours in a day, and setting priorities is an absolute must. Not everything is going to be accomplished. Some things will be left undone. Near the top of any priority list for a fundraiser working in a one-person shop is the importance of saying "thank you." You can never say "thank you" too often. It is important to be creative in your thanking. Thanking does not need to be expensive. A thank you note, a phone call, a card, a letter, an e-mail, a picture, a fax all serve the purpose. Timing is important. Nothing is better than to be able to say, "Thank you for your gift that we received today.*" The "thank you" is your first step in the cultivation process for the next gift.*

Rev. Gary L. Pohl, Executive Director, Lutheran Foundation of Texas, Austin, Texas

CHAPTER 17

International Fundraising

SIDEBAR BY DANIEL YOFFE

The practice of fundraising is growing dramatically around the globe. Within the past decade, the role of governments has been measurably reduced because of the emergence of new democratic cultures, technological advances in communications, and the inability of many governments to keep up with even basic services to its populations. Therefore, there has been a rapid development of nongovernmental organizations (NGOs)[1] that can be service providers while also acting as advocates for reform. The authors of a definitive volume on this topic explain, "The final decades of the twentieth century have witnessed an extraordinary shift in the social and political geography of the world."[2] Furthermore, as explained in another important text, this shift has "created the opportunity and indeed the necessity for citizens to become more engaged than ever before in the political, social, and cultural lives of their nations and of the world as a whole. Civil society in every region today is providing a broad and powerful means for mobilizing such citizen participation."[3]

What does all this mean to a fundraising professional in the United States? Perhaps the answer is best phrased by the authors of *The Nonprofit Sector in the Global Community:* "national boundaries will not be as important as either international cooperation and collaboration or cross-national public understanding and support."[4] The significance of NGOs, philanthropy, and voluntarism in other nations is growing, and Americans who have fundraising expertise are "being sought around the globe as nonprofit organizations increasingly seek to raise private funds to bolster their activities

and lessen their reliance on government funds. And as more and more countries are creating tax incentives to encourage giving to those organizations,
demand for Americans who have experience showing donors tax-savvy ways
to give is on the rise."[5]

A Johns Hopkins University research team twice studied international
NGOs in 22 countries in Central and Eastern Europe, Latin America,
Western Europe, Oceania, and North America as part of its Comparative
Nonprofit Sector Project. They found a surprisingly large scale of nonprofit
activity in almost every place that was researched. The reports confirmed
that NGOs everywhere are seeing astonishing growth, employing increasing
numbers of people, and collecting and spending more money than at any
previous time.

The research team found that NGOs are big employers; on the average,
the sector employs close to 19 million full-time equivalent paid workers,
which is about a ratio of 6:1 when compared with private business employment. Gifts account for 11 percent of nonprofit revenues, with the balance coming from fees for services, earned income, and government support.
The reports conclude that NGOs and civil society organizations (CSOs)
are a far more significant economic force than has generally been recognized, while the surge of voluntary activity has come amid a crisis of confidence in the ability of governments to deal with social problems.[6] Not
surprisingly, NGOs are having difficulty meeting growing needs, as governments cut back on direct aid to citizens.

The range of international NGO development is impressive. According
to the Social Information Agency in Russia, 40,000 nonprofit groups have
formed in Russia since the disintegration of the Soviet Union.[7] Countries
such as Croatia, which has a long-standing tradition of nonprofit activity,
are seeing a re-emergence of arts and cultural societies and other traditional
NGOs, and also an increase of organizations that meet needs engendered
by war. Charitable efforts in Turkey range back to the previous century,
when foundations were formed to care for specific causes. Now the face of
the Turkish nonprofit sector includes educational institutions, cultural organizations, hospitals, homes, and programs for street children. The former
Yugoslavia has seen tremendous growth in refugee causes, but other interests are also in evidence, for example, environmental concerns. In Argentina,
while well-known organizations including the Red Cross, Greenpeace, and

SOS Children's Villages are prevalent and active, many nonprofit causes such as museums of Jewish history and organizations benefiting the Pampas Indians are part of the NGO movement that began in the early 1980s. China began moving toward NGO ideals perhaps 15 years ago, when organizations such as science foundations were established.

Money from the United States has aided in NGO development internationally to some extent at least. U.S. foundation dollars to overseas causes totaled $1.6 billion in 2001, a $639 million jump from 1994.[8] Corporations tend to give where they have a direct investment, which means that the poorest regions of the world may not benefit from this source; however, corporate contributions to U.S.-based international organizations increased by 13 percent from 1998 to 1999, and this does not include giving by corporate offices at international sites.[9]

International philanthropy is complex because even in established democracies, charitable organizations are different from those in the United States. This is even more true in the fragile, emerging civil societies. According to Stanley N. Katz, president of the American Council of Learned Societies, grant-makers and, by implication, fundraisers should not try to duplicate the U.S. system but should ask what types of social organizations do the most for the common good. "The critical question is whether we are sufficiently aware of cultural differences, whether we are sure that foreign legal and political environments will not produce different philanthropic outcomes than we intend."[10] This concept is echoed by an article on international fundraising job opportunities, which warns, "Charities overseas are looking to American experts in large part because the United States has a long-established tradition of raising money from private sources. However, tactics that work for U.S. fundraisers at home may not necessarily always translate abroad."[11] There is concern that countries that are experimenting with civil society and democracy may be overwhelmed by expectations, perceptions, and the imposition of the U.S. model.

Therefore, philanthropic fundraising principles are universally adaptable, while at the same time they must be culturally and situationally appropriate. Within universality of principles and generalizations about fundraising, differences and similarities between U.S. and international fundraising must be noted. This can be accomplished by professional sharing and understanding of problems and successes. It is useful for the fundraising practitioner to know which concepts and principles of fundraising can be universally applied. Some of these are:

- The need and art of making a strong, compelling case for funding, and expressing this case in differing ways to different markets are concepts understood everywhere.

- Donor motivations, when discussed as part of both training and practice, are surprisingly universal. Some differences do exist, but the desire to help others is often a motivation that can be aroused or tapped.

- International fundraisers also understand the need to research and know the potential markets, to practice the exchange relationship in determining why a donor might give, and to diversify funding sources whenever possible.

- Without a doubt there is common understanding of the impact of a nation's and the world's economy on asking for and giving funds.

There are also issues that may make it difficult for a U.S. fundraiser to function effectively in another country. Some of these are:

- Professional compensation, such as the prohibition of working for a commission, is not understood as an ethical issue in many cultures.

- Prospect research may be difficult to carry out in some places because of lack of research resources as well as prevailing attitudes toward privacy. Consider, for example, the impact of nearly 50 years of KGB activity in the former Soviet Union, when personal information was sought about large numbers of citizens and often used in highly damaging ways.

- Board responsibility is uneven in many countries, and the idea of board members seeking funds still brings some horrified looks from England to Uruguay.

- Tax deductibility and the concept of planned gifts are unfamiliar in many nations.

- The habit of giving may not be infused in a country and its culture.

- Expectations of a U.S. fundraising professional may be excessively high, while at the same time the fundraiser may be starting from ground zero. This can be demoralizing to all parties, and exhausting to the fundraiser.

There are several positive aspects of working internationally. First, fundraising professionals may have opportunities not available in the United States. They may be able to find unique ways to work and accomplish goals, or use creative ideas that may not be welcome in a traditional setting in the United States. There is also the opportunity of fostering the growth of local personnel by sharing information and providing opportunities to learn. Above all, understanding international NGOs and fundraising helps us comprehend what is happening in the culturally diverse world inside our own borders. That is to say, understanding diversity on a global scale helps us understand what is happening in our own communities and with our own prospects, volunteers, and colleagues. In addition, philanthropy and the securing of funds to benefit others is an ancient practice, and the United States represents only a portion of this rich history. Although we in the United States have perfected many fundraising techniques and have much to offer in terms of sharing our expertise, we also have much to learn. International understanding enriches the global community of fundraising practitioners; we are part of a global system.

How would a fundraising professional find employment overseas? Actually, the range of international opportunities is broader than one might expect. The easiest way to get started is by volunteering; this does not necessarily mean working without wages. Some organizations provide a salary, others pay a stipend, while some expect the prospective employee to come up with his or her own financial support. There is no one single source for finding an international fundraising job. One way is to search the Web pages of international nonprofit organizations, another is to network with international consultants. One current source is DevJobs (see readings at end of this chapter), and similar Web pages are likely to crop up. Sometimes universities have international centers that can provide employment information, or their international student services departments might assist with making contacts.

Increasingly, we who are professionals in the United States are part of a growing scene. Fundraising is increasing daily on a global scale. In fact, "(w)hile many American fundraisers are happy to share their knowledge abroad, they say that in the long term, nonprofit groups based in other countries will nurture their own development professionals who are familiar with the language, culture, and traditions of local donors."[12] Our international colleagues embrace the need for and value of fundraising even while dealing with issues that U.S. practitioners rarely face. And they are coming up with solutions from which we can learn. U.S. professionals can be more competent by understanding the global perspective.

Fundraising as a profession is enriched by its proliferation and adaptation across nations and cultures, awareness of cultural issues, sensitivity toward differences, and the expression of a genuine appreciation of our international fundraising professionals efforts and achievements.

■ FURTHER READING

DEVJOBS. To subscribe, send·e-mail to devjobs-subscribe@yahoogroups.com.

This is a mailing list to post and receive international job announcements that are related to various development fields: microfinance, poverty alleviation, community development, institution development, governance, health care, population, food security, agriculture, human resource development, natural resource management, information technology, and rural development.

Fox, Leslie M., and S. Bruce Schearer. *Sustaining Civil Society: Strategies for Resource Mobilization.* Washington, DC: World Alliance for Citizen Participation, 1998.

A survey of the many strategies and tools for resource generation for NGOs that reflects the perspectives from many parts of the world.

Harris, Thomas, ed. *International Fund Raising for Not-for-Profits: A Country-by-Country Profile.* New York: Wiley, 1999.

A thorough survey of fundraising practices in 18 countries, ranging from Japan to Estonia. The chapters cover topics such as the history of the nonprofit sector, sources of funds, strategies for raising funds, and what a fundraiser should know when working in another country.

Ilchman, Warren F., Stanley N. Katz, and Edward L. Queen, eds. *Philanthropy in the World's Traditions.* Bloomington and Indianapolis: Indiana University Press, 1998.

Though voluntary association for the public good is often thought of as a peculiarly Western, even Christian concept, this book demonstrates that there are rich traditions of philanthropy in cultures throughout the world. Essays study philanthropy in Buddhist, Islamic, Hindu, Jewish, and Native American religious traditions, as well as many other cultures.

Kocher, Eric. *International Jobs: Where They Are and How to Get Them,* 5th ed. Reading, MA: Addison-Wesley Publishing Company, 1999.

Covers topics such as international career planning, how to research for the right jobs, what the right qualifications are, and types of jobs that are available.

Krannich, Ronald. *Almanac of International Jobs and Careers.* Manassas Park, VA: Impact Publications, 1994.

This is a guide to over 1,001 employers. It includes bibliographical references.

Krannich, Ronald. *Complete Guide to International Jobs and Careers*, 2nd ed. Manassas Park, VA: Impact Publications, 1992.

Discusses international jobs and careers available in foreign countries; a useful handbook to survey possibilities for employment overseas.

Lewis, Nicole. "Have Expertise, Will Travel: U.S. Fund Raisers Abroad Find Hot Job Market, Big Challenges," *The Chronicle of Philanthropy* (July 13, 2000).

This article contains views of Americans working as international fundraising professionals and includes suggestions for how to be successful and cope with challenges that make the job difficult, and describes the positive aspects of including this type of experience in a career track.

McCarthy, Kathleen D., Virginia A. Hodgkinson, and Russy D. Sumariwalla, and Associates. *The Nonprofit Sector in the Global Community*. San Francisco: Jossey-Bass, 1992.

Addresses several issues and questions about the roles and functions of nonprofits in many nations. The authors describe and analyze the functions and significance of nongovernmental organizations, philanthropy, and voluntarism within their own nation or in comparison with other nations.

Roberts, Elizabeth, ed. *The Directory of Jobs and Careers Abroad*, 10th ed. Oxford: Vacation Work, 2000.

This book is a thorough look at employment in foreign countries.

Salamon, Lester M., et al. *Global Civil Society: Dimensions of the Nonprofit Sector*. Baltimore, MD: The Johns Hopkins Comparative Nonprofit Sector Project, 1999.

This book provides a comprehensive country-by-country analysis of the scope, size, composition, and financing of the nonprofit sector in 22 countries in North America, South America, Europe, Asia, and the Middle East, with new data on nonprofit employment, volunteering, expenditures, and revenues. In addition, it provides a comparative overview and documents recent trends in sector size and composition.

Transitions Abroad: The Guide to Learning, Living, and Working Overseas. A bimonthly guide to practical information on working in a host country. Order by calling toll-free 1-800-293-0373 or e-mail at business@TransitionsAbroad.com.

Wagner, Lilya. "U.S. Models and International Dimensions of Philanthropic Fund Raising." In Dwight F. Burlingame, ed. *Critical Issues in Fundraising*. Baltimore, MD: Wiley, 1997.

The universal aspects as well as distinctions of fundraising in other countries are addressed in this chapter. A useful reference for guiding the initial steps of fundraising practice because it refers the reader to considerations that deserve a closer look.

Work Abroad: The Complete Guide to Finding a Job Overseas. Order by calling toll-free 1-800-293-0373 or e-mail at business@TransitionsAbroad.com.

Fundraising expertise and professionalism acquired in the United States is part of a cultural context in which philanthropy has been developed to a level that cannot be compared with the rest of the world. At the same time, the phenomenon of globalization reduces distance and tends to create a misleading perception of a unified world. Nevertheless, we must recognize and manage diversity in fundraising practice if we are to become successful on an international scale.

It is interesting to observe the similarities of opinion by experts who have carried out fundraising activities in countries such as Argentina, Brazil, Germany, India, Japan, Mexico, Singapore, Spain, and Switzerland. When we read their opinions, we can see the chief elements about fundraising in their societies or cultures. Here is their advice:

- Speak the language. In some countries this is a basic requirement. Without this skill, a barrier is created between the professional and the organization.

- Understand the culture, its values, and the differences from ours. This is a difficult task. The way of doing business, for example, can be very different from what we are used to. The idea that "time is money" can be taken as an offense in cultures where the creation of a personal relationship is the starting point of any activity.

- In many countries the needs are great and the amount of time is limited. This often interferes with the educational process that every fundraiser must carry out with NGO leaders.

- If one goes to work in an unfamiliar country, the best thing to do is immerse one's self in the culture.

The professionals are not only helping finance NGOs; they are also contributing to the development of a new philanthropic culture in that society.

DANIEL YOFFE is a professor in the postgraduate management for non-profit organizations program at the Universidad St. Andrew, Universidad Di Tella, and Universidad Catolica from Cordoba. He is also a professor in the school of education at Universidad Austral. He works as a resource development consultant for various universities and institutions and was a consultant for the International Red Cross Federation (Southern Cone: Argentina, Chile, Bolivia, and Paraguay). Daniel established The Fund Raising School affiliate based in Argentina and is executive director. The school operates in Argentina, Brazil, and Chile. He is a member of the Research Center of Studies for State and Society.

PROFESSIONALS SAY . . .

Just as goods now move freely from one country to another, charitable donations, likewise, cross international borders. The largest volume of foreign donations to U.S. charities comes from Canada, which also continues to be our largest trading partner; however, the volume of gifts from European and Asian countries is increasing. Philanthropy is also becoming more important within many of those countries, and charitable organizations, which previously relied on governmental revenues, are now turning to the private sector for supplemental support. In the practice of fundraising, they often adopt the U.S. models and advocate tax incentives similar to those that exist here. Development officers who work for universities and other charities with international donors will need to become familiar with the rules governing cross-border gifts. Those willing to venture beyond U.S. borders will also find expanding job and consulting opportunities in other countries.

Frank Minton, President, Planned Giving Services, Seattle, Washington

CHAPTER 18

Pressures and Stresses of the Profession

SIDEBAR BY TED R. GROSSNICKLE

The popular humorist, Dave Barry, has been known to state that people are the single biggest cause of stress. "That's why I seldom venture out of my home office," he has said. He cites three major sources of stress and overload: other humans, children, and spouses or significant others. His "tried and true" methods for relieving stress are:

- Avoid contact with others (if you don't already work at home).
- Wear camouflage clothing, perhaps disguising yourself as a filing cabinet.
- Learn to work from under your desk.
- Avoid the humor-impaired.
- Don't answer the telephone.[1]

If what Dave Barry says is even half-true, then fundraisers have a greater than average chance for experiencing and having to deal with stress, because their jobs consist of being with people constantly—donors, volunteers, colleagues, staff, board, supervisors, CEOs, and others—and their success depends on good human relations. Fundraising professionals continually interact with other individuals and populations groups, and they can hardly avoid answering the telephone or being publicly visible.

CAUSES OF STRESS

The pressures and stresses of a fundraising job vary greatly, depending on where you work or with whom you work, but there are some general issues that most commonly surface.

Evaluation of dollars raised, increased goals, cost to raise a dollar—these are just some of the aspects of fundraising that may cause stress. If expectations are too high and unrealistic, if for some reason the projected goals aren't achieved, if an unexpected postage hike causes expenses to flare out of sight, then fundraisers are often blamed and many accusations are made, both by staff and supervisors and by our external constituents. Therefore it is important for a professional to set goals that are achievable, to be accountable, to inform, and to substantiate any expectations on charitable income. For this reason it is also important for the professional to receive training and mentoring, so that fundraising practice is credible and verifiable (as discussed in previous chapters).

Dealing with rejection and refusal is another cause of stress. Naturally, some of our invitations to contribute to a cause will be declined. The point to remember is that we are asking on behalf of a cause, for our organizations, and the rejection is not personal. The donor has the right to say no, and as professionals we should consider why this might occur. Is the timing wrong? Have we approached a donor who is not really interested in the cause we present? What can we learn from the experience? Of course no one likes to be rejected—this is a universal fear; however, the rejection must be put into perspective and handled with sound reasoning and practice.

Feelings of inferiority may be another problem. Regular contact with those who have money and, sometimes, power may cause the fundraising professional to feel demeaned. It is significant to remember that we raise funds because we serve noble and worthy causes. We who ask others to join us in supporting an institution can be proud of our efforts!

Sometimes there is a lack of understanding of our role and the purpose we fulfill in our organizations. CEOs or presidents do not always participate in fundraising, nor do they grasp the complexity and multitude of responsibilities that accompany a fundraiser's job. Therefore, their expectations might be very high, but their encouragement and assistance may be nonexistent. Our job is to appropriately inform and educate, as well as to seek their presence on the fundraising team.

Board members and volunteers may be unaware of the importance of fundraising, or may actually use the often-heard phrase, "I'll do anything but fundraise!" Or they may give lip service to the program while refraining from involvement. Worse yet, they may treat staff with disdain and lack respect for their efforts. Volunteer and board training is crucial for building success in fundraising, as is frequent information sharing. The fundraising professional has to exert leadership in motivating, creating awareness, and building a team that includes volunteers.

Budgets may be inadequate for carrying out the expected tasks and reaching the defined goals. Helping bosses, colleagues, and volunteers understand that it costs money to raise money is at times a difficult task. The professional has to have knowledge of appropriate fundraising costs, when a department should be frugal and when it should spend extra money to raise even more money, and to be publicly accountable for financial operations in the fundraising office.

Office management may be difficult if support staff are lacking or inadequate, not well trained, or not well suited for the tasks of fundraising. Sometimes equipment is lacking, or physical space is limited. Such conditions may hinder the operation of a good fundraising program.

Lack of understanding by our friends and family—never mind the general public—of what fundraising is may cause some to become apologetic or even embarrassed. As noted earlier in this book, there are some myths and misperceptions that plague fundraisers—such as the dreadful "tin cup" image (i.e., fundraising is akin to begging). If the constituents we interact with don't understand that our phone calls are for the purpose of carrying out a mission and serving a defined group of people, or that the mail that clutters up their mailboxes really serves a significant purpose, then they may demean us who are seen as the guilty party for disrupting lives. This is why continual reference to the mission, purpose, and outcomes of our organization's activities is important. We are educators and relations managers for our organizations.

SIGNS OF BURNOUT

When problems pile up, we may experience burnout. The warning signs for such a condition are:

- Increased detachment as a means of emotional protection
- Impatience with others
- Assigning blame to others for your problems
- Mechanical performance of duties
- Poor judgment and therefore poor decisions
- Stereotyping of others
- Reducing the amount of time spent with others
- Venting at the expense of others
- Experiencing symptoms of illness
- Feeling no one appreciates you
- Depression[2]

Through all these possible challenges, we must remember that while the practice of fundraising may have any number of problems and difficulties, we are charged with making possible the operation of causes that benefit other humans and meet their needs, and therefore we are carrying out important work. Sometimes problems are solved by a change in our own attitudes; sometimes they can't be solved and we have to find a new position.

TOOLS FOR HANDLING STRESS

Some suggestions for how to handle the possible stresses and pressures of fundraising are quite concrete; others involve subjective matters such as changes in attitude. Here are some guidelines for how to navigate through both the positive times and the disturbing elements.

- Be a good planner, so that there is ample evidence of how you will meet goals, who will help you, who advises you, and how you will evaluate and prove results.
- Do not worry too much about the future. Live for the present where the action is, and handle those situations closest at hand. Mark Twain supposedly said, "I am an old man and have known a great many troubles, most of which have never happened."

- Analyze problem situations and define what can be solved and what you have to live with. Understanding the situation is the first step toward reaching a solution.

- Be realistic about what you can do and don't overpromise. Achieve the goals you set, then strive to raise them.

- Be a team player internally and seek collegiality and understanding of what you do. Develop an external network of trusted peers who can provide advice and, if necessary, sympathy!

- Accept the fact that you will not be 100 percent successful, nor are you perfect. You will get overworked, tired, discouraged. You will meet with failures—at times, colossal ones. You need to realize this is part of the road toward success—those dips along our career path help us appreciate the times when we are energized and everything is going our way.

- Keep yourself in good physical condition. Eat right, exercise, get enough sleep—those basic practices that maintain both physical and mental health.

- Perhaps get away from it all for a while. Provide a setting and time for relaxation. Sometimes this will give a new and different perspective on the problem.

- Strive to manage yourself better. Become better organized, track your tasks to see if there is a way to streamline your work, or increase your skills. Reprogram your thoughts and emotions, and build your confidence.

- Manage your fears. Understand what is causing your unease, worry, or even distress. Put a realistic perspective on those identifiable fears. As the saying goes, what happens to us matters less than how we react to what happens to us.

Of course, it would be arrogant to say that managing stress and dealing with pressures are up to us to handle and conquer. There are times when we must seek help, whether from friends or colleagues, or through professional counseling. There are also times when we should find another job. Perhaps the match was not right, or that situation was unworkable, or the organization was dysfunctional and on its way out of existence. Above all, therefore, it is necessary to analyze the situation as objectively as possible, and then determine the appropriate steps for managing the stress.

A bit of poetry by an unknown writer perhaps expressed our possible relationship to stress in the best way:

One can feel
at times like a
spinning leaf
blown along a
dirty street,
one can feel
like a grain of
sand stuck in
one place. But
nobody has
said that life
was a calm
and orderly
thing; it isn't.
One isn't a
tattered leaf
nor a grain of
sand: one can,
to a greater or
lesser degree
draw his road
map and
follow it.[3]

SIDEBAR   **TED R. GROSSNICKLE**

Successful people have the ability to focus their attention on achieving their goals. Unfortunately, this quality can sometimes turn counterproductive when warning signs of stress are ignored. Some degree of job-related stress is normal. Letting it throw your life off-balance is not. Watch for these three warning signs that may indicate that stress is gaining control of your life.

1. *Irritability.* Are people or things that you used to take in stride starting to annoy you? Do you find more and more aspects of your job unduly frustrating? Are you quick to anger?

2. *Loss of concentration.* Are even simple tasks difficult to complete? Are you increasingly forgetful? Has making a decision become agonizing work?

3. *Loss of perspective.* Are you losing sight of your goals and getting stuck on unimportant details? Are you forgetting how your work impacts others—and how theirs impacts yours?

If you notice—or if others notice—any of these warning signs, take these four basic steps to control your stress and regain balance:

1. *Prioritize.* You're not going to be able to meet all the demands placed on you, so don't try. Instead, determine and complete the key tasks for achieving your goals. Let other things fall by the wayside, if need be.

2. *Get enough sleep.* In the long run, skimping on rest in order to "get more done" will only lessen your productivity.

3. *Exercise.* If you do not have time to exercise, find time. A brisk 15-minute walk at lunch will give you enormous benefits in terms of stress relief and mental clarity.

4. *Take time for yourself.* This is not "wasted time." This is self-renewal. Make a commitment to yourself to pursue your favorite hobby, play sports, or read a good book—whatever you enjoy. You'll come back refreshed and ready for the challenges of work.

TED R. GROSSNICKLE, CFRE is president of Johnson, Grossnickle and Associates. Prior to co-founding JGA in 1994, Ted Grossnickle served for 10 years as vice president of development and public affairs at Franklin College. In 1993, he served as acting president. Before his work at Franklin College, he held positions at Northern Illinois University, Wabash College, and Procter & Gamble. He was named "Fundraising Executive of the Year" in 1994 by the Indiana Chapter of the National Society of Fund Raising Executives (NSFRE). Grossnickle serves as managing counsel to JGA's clients in the United States and Western Europe and also is a team leader for JGA's evaluation projects for private foundations.

PROFESSIONALS SAY . . .

Every fundraising professional whom I meet or work with complains about how busy they are with day-to-day activities. It seems that the "management" keeps them from doing the important stuff (i.e., meeting with major donors, strategic planning, etc.). This is what I usually suggest. For every new fundraising technique or trend you're going to try, choose something that you're not going to do. As professionals we can't keep adding to our workload if we don't simultaneously remove things. Set priorities and learn to let things at the bottom of this list go!

Clay Myers-Bowman, Executive Director, American Red Cross, Riley County Chapter, Manhattan, Kansas

The stresses of fundraising are both external and internal. Within the organization, it is the lack of comprehension about how fundraising actually occurs. You may have to deal with a board and a boss who "needs it now," irrespective of the lack of donor relationships. Outside the organization, you may have to represent a cause which is not understood, which duplicates service, which has outlived its usefulness or has bad PR. In short, it may have a weak case for support.

C. Edward Wardle, CFRE, Executive Director, The Foundation For Health, Owensboro Mercy Health System, Owensboro, Kentucky

PART FIVE

Conducting the Job Search

V oltaire wrote in *Candide,* "Work keeps us from the three great evils, boredom, vice, and poverty."[1] This may be true, but perhaps more important is to focus on what work helps us experience, not what work keeps us from experiencing. Perhaps Thomas Carlyle said it better. "All work is as seed sown; it grows and spreads, and sows itself anew."[2]

Because fundraising is like a seed sown, and its effects grow and spread, finding the right job to match a professional's qualifications, whether entry-level, mid-career, or seasoned pro, is important. This section deals with the realities of a job search—where to look, how to interview, and how to not be a loser at a no-win job. It also includes a chapter that will be useful to persons doing the hiring.

Chapter 19 discusses where the jobs are and how to find the right one. A listing of information sources regarding fundraising positions is provided, as well as suggestions on how to seek out a position that is an appropriate match between the organization's needs and the qualifications and characteristics of the applicant.

Interviewing is a critical professional activity. It is an important skill to acquire, and Chapter 20 offers suggestions for a successful interview, focusing in particular on preparation for questions regarding the desirable qualifications for a fundraising professional. This chapter can serve as a "coach" for interview preparation.

Even the best professionals at times forget to ask relevant questions and ignore or do not notice warning signs of a problematic job situation. Listed in Chapter 21 are the major warning signals that there may be a problem with the position or the organization. The optimists can sometimes overlook danger signs, while the pessimists may see negative aspects in everything and therefore assure themselves that perhaps it is their pessimism that caused those danger signs to surface. Achieving the right balance between seeing possibilities and understanding realities is important.

When it is time to move on and seek or accept a new job, the professional carefully considers how to do so in a way that maintains good relationships with the current organization and its personnel. Knowing when it is time to find a new position, challenge, or opportunity is part of professional development and taps into a different set of professional skills. There are many reasons for leaving a job. Sometimes the fundraiser may have accomplished all that is possible within a current setting. At other times, advancement opportunities are only available elsewhere. And there are occasions when the professional is asked to leave. Chapter 22 discusses the issues, behaviors, and attitudes that are vital in maintaining good relationships with employing organizations. Additional professional issues such as donor relations and communications need to be considered when making a transition, and to what extent ties with the previous organization can or should be maintained.

The final chapter in Part Five will be useful for readers who wish to hire the right professional for their organization. It includes a summary of expertise, training, and personal qualifications important for a successful fundraising professional to possess, and how to look for the right match between the organization and the professional.

Joseph Conrad wrote, "I don't like work—no man does—but I like what is in work—the chance to find yourself."[3] The fortunate thing about fundraising is that as a person finds himself or herself, the outcome is also finding ways to help others. Therefore the just-right job is a goal worthy of all fundraising professionals.

Where the Jobs Are, and Finding the Right One

SIDEBAR BY DAVID STERNBERG

"**M**any more development positions are open than there are qualified fundraisers to fill them. And the ability for fundraising executives to pick and choose jobs is greater than we've ever seen," said Rick King, a leading executive search consultant, in an article published by *Advancing Philanthropy,* the journal of the Association of Fundraising Professionals (AFP).[1]

A special publication produced by *The Chronicle of Philanthropy* in early 2001 states, "Times have changed. It used to be, you could run an ad and get a stack of qualified resumes in just a few days. No more."[2] The job market has changed for several reasons: unemployment is at record lows, corporations are offering larger salaries and benefit packages, and more nonprofit organizations are competing for funds.

It is true that some in the fundraising profession are fortunate in being at the right place at the right time, and in knowing the right people. This, in particular, is the case for seasoned professionals. They don't go searching for the job; the right job finds them. For many others, switching jobs, finding the right one in the first place, or even entering the fundraising job market may be a bit more difficult.

For example, many job ads, including those found in *The Chronicle of Philanthropy* and *The NonProfit Times,* indicate that at least three years of fundraising experience is the minimum requirement. Because many organizations have limited resources (e.g., time, money, and opportunities) to foster the growth of entry-level candidates, the entry-level fundraiser may have to take extra measures to acquire the first-time position. A 1997 survey conducted by The Development Resource Group in New York stated that while numbers of nonprofits are increasing, and there is a smaller pool of qualified and experienced candidates for fundraising positions, most organizations preferred to hire experienced professionals.[3]

Therefore, while it is true that "development jobs are available in great profusion," as stated in an article in *NSFRE News* in January 2000, the job search for the novice will be somewhat different than for the experienced professional. This chapter covers the following points and suggestions. For the most part, these are worthwhile suggestions for professionals at all levels who are seeking fundraising positions.

- Developing a plan and setting goals for a job search
- Identifying resources and gaining an understanding of the possibilities; building a network of people and organizations
- Preparing a résumé
- Preparing for an interview and developing questions to ask (the following chapter covers the topic of interviewing in detail)
- Developing a strategy that builds on your preparation, as described previously

At the close of the chapter there is a listing of printed materials and Internet resources to aid the job seeker.

DEVELOPING A PLAN AND SETTING GOALS FOR A JOB SEARCH

As Alexander Pope said, "Know then thyself."[4] Make a case for yourself. That should sound familiar to even a novice in the fundraising profession. Assess your experience, and while doing so, determine the aspects you liked best about the jobs you have held or the job you would like.

Then write your own case, concentrating on how you qualify for what you consider an ideal position. In other words, write your preferred job description; it is the best way to determine what you know and what you want.

While preparing your personal case statement, you might ask yourself the following questions:

- How do I describe success? How can I or others measure it?
- What makes me good at what I do? What skills, knowledge, and talents do I have?
- What do I most enjoy doing? Least enjoy?
- Can I describe the perfect role for myself?
- What have I enjoyed in previous work experience?
- What are my weaknesses?
- What goals do I have, short-term and long-term, for my career?
- What praise have I received? Why was it meaningful?

After you've written your personal case statement, test it against reality. Be specific about what you are looking for, or you won't be memorable—you will become one more talented but vague figure in the prospective employer's mind. In short, you need to make a case for yourself so that you can market yourself! While taking a good look at yourself—and accepting yourself—you will assess the areas in which you excel as well as your weaknesses. In the right job setting, you might even turn these weaknesses into strengths.

At this stage of your job search you should try to define what kind of job opportunity you are looking for, the type of organization and cause, geographic area, salary that you need, and a timetable for your search.

IDENTIFYING RESOURCES AND GAINING AN UNDERSTANDING OF THE POSSIBILITIES

A most important technique to use in developing job leads is using your personal contacts. It has been said that you are never more than six people (some optimists reduce that number to four) away from the individual you want to reach. You want to build a network of people and organizations.

Some job-search specialists state that as many as 40 percent of all jobs are obtained through personal contacts. There is general agreement that networking—the word-of-mouth approach—is more effective than seeking a position through newspaper ads or by making "cold calls" yourself.

Tap your circle of friends and acquaintances. Contacts may include former teachers, colleagues, people in your clubs, church, or social group, and friends of friends. Although these might not be people who are connected with organizations for which you'd like to work, each one may know someone else who can help you get the job you want. Seek advice. Follow up every lead, because leads can proliferate.

Keep these points in mind as you develop your network of significant people.

- *Join professional groups.* Increase your contacts. Be genuinely friendly and interested in wanting to get acquainted with peers and colleagues in your field.

- *Find a mentor.* Mentors may be senior professionals and often can be found through professional associations. AFP chapters frequently have formal mentoring programs. An inexperienced fundraiser can also seek out a mentor by making personal contacts. Most people are willing to assist colleagues, whether inexperienced or established professionals. Be sure you are specific about what you desire from the mentoring relationship, and don't wear out your welcome!

- *Maintain contacts.* Keep in touch with people who have been significant in your career in the past. Take the initiative in writing or calling.

- *Attend workshops, seminars, conventions, and conferences.* Determine to become acquainted with at least one person during the conference, and select this person carefully. College or university courses related to nonprofit management (which usually includes fundraising) will also bring a person in touch with established professionals. In addition, more university placement centers are providing information about nonprofit employment. Students seeking information and contacts are often allowed access to organization and professionals to a greater degree than established professionals. Therefore, students should be encouraged to do academic work in such a way that they draw on the community and professional resources.

- *Volunteer.* Volunteering may provide valuable training for a new fundraising professional, although sometimes the experience does not reflect reality as much as it should; however, volunteering does provide visibility and contacts, and an overall view of at least some portion of the nonprofit sector. It can be included on a résumé as credible experience. Sometimes organizations are highly dependent on volunteers, and these individuals can gain actual job experience that serves as a basis for their résumé.

- *Become an intern.* Internships may be the best solution for acquiring on-the-job experience. Internships are available at many nonprofit organizations, some foundations, and some corporations. I have personally known a number of students whose internships landed them jobs at the same organizations, such as foundations, or who were more marketable as a result of this experience.

PREPARING A RÉSUMÉ

When making a case for yourself, concentrate on *achievements,* not responsibilities or duties. Write down or talk about measurable accomplishments, not vague feelings. State in concrete terms the results of your work.

Your personal case statement should then be translated into your résumé. While a great deal of advice is available on this subject, a few points are worth remembering. Make your résumé pass the "So what?" test. This doesn't mean ignoring good, basic standards of résumé writing. It does mean that you will specify what actions or activities you undertook in previous work, and the results you achieved. Your prospective employer doesn't really care about your responsibilities or tasks in your previous position. The employer *does* care about the outcomes.

Make your résumé brief, uncluttered, and to the point. Avoid the "ho-hum" syndrome. Also, tailor your résumé to be job specific. Giving all prospective employers the same résumé is equal to crossing your name off their list of candidates; in most cases, the prospective employer can spot signals that you cranked out your résumé from your computer without giving it a second thought.

If there are gaps in your job history, or if you need to give evidence of short-term employment, place these in a positive light. Maybe you were volunteering, or going to school, or were hired for a short-term assignment. Be prepared to explain these, as well as any incongruous changes in career. You might be able to explain any irregularities in your career in your cover letter; if so, do it succinctly.

Above all, remember that the average time a prospective employer takes to scan a résumé and determine if the prospect should be interviewed is just

20 seconds. Your résumé should therefore project a professional image, present your abilities and accomplishments, and make the reader want to meet you.

Make sure your résumé is easy to read. Keep the length short. Begin accomplishment statements with action words. Be factual, and do not stretch the truth. Avoid irrelevant references, such as hobbies. Know your audience, and use the vocabulary and language that is appropriate for the organization and job. Let your personality shine through. Remember that employers do not hire résumés, they hire people. Rick King lists his ideas about what qualities the best fundraisers possess: "Exceptional people skills, a fearless attitude about approaching people for gifts, an ability to write well, and terrific organizational management skills."[5] These become the essence of your résumé—the verbal picture of yourself and what you can do.

PREPARING FOR AN INTERVIEW AND DEVELOPING QUESTIONS TO ASK

Conduct research about each organization before an interview. Find out about the organization, how it is doing, and who is in charge. You need to take time for detailed research if your job search is serious, and this is time-consuming.

Some questions you might ask about the organization and its fundraising program are:

- What cause does it represent?
- Who are the population groups it serves?
- Does it have a good image and track record of achievement?
- How many are on staff?
- Are there any campaigns in progress?
- What about the board? Who is on it, and are they involved?

Queries related to the vision, volunteers, collegial relationships, community image, and above all, the organization's mission will be helpful as you plan for the interview.

At the interview itself you will, of course, want to ask more specific questions concerning such things as working conditions, reporting and supervision, technological and secretarial support, salary and benefits, and other details of the job.

DEVELOPING A STRATEGY THAT BUILDS ON YOUR PREPARATION

In summary, prepare your plan. It must be flexible and open ended, because as you proceed with your job search, opportunities will present themselves. You will reassess your plan regularly as you meet people and explore possibilities. These steps may be helpful as you plan.

- *Build your morale.* Assess yourself and your goals. Write your personal case statement. Some organization is going to need you. Remain optimistic!

- *Evaluate how you want to be perceived, both on paper and in person.* Maintain a presence and become known by increasing your visibility and doing work that can bring recognition.

- *Determine your targets and assess your approach intelligently.* Aim to win!

- *Be enthusiastic.* Above all, be positive about yourself as well as the prospective employing organization. Make yourself memorable and someone who's good to have around.

An additional word about using consultants or recruitment firms: Frequently they are hired to seek out the right professional for a specific job. Consequently, consultants attend many conferences and professional meetings, looking for leads. They make it possible for the hiring organization to increase its pool of fine prospects, allowing administrators to concentrate on their own work rather than take charge of a time-consuming search to fill a position.

A person seeking a job needs to remember a few guidelines about consultants. Be wary about sending your résumé to a recruitment consultant. Above all, don't try to elicit information about a specific position opening from a firm. Consultants prefer to contact you. Most maintain a database on professionals in fundraising, identify candidates on behalf of clients, and approach these clients directly.

What's the best way to get noticed by a consultant? Most consultants would agree that you must be doing good work already. Give presentations, and increase your network. The consensus is that you should build your reputation by achieving results; strive for a verifiable track record that serves as proof of your competence and expertise.

Word of mouth is the most common means of becoming known. Here networking may once again be valuable. Although you may not be acquainted with any consultants, someone you know just might put in your name. If a consultant calls you, be helpful even if you are not asked to be a candidate. Positive contact may pay off when a different job search is being conducted. While you are helpful to someone you respect and like, you just might be helping yourself. Consultants do their best to make the right match between the organization and the professional. Your turn may come.

Most consultants are requested to seek personnel at the upper levels, such as vice presidential positions. In general, recruiters rarely see entry-level candidates, although some become involved in seeking personnel for mid-level openings, such as directors for corporate and foundation giving.

Finally, a job search can be either a painful struggle or an exciting adventure. Remember that it will take time, assertiveness, initiative, enthusiasm, and knowledge. Many people look back on their job search not as an excruciating experience, but as a rewarding time in establishing or continuing their careers.

FURTHER INFORMATION

Recommended Printed Materials

Bolles, Richard Nelson. *Job-Hunting on the Internet.* Berkeley, CA: Ten Speed Press, 1999.

Bolles, Richard Nelson. *What Color Is Your Parachute?* Berkeley, CA: Ten Speed Press, updated yearly.

The Chronicle of Philanthropy. Washington, DC (published biweekly).

Judy, Richard W., and Carol D'Amico. *Workforce 2020: Work and Workers in the 21st Century.* Indianapolis, IN: Hudson Institute, 1997.

King, Richard M. *From Making a Profit to Making a Difference: How to Launch Your New Career in Nonprofits.* Publisher: Planning/Communications, 2000.

Krannich, Ron, and Caryl Krannich. *Jobs and Careers with Nonprofit Organizations.* Manassas Park, VA: IMPACT Publications, 1994.

Lauber, Daniel. *Non-Profits' Job Finder: America's Job Finders for the 1990s.* Published by Daniel Lauber, 1992.

The NonProfit Times. Skillman, NJ (published monthly).

Wendleton, Kate. *Through the Brick Wall: How to Job-Hunt in a Tight Market.* New York: Villard Books, 1992.

Ten Speed Press also has other valuable resources on job hunting, ranging from creating your own mission in life to writing effective resumes and interviewing. Contact info: Ten Speed Press, P. O. Box 7123, Berkeley, CA 94707. For orders and customer service, 800-841-book.

Selected Internet Resources

ACCESS: Networking in the Public Interest
    www.accessjobs.org
Alliance for Nonprofit Management
    www.allianceonline.org Click on CareerBank.
Careerbuilder
    www.careerbuilder.com
Charity Channel, Career Search Online
    charitychannel.com/careersearch
The Chronicle of Philanthropy
    www.philanthropy.com
Council on Foundations
    www.cof.org/jobbank
The Foundation Center
    http://fdncenter.org
Job-Hunting on the Internet
    www.tenspeed.com/parachute
Job Safari
    www.jobsafari.com
Nonprofit Charitable Orgs
    http://nonprofit.about.com/careers/nonprofit

DAVID STERNBERG

Fundraising is a people business. Unlike many aspects of our high-tech world, fundraising remains largely a person-to-person venture. Large donations and thoughtful planned gifts are not likely to be acquired by letter or the Internet. Likewise, you're not likely to be offered that perfect position via e-mail.

The often overused and stereotyped word *networking* will be important to you as you build your career as a fundraising professional. Although you could very well spend countless hours at luncheons and educational seminars shaking hands, distributing business cards, and meeting fellow professionals, there is often an easier and more enjoyable way to learn about the fundraising job market in your area.

Get involved! Don't wait to be asked. Determine how much time you have to spend, and volunteer for the professional fundraising society or group in your local area. Find out if there is a committee, a local conference, or even an open seat on the local fundraising association that you can fill.

Your involvement will give you the inside track on current and potential job openings, provide insight about the health of local nonprofits, and even create personal contacts that may be helpful in future job searches.

Volunteering has a funny way of giving back . . . don't wait, start today!

DAVID STERNBERG a graduate of The Ohio State University, is a partner with Loring, Sternberg & Associates, an Indianapolis-based fundraising and nonprofit management consulting firm. Dave served as the chief development officer for the Phi Kappa Theta National Foundation and as assistant director of annual giving for Butler University. Dave has been a member of the Indiana Chapter of the Association of Fundraising Professionals since 1993 and has served as chair of Indiana Fundraising Day for two years. He is currently in his second term as vice president of programs for the chapter. Additionally, Dave serves on the Research Committee for the Center on Philanthropy. He is an alumnus of The Fund Raising School and has assisted with the instruction for The Fund Raising School's course on Annual Campaigns.

PROFESSIONALS SAY . . .

Different types of nonprofits offer widely varying environments for fundraisers. It may be true that the skills and techniques are the same. Nevertheless, how you apply them differs greatly depending on the type of organization. Even the organizational cultures are quite different, and you should be comfortable in your choice. For example, in a food bank operating on a shoestring, your office could be in a warehouse, there might be a great deal of camaraderie, and you might handle boxes with the rest of the staff. In a hospital environment, fundraising is a much smaller piece of the revenue pie, and you must fit into a large bureaucracy with lots of stress. In a large university, you will be one of many on a large staff, and your area of responsibility very narrow. Salary levels for these different jobs vary hugely, but going for the highest salary may put you in an environment you're not comfortable with.

C. Edward Wardle, CFRE, Executive Director, The Foundation For Health, Owensboro Mercy Health System, Owensboro, Kentucky

Keep yourself informed of what is happening in the field professionally, what are the current job opportunities, field-related publications, networking with colleagues and friends. Then make personal calls on anyone who could be influential in helping you secure a position regardless of whether or not they may have something in their own organization available. Being informed and networking are the two most important job search tools.

Linda Hardwick, Associate Director of Development, Purdue University

CHAPTER 20

Suggestions for a Successful Interview

SIDEBAR BY RICHARD M. KING

"You've got just seven seconds to make the right impression. As soon as you make your entrance, you broadcast verbal and nonverbal signals that determine how others see you. . . . You are the message, and that is never more true than in first impressions."[1]

Interviews are critical. All the hours that have been devoted to résumé preparation, making contacts, researching potential employers are just preparation for the most important step of the job search—the interview. Overall, the interview should follow this bit of advice: "Apply 'The Greatest Executive Job-Finding Secret' . . . find out what people want, then show them how to get it."[2]

The success or failure of an interview is often determined before the meeting actually takes place. As you read in the previous chapter, your performance will reflect the thoroughness of your research, as well as the thought and practice you have given to the process.

To prepare for an interview, first develop a statement that briefly describes who you are and your professional background. You will be asked to summarize your job interests and career path. Acquire information about the position for which you are being interviewed, such as job responsibilities, the role it plays in the organization, goals to be achieved. Evaluate your experience and abilities and be sure you know how they match the position. Be sure you can state achievements that support your experience. Learn as much as you can about the organization's interests and needs.

Some questions you might research beforehand are:

- What is the role of the president or executive director in fundraising? Does the board get involved?

- Is there a long-range plan? What would your place be in this plan?

- What are the fundraising goals, and how were they determined? How do they fit with the overall budget? Is an audited financial statement available for your perusal?

- Are there campaigns, events, or projects that are pending and that you will be expected to implement or complete?

- How large/small is the staff, and what responsibilities do they have?

- Is there a development committee, and if so, how will you be working with or relating to it?

- Can the organization share communications materials with you, particularly those used with donors?

- What about the person who previously held the job? What was his/her tenure? Why is he/she departing?

Although these questions are not exhaustive, they will help you determine as much as possible about the organization so that you can tailor your honest responses to interview questions.

Some general suggestions to consider when interviewing are:

- Rehearse your interview. Practice with someone you trust.

- Acclimate yourself. Determine the mood of your interviewer or interviewers. Are they excited, enthusiastic, distracted, skeptical?

- Listen carefully. Most of us talk more than we listen, and this is especially true in a stressful situation. Listen to each question or comment carefully to make sure you understand what is wanted. Do not interrupt. If you tend to talk too much, practice answering questions with a friend or mentor.

- Turn the focus off yourself and onto the interviewer. Talkative candidates give the impression that they are nervous or lack focus in their job search, or that they are self-centered and not team players.

- Dress carefully and appropriately for the situation. Understand the corporate climate as much as possible. Dress the part!

- Don't allow yourself to be rushed; arrive early. Give yourself every psychological edge. If your hands tend to become sweaty, get there early enough to wash them.

- Answer questions in job-specific ways. Try to reflect your interviewer's manner of speaking. If the questions are long and drawn-out, a clipped answer may not set well. Don't give too much information about yourself; remember that you're picking out your skills and traits to match the position.

- Remember that approximately 90 percent of all interviews include the phrase, "Tell me about yourself." This is not a time to indulge in sharing your life's history. The interviewer is really seeking out what skills you have that will meet the needs of the organization. How will you be an asset, and what problems can you solve? Again, tailor your answers to be job-specific. Facts are better than feelings.

- Be honest. Any misstatements or deliberate shading of the truth will catch up with you.

- Set the tone for the interview by appearing confident and friendly, but avoid too much familiarity, light-heartedness that may seem like you're not serious about the position, or irrelevant talk. Avoid being casual.

- Voice quality is important. Record yourself and learn to vary your pitch, tone, pace, and volume.

- Remember body language. Your body reflects your feelings. Although it may seem old-fashioned to consider gestures and other forms of bodily expression, take these seriously, since impressions are quickly made on the basis of eye contact, posture, and similar non-verbal displays.

- Demonstrate passion (see Chapter 24). Loving what you do is a quality that search committees and interviewers look for. Convey the enthusiasm you believe you will feel for the potential job.

- Indicate that you can be flexible and have the ability to change. Avoid the "we've always done it this way" syndrome by showing how you can be, or have been, innovative. You may be hired to help take the organization in new directions.

- No matter how many interviews you have, treat each one like it is the most important one you will have.

- Never be negative. Show loyalty to your former employers. Everyone knows that there is no such thing as a perfect job.

- Be prepared to ask questions yourself. Most interview sessions allow this privilege. You might wish to expand on the pre-interview information you acquired. Don't shrug and say, "None at this time." There may never be another opportunity. (See Chapter 21 for areas of potential questions.)

What questions do interviewers tend to ask? Many sources exist that give list after list. In general, questions by interviewers are geared toward finding out how different candidates might fit into the organization, the attitudes they will bring to the position, their career goals, their self-confidence, their abilities and skills, and their communication as well as people skills. Common interview questions may be:

- *What do you know about our organization?* Be sure you've done your homework!

- *Why do you want to work for us?* Tailor your answer so that you show you can contribute in positive ways, to provide a solution for what the organization needs.

- *Tell me about yourself.* Remember to point out those characteristics and qualities that suit the position. This isn't a time for a personal history.

- *What motivates you?* What are your personal goals? Indicate a desire to contribute to the organization in specific ways that you enjoy and do well, trying to make a match between the needs of the organization and your abilities.

- *Why are you leaving your job?* Be sure you have a level-headed answer for this one. Don't downgrade your previous position or boss. Indicate positive reasons for seeking advancement, a change, or a new challenge.

- *What qualities and experience do you have that are important for this fundraising position?* The interviewer has your résumé, but he or she wants to hear how you can express your success. This is also a time when the interviewer may test your communication skills.

- *What has been your greatest accomplishment in fundraising?* Remember to make your answer outcome oriented, focusing on the organization and its clients rather than your ego.

This is just a sample of the questions that might be asked, touching on the major points that normally are covered.

Salary and benefit information will generally be offered sometime during the interview. Be prepared to negotiate appropriately. That means you should know something about salary levels for positions such as the one for which you are being considered, and what is fair. Sometimes a contract is offered by the organization. Be careful to study any contract carefully. No legitimate organization will expect you to sign on the spot.

Keep in mind that when negotiating for compensation, the discussion should be a win–win for both sides. Be realistic and ready to make concessions, if necessary. Try to get the organization to at least give a hint about salary before you indicate what you'll work for (see Chapter 11 for salary and wage information).

What about job references? Opinion is divided as to when references ought to be offered to the potential hiring organization—when applying by mail, just prior to the interview, or during the interview. Normally, the organization requests references if it is serious about your candidacy. It is a good idea to have a list ready that you can tailor to the requirements of the job.

Be sure to request permission to use someone as a reference; no one likes to be caught off guard. You may be at a distinct disadvantage if your references have not had time to think about you positively. Your references are most likely to be contacted if the job is a high-ranking one, or requires excellent skills. And the contact will probably be in person or by phone; many people are reluctant to put anything in writing, even positive statements.

What should you do after an interview? Thank the interviewer for the meeting and emphasize your interest in the position (if, indeed, you are interested). Briefly review your qualifications, and indicate once again how they match the demands of the job.

Each interview is good preparation for the next one. Do a self-analysis:

- Do I feel good about how the interview went?
- What do I think I did or said well?
- What should I improve?
- Did I listen enough?
- Were my answers to the point?
- Did I create a positive image?

- What phase of the interview was the hardest for me? The easiest?
- What are my gut reactions?

This chapter is not an exhaustive overview of the interview process. It is intended to focus specifically on the interview for a fundraising job. Ample resources are available in print and on the Internet that address interviewing in general. Remember, once again, that "You can get anything you want in life if you first find out what people want, then show them how to get it."[3]

■ FURTHER READING

Cassiani, Robert. "Lead with Your Best—Tips for Successful Interviewing," *Association of Fundraising Professionals News* (February 2001).

> *This article, which is from the AFP newsletter that goes to all members, outlines suggestions for handling an interview. Questions and suggested answers are included.*

| SIDEBAR | RICHARD M. KING |

Regardless of the particular scope and duties of the fundraising position for which you are interviewing, there are several fundamental concerns the interviewer will most likely want to address with you. These concerns or questions will enable the interviewer to determine your readiness, relative ability, and even potential to succeed in the job. Be prepared to address these fundamental concerns in your interview.

- *Interpersonal skills.* Whether speaking to individuals, corporate executives, or foundation grant-makers, the ability to connect with people, to come across in a genuine and sincere manner, and to project appropriate enthusiasm are absolutely critical to fundraising success. The interviewer will want to assess how you communicate in the interview, how you speak, what body language you use, how well you listen, and how you engage the interviewer. These personal attributes will determine the nature of your interactions with donors and prospects, so the interviewer will try to gauge your fit with the constituency with whom you would be working.

- *Organizing abilities.* Fundraising is a highly multitask activity, particularly in a fundraising department with limited resources. But even in large development offices, your ability to organize your time and work is important for the interviewer to know. Talking about your prior job experience in high multitask accomplishments will satisfy the interviewer that you can fit into their culture.

- *Adaptability.* Successful fundraising professionals understand the importance of being flexible with constituencies and adapting to the circumstances. This is particularly true in developing and sustaining good volunteer relationships. If your job track record provides ample evidence of your ability to adapt to people and situations, the interviewer will not have a concern in this area.

- *Resourcefulness.* Because development offices will never have all the staff support and budget required, the ability of fundraising staff to be tactfully imaginative, to creatively solve problems, and to think independently yet support teamwork is important in reaching goals. An attitude of resourcefulness may also apply to certain donor interactions as well, so the interviewer will likely explore this area with you from that perspective.

RICHARD M. KING president of Kittleman & Associates, has more than 30 years of nonprofit management experience in association management, health care, and human services—as an executive staff member and an outside consultant. Mr. King joined Kittleman & Associates in 1984 with 15 years of nonprofit organizational experience in human services and health care association management. He has served as a volunteer and board member for several nonprofit organizations and is the author of *From Making a Profit to Making a Difference: How to Launch Your New Career in Nonprofits* (2000). As an adjunct faculty member of the Rosary College Graduate School of Business, he also teaches a course in organizational behavior.

PROFESSIONALS SAY . . .

The attraction of any new position will fade quickly if there is not a values-match. When considering a new position—especially if you have experience—the interview process works both ways; you should be evaluating the organization and the people within it with the same diligence they are evaluating you.

Bill Hallett, Ph.D., ACFRE, Vice President & Chief Development Officer, The Hospital for Sick Children, Toronto, Ontario, Canada

CHAPTER 21

How to Avoid the No-Win Job

SIDEBAR BY ROBERT L. THOMPSON

Many of us move from job to job for good reasons. Perhaps there isn't hope for advancement unless a move is made. Maybe compensation is better, or benefits are more attractive. Sometimes a new boss takes over and the chemistry just isn't right. There are even times when we feel that we have achieved our professional and personal goals and it is time to change the scenery.

A major reason for leaving a job, however, is because it is a no-win job. The position seems to be affected by the Murphy's Law syndrome— anything that can go wrong has! Despite glowing promises and statements, perceptions did not match. What the fundraising professional *thought* the hiring organization said turns out to be different or skewed. This chapter is designed to help you avoid getting involved in those no-win situations in the first place.

The symptoms and dilemmas of a no-win job can be the following. Fundraising may be a low priority. Support staff is nonexistent. The development officer is left out of the loop, and important information is hard to come by. The prospect base is weak or absent. There is an imbalance between cash donations and planned gifts; one is neglected at the expense of the other. Board members make promises but don't follow through. In fact, they *won't* raise funds. Records are in a mess. Marketing is not congruent with mission. The board is micro-managing and will not adopt a policy role. The fundraising professional is expected to perform miracles—and do it alone! When goals aren't reached, blame often falls on the unfortunate yet most obvious culprit, the development professional.

If we're going to maintain a steady and increasingly successful career path, promote professionalism in the field of fundraising, and maintain our sanity and self-concept, we need to be smart as well as wise in assessing a new job possibility.

What should a fundraising professional do to avoid a nonproductive, frustrating, futile experience—one that might even derail a career?

Here are ten points to ponder, keeping in mind that there are *no* perfect jobs. Some situations can be remedied, but we may just have to live with some dilemmas!

- *Visit the site, if possible.* What is the mood of the corporate culture? Are people busy yet seemingly content? Is there an indication of meaningful activity, or are people sitting around, staring out the window? It is usually apparent when employees are happy in their work. It does not take a psychologist to figure out mood. Place yourself in those surroundings and see if you "fit." Does the CEO introduce you to potential co-workers or ignore them? If employees interview you, how guarded are they? Are they asking you meaningful questions and sharing relevant information? What is their excitement level? There does not have to be a constant "high," but a prevalent enthusiasm should be present. Are you allowed to walk the halls without others hanging around? Are you allowed to talk with junior staff members without interference from senior staff members?

- *If you are more than entry-level, ask to meet with board members.* Find out as much as you can about each board member. Review the current and past board lists (former board members may be key volunteers or donors). What do they do? What are their connections? Are there any door-openers and check writers? What is their collective giving history? If there is reluctance in sharing this information, that may be indicative of a problem. If board members are overly enthusiastic about your coming, it may be they see you as the answer to their fundraising reluctance. If board members insist on your making a certain number of calls a week, they are engaged in micro-management. If they say too many nice things about you, watch out. Do they engage actively in fundraising, or just provide lip service? Board policies regarding giving and asking are of little use unless there is evidence they have been put into practice. If you are a senior development officer, meeting with the board's executive committee on a one-on-one basis is imperative. Also, as a senior member, determine whether you can attend board meetings and otherwise have access to the board.

- *Find out about the dynamics between the board and the chief executive.* If they get along well on a personal level, they may also work together on fundraising and therefore support you. If there is an acrimonious relationship, you may not get their cooperation. Try to have an opportunity to state that you will raise money *with* them, not *for* them. Some of this information may be acquired by observation and appropriate questions during the interview process; other sources may be your colleagues in the fundraising community.

- *Evaluate the potential relationship between you and your supervisor, particularly if your boss is the CEO.* Fundraisers need to support the chief executive, and they must be loyal to their immediate supervisors. If the CEO is a former fundraising professional, try to determine what his or her track record might have been. Will the expectation be that you will measure up to that record? Will the CEO or supervisor possibly be threatened by your potential success? Thorough preparation prior to the interview may provide you with indicators as to any personal issues that affect your eventual relationships, and guide you in the questions you will want to ask. Also, determine if the CEO is a gatekeeper and requires that all board and key volunteer contact be approved or managed through the CEO.

- *Ask to see an annual report that lists donors.* You won't be asking for sensitive information. Request this information in such a way that the CEO won't think you are a spy for the competition. What you want to know is: Are there prospects, are there donors, how much have they given, have feasibility studies been done, who's working with these prospects, and what are the fundraising goals versus the prospects? Have former and current donors been asked so often that they are exhausted, and yet the organization expects a significant boost in fundraising income overnight? Is there a program in place to cultivate new prospects?

- *Ask about expectations for your job, then ask again.* Be honest with yourself. Can you really, truly meet those expectations? Of course you want to stretch yourself. That's why you're looking at a different job. Of course you want a challenge. But are the expectations congruent with what the organization has done, both in fundraising and in general program delivery? Will you really have a chance to lead, or are there certain individuals controlling the process? Beware of being seen as the answer to all prayers just because you come with a good track record and stellar reputation; your reputation could be seriously damaged.

- *Check on the terms of your employment.* Are they contingent on certain goals being reached, on a grant running out, or are they (heaven forbid) commission-based? Is the job contract or letter clear on whether the position is temporary or term; are there any contingencies? What does it say about termination? How about job evaluation and review? How much, and when, can you expect increases in salary? Is there a bonus program, and how does fundraising fit into that? A senior professional should have a minimum of 24 months to make necessary changes. Find out if you have a contract that provides you with a reasonable window of opportunity to manage change.

- *Be wary of overly generous offers.* A very high salary, in comparison with others for your rank, may indicate excessive expectations, or that the leadership assumes that it will not have to assist you. In some cases, it may be a warning sign that something is wrong, and that you are expected to help the organization out of a crisis.

- *Ask to meet and talk with support staff and/or colleagues who have been assigned to work with you.* Do they seem interested in what you will do at the organization, or do they seem puzzled about your role? Or, do they talk about shopping and sports and ignore the workplace altogether? Will you possibly work with staff who wanted your position? If so, what have they been told about their future roles? Are staff being nurtured and mentored? If you are in charge, will you be allowed to terminate staff? What restrictions are there in creating your own team if the "chemistry" is not right or employees do not want to change with new leadership and new policies as well as practices? You need staff loyalty in order to succeed. If the support staff is inadequate, say so now. Later it might be difficult to get clerical or even collegial help. Competent as you are, you might inadvertently give the impression or hint that you can do it all.

- *Ask about office procedures.* How does the phone get answered, and by whom? Is there adequate computer, fax, voice mail, Internet, and other technical support? Remember, your success is highly dependent on how the organization represents itself to the rest of the world. If phone calls are treated haphazardly, then you'll have trouble communicating with the very people from whom you will seek donations. Are people willing to orient you, show you where relevant files and documents are, tell you about the quirks of the computer network, and point out the restrooms?

Most persons in a career and professional dilemma realize they should have taken more time to make the right inquiries. A good job might be passed up by such a logical and reasonable delay, but more likely, the *good* job will wait until the professional is in a position to ask the right questions, set up realistic expectations, determine the feasibility of teamwork, and find out just what is possible to accomplish.

It seems that organizations want more from us with each passing year. Job expectations seem to increase as the funding pool decreases. We are doing no one a favor, least of all ourselves and our profession, when we accept a no-win job. Of course we would not do so consciously, but sometimes we avoid the painful truth and find ourselves in a situation where no one wins. Use your head and choose what is realistic for your experience and talent.

▓ FURTHER READING

Watt, Charles V. "Ask the Right Questions Before You Accept the Job," *Fundraising Management* (June 1996), pp. 16–19.

   This article contains lengthy lists of questions that an interviewee might consider asking in order to acquire the necessary information on which to make a job decision. It is an excellent reminder of what a candidate should look for.

I am amazed at how often the "No-Win Job" pops up on the résumés of some very competent and qualified professionals in development. Of course it is always a red flag because the employment history shows a position that was held less than two years and a change of employers. This is often a one-time blip in an otherwise impressive employment history, and that may happen to anyone. On the other hand, if the "No-Win Job" shows up more than once on a résumé, a probable conclusion is that this applicant may have poor judgment.

There is usually a relatively simple explanation for a particular experience that has been a "No-Win Job," something quite specific that precluded the individual from performing up to his or her own expectations or the employer's expectations. And, more often than not, the problem "the fatal flaw," was self-evident before the position was taken, but was overlooked because so many factors or even all other factors were positive.

As just one example, we have all run into organizations that are dominated by a founder or by a large donor who has become quite used to micromanaging a development operation. Overcoming this situation obviously requires a total change in culture, which usually cannot be effected by development staff, and to believe otherwise is really wishful thinking.

In the application process, I would underline asking about and understanding expectations, and having contact and discussion with others who have held the position or who have supervised the position. If we are talking about a new position, it is critical to determine that you will have the authority and the latitude to be effective. If it is replacing someone in an existing position, the organization will likely be looking for a steady if not dramatic increase in the level of production and the assessment must be whether the objectives are realistic. Once you have established the parameters of expectations, you need to determine what is needed to achieve those objectives, whether there is something missing that might preclude achievement of those objectives and what has contributed or might contribute to preventing those objectives from being attained.

We who are part of this wonderful enterprise are extremely fortunate to have a very specific mandate—to help organizations raise money. And we are able to cut to the chase relatively quickly in evaluating the factors that affect that mandate. It is difficult to sort out all of the dynamics that will affect our ability to perform in a given situation, but recognizing "the fatal flaw" for what it is can often preclude getting stuck in the "No-Win Job."

ROBERT L. THOMPSON is the former Chairman of Ketchum, Inc. and has 38 years of experience in fundraising counseling, 32 of those with Ketchum. He retired from Ketchum in 1995 to focus on planned giving programs and personal counseling for clients in capital campaigns and strategic planning. Thompson has been a frequent speaker and trainer on fundraising and philanthropy at national, international, regional, and local conferences. He has served as counsel to more than 200 schools, colleges, universities, medical institutions, churches and church-related organizations, national and international groups, and other nonprofit organizations. He broad services includes the Association of Fundraising Professionals (formerly known as NSFRE), the Association for Healthcare Philanthropy, the Advisory Council of the Center on Philanthropy, and as Chairman of the American Association of Fund Raising Counsel. Thompson continues to serve as a fundraising consultant to a limited number of educational, healthcare, religious, and social service organizations.

PROFESSIONALS SAY . . .

While it's obvious that it's important to research the personnel related to the job, both your prospective colleagues as well as the organization's base of donors, the technical aspects are harder to determine . . . and can make your job much harder if proper systems aren't in place! Of course, donor records are confidential, so you truly cannot learn the full extent of the database's accuracy and accessibility until you're on the job. Try to gauge this beforehand, however, by asking some questions during the interview: Is the database regularly subjected to an electronic screening for updates? How are files updated? How many people have access to the database? What type of information is captured in a donor's record? Who runs queries of the database and what types of reports are readily available? While it's readily apparent this information is necessary to conduct a successful annual fund, a reliable, responsible database is critical for every aspect of fundraising.

Shelley Murphy Strickland, Director of Alumni & Foundation Relations, Kennesaw State University

Without question the single most important factor in taking a new job is in the person you'll work for. Your boss (hopefully the CEO) can make or break your efforts. You must try to get a feeling during the interview process about how your boss will view your access to the board and important donors; about the process of making a plan and following it, rather than jumping from need to need in midstream; about how much your boss actually knows about fundraising; about how committed he or she is to participating in the process. I once had a boss who said, "I'm offering you the job. I don't want to fool with it, so you do it."

C. Edward Wardle, CFRE, Executive Director, The Foundation For Health, Owensboro Mercy Health System, Owensboro, Kentucky

To avoid the no-win job, and a reputation as an opportunist, be thorough in your analysis of your prospective employer. A few of the questions that require your positive response are: Do the values of this charity align with mine? Does the mission of this nonprofit resonate with my philosophy? Is the vision of the charity achievable, while still offering considerable challenge? Is the leadership of the organization committed to philanthropy? Are they as energetic and passionate as I am? Will the culture of the organization allow me to have a significant impact? Will this position satisfy my career objectives now and for the long term? Does this position provide opportunities for professional development? Will I be able to experience joie de vivre *in this position and with this organization? If the answers to these questions are positive, then you're ready to consider remuneration.*

Bill Hallett, Ph.D., ACFRE, Vice President & Chief Development Officer, The Hospital for Sick Children, Toronto, Ontario, Canada

CHAPTER 22

How to Exit Gracefully

SIDEBAR BY ANGELA LANE

If you have a career, then you have a career clock. It is a sense within you that keeps time with your ambition versus your comfort level, your potential versus a plateau, progressive achievement versus status quo.

One day the clock says 4:00 P.M. Your heart and head pound, you remember too many challenges, frustrations, lapsed donors, lost records, and domineering board members. No matter how hard you try, your successes, ideals, and feel-good moments fade under the gloom. Your eyes glaze and wander toward the window. You untangle your phone cord, or worse yet, make a mental note to do it sometime. You finally wonder, "Have I stayed here too long?" Maybe you have. Maybe your career clock says that, for good reasons, it is time for a change.

Then again, someday it may be 4:00 P.M. and you have been told your services are no longer needed. You never thought you would hear your career clock ring quite so soon—and ring like a death knell. If you are like most people, you feel like a loser, no matter how logical the reasons for your dismissal, and you ask divorcelike questions: What about all the time I invested in this organization? Did anyone ever consider how many impossible tasks I accomplished? Is this really good-bye?

If you are experiencing a career crisis, you probably find other means of employment attractive. The job you turned down a year ago suddenly seems like a missed opportunity rather than a poor fit. Or you even flirt with the idea of leaving the profession entirely.

If you were asked to vacate your position, you might linger in despair, wondering where you went wrong and why no one likes you. You become despondent, and rational thinking isn't your strength at this moment.

Whatever the reason for your impending departure, and whether or not it's self-imposed, you are headed into a change mode.

Career-development experts generally concur that there are various steps or phases in any career. It begins with exploration, where you understand possibilities and how you fit them. Trial is the stage when you experiment with whether the match between the job and you is a good one. At this point career change may also take place, and you may step back into the exploration phase. The formation stage is a time when you establish your credibility, build a track record, and move toward the maintenance stage, which is the stable part of your career path. All goes according to plan, your achievements are notable, and you are content in your work. Then you might move toward disengagement, the letting go time. Perhaps this means retirement, but more often than not, people in the last 20 or so years have seen disengagement long before retirement. That's because, contrary to our parents' and grandparents' time, when one could expect to hold one job for a lifetime, now we might have several careers.

This chapter addresses three major questions. First, how can you determine that it is a logical time to move on? Second, what should you do if you are forced out? And third, regardless of your method and reasons for exiting, how should you leave a job and your current environment? A career management guide will be included at the close of the chapter.

DETERMINING WHEN IT IS TIME TO MOVE ON

Knowing when it is time to move on means coping with change. Although change is inevitable, many people would rather avoid it. They make safe choices, react rather than take risks, talk about change instead of taking action. Making a change means taking the initiative and overcoming fears. Making a change requires taking stock of what is and what can be. Asking questions such as these can be valuable in determining whether it's time to find a new job and take a different or new career path.

- What are my priorities now? What are my top values? Why do I do the things I do? Do I have a sense of purpose?

- Am I tied to a routine? Can I afford to be flexible or do I feel I am so valuable to my job that it consumes my time?

- Did I choose my career, or did it just happen? Does my current job match my needs and wants? Am I seeing continual growth, or have I become stagnant?

- On most days, do I look forward to going to work in the morning?

- Are my abilities used well in my work?

- Does my job give me the mental challenge I need? Does it have the excitement I want?

- Has my work become tedious?

- Am I proud of the work I do?

- Could the organization get along without me?

- Do I feel that my work contributes to the well-being of my community and society?

- Am I a workaholic or an underachiever?

- Have I done what I aimed to do when I took this job?

These questions can become a guide toward assessing why you might stay or move on to the next step in your career, and therefore the next job. You need to discover how content or discontent you really are with your current job before developing a strategy for change. There are some common symptoms for when it is time to heed the clock:

- The pile of phone messages increases daily, and by quitting time, you have barely made a dent because you just didn't have the energy or motivation.

- The trade publications and professional journals stack up, while you fight the urge to indulge in a good mystery.

- You eat lunch at your desk and avoid a friendly chat with colleagues.

- You are tired in the morning, and the caffeine needs become more serious.

- Your vision has faded. If someone were to ask you for your vision of your organization and your role in it, you mumble and speak in sentence fragments.

- You lose patience with all those people who "just don't get it," will not cooperate, and have their own agendas.
- You have trouble sleeping at night, and you snap at your friends.

A career is not just a job. It is a life. Any symptoms that indicate a need for change should be taken seriously, and a career management plan should either be revisited or revised—or even drafted. It is never too late. (See the suggestions on a career management plan at the end of this chapter.)

RESPONDING TO TERMINATION

When you are asked to interrupt your career, and therefore your life, it might take a while to gain perspective. It won't be easy, especially if you have been at your current job for a while.

Reasons for being terminated may stem from organizational dysfunction, financial difficulties, personality conflicts, or changes in organizational leadership. They may also be because you did not meet expectations or goals, or simply did not fit the environment. The first step when you are let go is to take stock.

First, of course, determine the severance implications. Will you continue to be paid for a certain amount of time? Will career search assistance be available? What goes on your personnel record?

Second, assess as objectively as possible the reasons you were terminated. What were you told, compared to what the office gossip indicates? Were your successes acknowledged? Were you counseled about your weaknesses? What responsibility for this divorce should you assume, and what are the circumstances for which you are not largely responsible? Answering these questions for yourself allows you to get a perspective and move on. Most importantly, do not assume blame, or put the entire blame on others. The reasons for your being discharged may be very logical, such as a downturn in the economy or a grant not coming through, or they may stem from human relations issues. Your reaction determines how well you can go on to finding your next career step.

Third, start a job search, following the steps outlined in Chapter 19. Determine what you want to do next, balance your desires against the job market, get advice, get counseling if the situation was traumatic, network with trusted colleagues, get in touch with people who can help you and seek their advice, do research—and above all, think big and think different! Do not expect a quick-fix; you may end up in a worse situation than unemployment.

Regardless of how and why you leave a job, whether it is your choice or someone else's, maintain your dignity and integrity. For the fundraising professional, there are some serious considerations, both practical and ethical:

- *Burn no bridges.* Even if your parting was less than cordial, avoid any negative talk. You may need to vent and air feelings, but do so privately. Maintain your professional demeanor. Remember, who wants to hire a complainer? You protect your own reputation by behaving in a respectable way.

- *Leave all records and materials well-organized and in good shape.* You want them to be understandable to your successor. Leave your work in such a state that a minimum of questions need to be asked of you after your departure. Do not feed your sense of importance by making it necessary for the organization to hunt you down and ask you questions you should have left answered.

- *Remember that donors belong to the organization and not you.* You have developed relationships on behalf of the cause. Although some friendships will be natural, in general donors should always understand that they have chosen to support the organization, and that future funding choices are also theirs.

- *Maintain good will.* Whether you are aiming for a job in the same community, or are heading out of state, your past will follow you. You may need to use former employers and colleagues as references. These individuals may be contacted whether or not you list them as references. Leave no enemies.

- *Leave appropriate evidence of your achievements.* Remember that what you accomplished was on behalf of the cause and the organization, while at the same time you built your career. Document goals reached, new donors acquired, volunteers recruited, projects accomplished. You can provide a solid base on which your successor will build, and you will both look better for that.

MOVING ON

Career management needs to be proactive. Assuming you have a plan, follow it—but also determine to be flexible. Be adaptable and make changes or adjustments as needed. Change is inevitable; include the possibility of change in your plan. In general, the best career plans include these components.

- State your career goals and objectives. Outline what you intend to achieve. Set a tentative long-range and short-term schedule for yourself. Do this even though you know the unexpected can always happen; it will provide you with a focus that others will notice.

- Inventory your skills and experience, and keep this list up to date. Also keep a record of your achievements.

- Research the job market, set your goals to fit the right job, and be knowledgeable of changes in career opportunities.

- Determine what training, education, and experience you need in order to reach both short-term and long-term goals. Then take action to build your knowledge and skills.

- Become active in professional organizations. This allows you to be more knowledgeable than average, to network, to learn of job opportunities, and to acquire new ideas. What you get from others, be willing to share as well. Be generous with your advice and ideas.

- Learn how to market yourself. Know how to be self-confident and assertive without being seen as egotistical and self-centered.

- Build your reputation. Write, speak, serve on committees, provide leadership in your profession. Document your credibility as a fundraising professional. Report your achievements appropriately, giving recognition and credit as deserved.

- Provide checkpoints for yourself. Assess as objectively as possible whether your career path is moving according to plan, whether you should detour or even step out of it for a while, and what changes you should make. This means, of course, that you will be ready to address a job change, whether or not you are required to do so.

- Share your plan with a trusted colleague, friend, or mentor. You will not only gain confidence in your plan, you will also glean excellent insights and suggestions.

Few careers proceed smoothly. Fewer still are planned, and the plans followed. Change may be difficult, but risks make the career path worthwhile. A lesson may be learned from one of America's poets, Edgar Lee Masters, who wrote the *Spoon River Anthology*. The Spoon River runs through central Illinois and was immortalized by the poet because he made it the setting for his perceptive writings. The *Spoon River Anthology* is a series of epitaphs that the dead of a small Illinois community speak from their graves. Their subject matter is interesting and simple, yet it speaks of the frailties, eccentricities, and failures of people. One poem in particular, "George Gray," focuses on the need to risk in order to live life with meaning.

I have studied many times
The marble which was chiseled for me—
A boat with a furled sail at rest in a harbor.
In truth it pictures not my destination
But my life.
For love was offered me, and I shrank from its disillusionment;
Sorrow knocked at my door, but I was afraid;
Ambition called to me, but I dreaded the chances.
Yet all the while I hungered for meaning in my life
And now I know that we must lift the sail
And catch the winds of destiny
Wherever they drive the boat.
To put meaning in one's life may end in madness,
But life without meaning is the torture
Of restlessness and vague desire—
It is a boat longing for the sea and yet afraid.

SIDEBAR   ANGELA LANE

So you've done your homework, the job looks perfect, and you're ready to take the plunge. Six months later, while popping Advil behind an avalanche of paper, you ask, "What did I do wrong?" Perhaps nothing. A new job is a new relationship, and slowly comes into focus over time. Sometimes uncontrollable factors can make a good fit a disaster, no matter how much you try. It is important to recognize the warning signs and know when to start crafting your exit strategy.

(continued)

For example, a new boss takes over and the chemistry between you stinks. As the subordinate, you are patient, explore various means of communicating, and try your best to make it work. After sufficient time banging your head against a wall, however, you may start feeling hopeless, trapped, or exhausted all the time, with a sense that no matter how hard you try you will never succeed.

When you start to feel this way, take a deep breath and reassess the relationship. *Don't wait!* Your internal alarm system is going off. Look objectively for some fundamental and immutable attributes of your job to confirm that it's time to go, or to provide a reality check on your expectations and goals. You . . .

- don't fit in with your coworkers or team,
- find yourself continually left out-of-the loop,
- repeatedly take the blame for others,
- are given unrealistic and ever changing performance expectations,
- realize that the organization has financial problems or an uncertain future,
- discover that the organization's plans, mission, or goals don't match yours,
- receive much more negative than positive feedback.

If you truly have tried to make it work with no hope of the relationship improving, you may be better off leaving. As rewarding as a new job can be, recognizing a bad situation and escaping can be just as empowering and fulfilling.

ANGELA LANE works in international fundraising for the American Red Cross, serving as liaison between the development department and international services, and coordinating fundraising activities for international disasters and programs. Previous to joining the Red Cross, she acquired several years' experience working in communications and fundraising at nonprofit organizations such as Girls Incorporated, CIVICUS: World Alliance for Citizen Participation, and the Multi-State Filer Project. She holds a master's degree in public communication from American University and will complete a master's in philanthropy from Indiana University in Spring 2001.

PROFESSIONALS SAY . . .

It is said that any fundraiser worth his salt will be fired from at least one job. Apparently I'm worth my salt—in the course of my 20-year career and seven different jobs, I was fired once. It really hurt, especially because I didn't see it coming. I cleaned out my desk the same day, but left all donor records intact—even the Rolodex. After all, as a development professional, I knew it was the ethical thing to do. A colleague, however, noted this and praised me for my professionalism in the face of losing a job under extremely stressful conditions. She remarked on my integrity for leaving my part of the development department with records, files, and upcoming deadlines that needed to be addressed. No matter what the circumstances, it has always been my custom to leave my job in that way. I just never thought anyone would notice! My colleague helped me to realize that others do notice my personal ethics. I do it for the organization and the mission for which I worked. I do it for the donors with whom I developed relationships. I do it for my peace of mind, which speaks volumes about the values I hold dear.

Roberta L. Donahue, CFRE, Director of Development, Lutheran Child and Family Services of IN/KY, Indianapolis, Indiana

CHAPTER 23

What to Look for When You Are the Employer

SIDEBAR BY ROBERT J. SIMONDS

A major university on the West Coast hired an executive search firm to find a vice president for advancement. After conducting a national search, several candidates were suggested, who were then interviewed by a university committee that included board members. The winner was announced with much excitement and great hopes. Six months later, he was gone. He had come with great fanfare and left under a cloud.

A fundraising professional left a children's home to accept an offer by a large Midwest health care institution. He had just won the Fundraiser of the Year award, and everyone felt optimistic about what he could do for the organization. On the heels of National Philanthropy Day, he was fired for not reaching goals and meeting expectations. This was just three months after being recruited, interviewed, and hired.

More than 100 people answered an ad for a fundraising professional placed by a nonprofit human services agency. More than half had no fundraising experience. The person who was hired lasted only two months. In this case, the organization probably wasn't prepared to employ a fundraiser. Also, the ad was confusing and poorly written, thereby drawing people who truly didn't know what it was all about but thought they were qualified.

A large international relief organization based on the East Coast called a fundraising consultant with this question: "Is it better to hire a young person fresh out of the university who has learned about fundraising and train that person, or to hire a seasoned professional who knows the ropes but may have his or her own way of doing things?" The answer, of course, is, "It depends."

There is a lot riding on the hiring process. The success of an organization ultimately hinges on who becomes the person in charge of fundraising, or who joins a fundraising team. This chapter contains suggestions for those who are doing the hiring, or those who someday plan to be in a position to do so. Of course, this perspective may also be helpful for those being hired.

According to a special publication issued by *The Chronicle on Philanthropy* in 2001,[1] the first step in hiring is to understand the market. Many nonprofit organizations have been slow to understand that currently fundraisers, even recent graduates, have more options than ever before. Often boards and search committees as well as nonprofit CEOs think candidates should be lining up for the chance to work for their organizations. But the job market is in constant flux, and change is inevitable. Suggestions for this step are to educate those doing the hiring about job-market realities, plan for a long search but move quickly if the right candidate surfaces, and be aware of appropriate salary levels.

The second step, according to *The Chronicle on Philanthropy,* is to consider what you need and what you can offer. Define exactly what your needs are—a top fundraiser with proven experience? Someone with technological expertise? A researcher? A generalist? A major gifts officer? Once there is a clear picture of the position requirements, salary and benefits should be considered and be competitive. Then, promote your organization; show candidates that you have something special to offer. Ask yourself, "Why should anyone work for us?" Action to take at this step is to develop a job description, evaluate what you can offer in terms of compensation, and promote your organization and location, not just the job itself.

Step three is to launch your search. Run classified ads, do networking, attend job fairs, conferences and other meetings, and be listed online. Accept that the competition is stiff, that many other jobs are available, and that you will need to promote your strengths.

The most important thing that a nonprofit can do when conducting a search is to ask tough questions, states an article on "Finding the Right Fundraiser."[2] Gary Kaplan, from a recruiting company in California, is quoted as saying,

"When I interview a development professional, I often feel like I'm cast in a pen with a greased pig . . . I can't get my arms around what they've done. They have the ability to talk about gifts using the collective 'we,' but when you ask them what their significant accomplishments are, it's hard to pin them down."

Kelly Beamon writes that "selection committees are looking for experience in fundraising, advocacy or policy programs, evidence of broad, strategic thinking and an ability to negotiate with nonprofit board members."[3] Executive search consultants often say that the ability to manage people is highly significant, with financial management coming as a close second. Energized and motivated individuals are usually in demand, and boards look for those who can get the job done.

CHOOSING A SEARCH METHOD

There are several ways that nonprofit organizations can recruit, select, and hire fundraising professionals. Some work through the human resources department. In other organizations the search is managed by the CEO, with some input from other professionals, particularly if a fundraiser or department is already in place. Other organizations work with search committees, on which representatives from board, leadership, and staff are included. Larger organizations searching for senior staff often utilize recruiters or search firms.

In most cases the job is advertised; just how widely depends on the level of the position, requirements of the job, and perceived pool of applicants. Networking or word-of-mouth is also a way to bolster the applicant pool; usually, this is done in addition to advertising. If recruiters are used, they search for specific applicants and screen résumés already on hand, or contact candidates who have already come to their attention. The advantage of using search firms is that they look for specific candidates and can approach the process objectively. In addition, their expertise in filling positions may make a good match likely. More recently, search firms are identifying promising professionals coming up through the ranks instead of relying on experienced professionals with whom they have maintained contact. Search consultants are also expert in weeding out those who aren't well qualified or who don't match the requirements of the position.

When engaging a search firm, it is important to select carefully, the same as when choosing a fundraising consultant or fundraiser. References should also be checked prior to hiring a firm, and the expectations clearly laid out, such as frequency of reports. A written contract protects both the firm and the nonprofit doing the hiring of the firm.

Even though interviews are important, some doing the hiring depend too heavily on them when they should be checking out references.[4] The savvy employer will check not just the references provided by the candidate but will also ask each reference for additional ones. Getting references from a variety of persons, not just those in fundraising, can be helpful.

Search committees may provide good perspectives that reflect the needs of the organization, but they can also slow down the process due to personal preferences, politics, or simply the slowness that is a characteristic of committees. The best use of search committees is for screening applicants, then leaving the ultimate choice up to the senior professionals doing the hiring.

INTERVIEWING JOB CANDIDATES

When the search method has been identified, needs specified, compensation determined, then conversation with the candidates takes place. The key to making the right selection is to ask the right questions and to secure important information prior to the hiring. The categories of questions might be the following:

- Personal traits and ambition
- Fundraising knowledge
- Credibility and track record
- Interpersonal relations
- Communication skills
- Planning ability
- Financial expertise

From these broad categories, some more specific questions will help reveal important qualities of the candidate.

- *What is your greatest weakness?* Strong candidates will generally identify something they're good at but could still improve. Weak ones might respond "None," or try to change the subject.
- *What are your greatest strengths?* The best candidates highlight strengths as they relate to the requirements of the job. Those who give an un-

focused answer, or claim a multitude of strengths, are probably not well prepared.

- *What has been your greatest failure?* A candidate may claim that he or she has none, which is probably false. Best prospects usually give details on something specific but go on to explain how they rescued the situation.

- *What achievement makes you most proud?* Candidates who show results, explain how they did it, and back up their claims with evidence are the most likely to succeed. These achievements should always be a good match for the job requirements that the applicant claims to meet. Those who express achievements of a personal nature or who are hesitant may not be prepared or actually may not have noteworthy achievements.

- *What motivates you?* If the answer is money, which is a legitimate but generally unspoken motivator, there should be concern. Most candidates would not be this crass, however. They may hide behind saying that they need a challenge. That is too simple. Devotion to a cause, the satisfaction of making a difference because fundraising goals are reached, the chance to improve society, may be a combination of answers that indicate appropriate motivation for a fundraising job.

- *What frustrated you in your last job?* The ideal candidate will relate an incident or describe a situation, then explain how he or she handled it effectively.

- *If I called your boss, what would he or she say about you?* Strong candidates give answers that indicate a good relationship. Hesitation may be a warning signal; the person may be more interested in leaving a previous job and not have a burning desire to do the job for which he or she is being interviewed; however, it should be noted that some people who turn out to be excellent employees are shy about touting their achievements; body language is often a strong indicator in this case.

- *What can you tell me in five minutes that would persuade me that you should have the job?* This question may catch applicants by surprise, and they may ramble or be unfocused. As indicated in Chapter 19, a strong candidate will have prepared for this, and part of that preparation should include the ability to express it succinctly.

- *How would you solve this problem?* Asking a candidate to respond to a case study and provide suggestions for solving the problem or situation can test reactions to situations that may be challenging in your organization.

PREVENTING HIRING MISTAKES

What are some of the mistakes that are made when hiring personnel? The most serious may be the organization's lack of readiness for fundraising and, therefore, for a professional to do the job. Job descriptions may be missing or be fuzzy. The board does not understand the full array of responsibilities required in a successful, ongoing, philanthropic fundraising program. Interviews lack preparation, and those doing the search are distracted by other duties or interests.

You should watch out for these serious hiring mistakes, as listed by a corporate human resource professional:

- Not understanding what the successful candidate will "look like"
- Unintentionally limiting the sources for candidates
- Failing to interview candidates thoroughly
- Falling for the "halo effect"
- Wishful thinking
- Ignoring intuition
- Failing to check one more reference[5]

Finding the right person for the job you need done is both a challenge and an opportunity. Careful preparation pays off. Not surprisingly, hiring the right person for a fundraising position is not much different than hiring for any other meaningful job. Some of America's notable individuals expressed their employee preferences in ways that are easy for nonprofit executives to relate.[6]

John D. Rockefeller III said, "I will pay more for the ability to deal with people than any other ability under the sun."

"Success is not measured by the heights one attains," said Booker T. Washington, "but by the obstacles one overcomes in its attainment."

James M. Barrie said, "The secret of happiness is not in doing what one likes, but in liking what one has to do."

Thomas Edison outlined the following qualities of success: "The three great essentials to achieve anything worthwhile are, first, hard work; second, stick-to-itiveness; third, common sense."

Brian O'Connell, founder of INDEPENDENT SECTOR, said, "Raising money takes dogged persistence, bullheadedness, salesmanship, year-round cultivation, board support and encouragement, a plan, an attainable goal, and lots of excitement."

Finally, Bernard M. Baruch gave this advice for professional achievement. "Whatever task you undertake, do it with all your heart and soul. Always be courteous, never be discouraged. Beware of him who promises something for nothing. Do not blame anybody for your mistakes and failures. Do not look for approval except the consciousness of doing your best."

Katharine Graham wrote that people who succeed do so by working harder, knowing more, taking risks, and being better than their competitors. "I suspect both men and women who get to the top in whatever field they choose will be rather single-minded, love what they do, and pay a price—often a heavy one—for their success. The difference is that today's generation has not only the freedom to succeed but the freedom to choose where success shall lie."[7]

▪ FURTHER READING

Slaymaker, Michael, "How Good Human Resources Improve Performance." *Advancing Philanthropy,* Vol 6., No. 1 (Spring 1998).

> *The author outlines steps in human resource management that will ensure both the supervision of a fundraising professional and the circumstances that help such a professional achieve on behalf of the organization. Excellent source for those who will manage fundraising professionals.*

SIDEBAR	ROBERT J. SIMONDS

When hiring a fundraising professional, the following steps are recommended.

Defining the Position

The first step in hiring a fundraising professional is to define the job to be filled, get appropriate approvals (human resources, legal counsel, etc.), determine the salary range, and name a search committee to coordinate the process (or retain an executive search firm to handle it).

(continued)

Some of the questions to be considered in describing the position are:

- What is the specific focus of the job? Annual giving? Planned giving? Major gifts? Capital campaign? Prospect research? Special events?
- Is an advanced degree required? Desirable?
- Is travel required? If so, how much?
- How many years of experience in the field are required?
- What are the required communication skills, written and oral?
- What is the deadline for application?

Advertising the Position

A variety of channels, including the following, should be considered:

- Notices on the institution's bulletin boards
- Local newspapers
- *The Chronicle of Philanthropy*
- AFP publications (and those of other professional associations)
- Major national newspapers (budget permitting, and if it is a national search)

Selecting Candidates

Working on a specific timetable, the search committee or executive search firm should review all applications, check references, and winnow the candidates down to a "short list" of four or five. This group would be invited to on-site, face-to-face interviews with the committee and other appropriate persons (CEO, chief development officer, key volunteers, and so on.) The selection process should be designed to reach consensus on first choice, second choice, and so on, and a written offer should be extended to the preferred candidate.

Communication

All applications should be acknowledged, and the "short list" of candidates (who are probably looking at other positions) should be kept posted on developments in the process.

ROBERT J. SIMONDS is president of the North Group, First Counsel, Inc., which includes the Midwest, Northeast, and New England areas. He also chairs FCI-International and is a member of the firm's board of directors and executive committee. His past experience includes a lengthy tenure with Ketchum, Inc. He has served private educational institutions and numerous community regional health and human-service organizations. Actively involved in professional affairs, he has held leadership positions in AAFRC, CASE, NSFRE (now AFP), and AHP.

PROFESSIONALS SAY . . .

What contributes to one's success as a fundraiser? Excellent interpersonal skills, strong writing abilities, attentiveness to detail, good detective work, and a genuine heart for people. Why are these important? "People give to people." They also give to trustworthy organizations that they believe can accomplish things that are important, projects and programs that will leave a legacy. Good relationships are built on respect. Respect that donors want to be good investors of the funds entrusted to them (don't be too quick to immediately push your needs on them), that they have dreams to be brought to fruition, that they be treated with courtesy in both the small and large matters of life. In fundraising, as in all of life, the "Golden Rule" provides helpful guidance. Treat others as you would like to be treated—with respect and courtesy. By working together to make exciting things happen, those on the giving and receiving end of gifts can experience synergy as both feel equally thrilled!

Karen A. Longman, Ph.D., Vice President for Academic Affairs and Dean of the Faculty, Greenville College, Illinois

PART SIX

Maintaining Excellence and Equilibrium

T o live is to function. To live well is to function well. Every person's working life, whether in the arts, in business, in sports, or in anything else, is a portrait of him or herself. Life is not a rehearsal. Life is an end in itself. Therefore, every professional—including those who engage in fundraising for the benefit of civil society, for the benefit of a philanthropic society, and for the benefit of each nonprofit that serves a human cause—must work with excellence. This excellence requires an awareness of success factors and accompanying attitudes that shape success.

In the final section of this volume, the discussion focuses on how a fundraising professional can maintain the high level of work that has been achieved, and what factors shape a professional's success. Paramount to all this is the concept of being true to one's mission in life and in work, and performing with a passion.

The fundraising professional is often faced with attitudes, myths, and perceptions about fundraising that may be less than favorable. Chapter 24 offers ideas for how to develop and maintain a winning attitude in most, if not all, situations. Because fundraising depends on an enthusiastic and committed approach, this chapter also lists traits that lead to success and provides ideas and evidence on what it takes to make an exceptional leader in the profession, regardless of rank, pay, or title.

Development of and adherence to a personal mission is crucial for fundraising success. Such a mission must be compatible with the organization's mission. Suggestions are included in Chapter 25 for an introspective process that includes examination of values and setting of priorities. This is a discussion on how to move from being a technician to being a visionary leader who has great commitment and passion for the cause being served, and why this is important for fundraising success.

Being a Winner in the Fundraising Profession

SIDEBARS BY EDWARD C. SCHUMACHER
AND JAMES E. GILLESPIE

In a telegram to the Reverend Milton Wright, sent from Kitty Hawk, North Carolina, on December 17, 1903, the Wright brothers wrote, "Success. Four flights Thursday morning. All against twenty-one-mile wind. Started from level with engine power alone. Average speed through air thirty-one miles. Longest fifty-nine seconds. Inform press. Home Christmas."

Success is relative and subjective. Perceptions of success change with time and through the influence of greater achievements than those of the moment, as can be seen by the Wright telegram. What was a great accomplishment at the time still retains its greatness but has also been surpassed by even greater achievements. This truth holds for fundraising, as well.

When surveying the successful lives of many noteworthy figures of the past and the present—personalities such as the Wright brothers—10 core beliefs that are unique to these men and women become apparent:

- Winners are not born, they are made.
- The dominant force in your existence is the way you think.
- You can create your own reality.
- There is some benefit to be had from every adversity.

- Each one of your beliefs is a choice.
- You are never defeated until you accept defeat as a reality and stop trying.
- The only real limitations on what you can accomplish are those that you impose on yourself.
- You already possess the ability to excel in at least one key area of your life.
- There can be no great success without great commitment.
- You need the support and cooperation of other people to achieve any worthwhile goal.[1]

These may seem like warm fuzzy platitudes, but when applied to fundraising they do indicate qualities that are success generators; however, achieving success is not as easy as listing success factors. "The road to success can exact a high toll from everyone in a business," wrote Paul Huff of Partners in Success, a consulting firm based in South Carolina. He lists several myths of success that often stand between individuals and the accomplishment of their goals. Companies that have looked beyond the myths to embrace truths generally experience extraordinary success.[2]

The first myth is, "The harder you work, the better your result." People often think that attaining success is a painful process that requires time, self-denial, willpower. Huff maintains that a mindset or mental momentum can help peak performance. Therefore choices, habits, and beliefs support or diminish your efforts, which leads to the second myth: "Power, prestige, and security are ultimate goals." These goals, however, are hollow. Goals that focus on how we can make a difference and affect the lives of our clients increase our self-esteem and create passionate work environments. They draw on humans' innate desire to help others.

CONFRONTING NEGATIVE PERCEPTIONS

The fundraising professional generally wishes to believe that hard work coupled with a positive attitude will shape success, and that there is an underlying desire to make a difference that influences the drive for success.

Perceptions both inside and outside of the field affect the mastery of success, however, and these should be addressed before the opinions of veterans in the field are examined. Duronio and Tempel enumerate some perceptions that affect the fundraiser's success:

- *Lack of understanding by the public.* For most, fundraising includes everything that involves asking for money, from bake sales to producing direct mail pieces. Although the lack of understanding by the public shapes the ability of a professional to produce results, more significant is the internal ignorance of CEOs, board members, and colleagues about fundraising. This lack of understanding and, therefore, lack of support limits the ability to effectively carry out an organization's fundraising program.

- *Negative public perceptions of fundraisers.* Some of these include jokes, such as "Who is he hitting up today?" or "You had better hang onto your wallet!" Others are comparisons that are not complimentary, such as comparing fundraisers with used car salesmen. A great conversation stopper, in many cases, is to admit that you are a fundraiser. People back off. It is true that some unprincipled and unethical fundraising practices have caused these perceptions, but fortunately, many professionals think these are changing. Fundraisers are often comfortable in talking about what they do because they can describe the role they play in the nonprofit sector.

- *Negative perceptions of fundraising by fundraisers.* Perhaps a more serious issue is the negative perceptions that fundraisers hold of themselves. Some have discomfort about asking for money, some feel negative about others in the field who seem to be doing it for self-aggrandizement, and others decry the big talkers who actually don't know what they are doing.[3]

Fortunately, there is progress and the majority of fundraising professionals understand the negative perceptions while they move ahead to extraordinary success. They do this by dispelling myths and focusing on professionalism, such as commitment to the profession, collegiality, education, service orientation, and focusing on special skills and knowledge that support successful practice.[4]

RECOGNIZING CHARACTERISTICS OF SUCCESS

The following, which reflect the collective views of many professionals in fundraising, may be the characteristics of success:

- The ability to inspire confidences, to lead regardless of rank or position
- Passion for the cause, an allegiance of the heart
- The ability to speak and write well
- The ability to motivate individuals and teams to get great results
- Knowledge of development practices
- A vision of the future and what must happen to secure it
- The ability to identify priorities, and to be able to see the difference between what is urgent and what is important
- Knowing how and when to act (Courage and decisiveness are essential if organizations will attract resources.)
- Exemplifying personal skills and commitment in implementing plans

Jack Schwartz, a leading member of the profession, summarizes well the success factors of a good fundraiser—the ability to care about our society, have deep and durable integrity, earn the respect of others, and develop an enthusiasm for the organization's mission.[5]

Moving to experts in career strategies, not just those in fundraising, it might be good to review suggestions by some who are esteemed in the field of management. Success secrets from a master, Tom Peters, who compiled these guidelines based on "51 Years of Painful Experience," also relate well to the fundraising profession:

- *Thank people.* Never forget to say thank you to someone who has done something for you. A written note is one of your best success tools.
- *Show up.* Nothing beats a face-to-face meeting. Communicate in person whenever possible.
- *Do not delay.* Deal with today's molehill before it turns into tomorrow's mountain.
- *Work your Rolodex.* Keep in touch with people and build relationships that will profit everyone.

- *Build credibility.* Talk to the experts in your field. They will be more helpful than you think.

- *Communicate your commitment.* If you cannot show people that you are committed to the mission and cause you serve, they will not be willing to expend much energy in helping reach common goals.

- *Manage your time.* Focus on what you need to accomplish.

- *Mind your manners.* It is the little things that position you better in getting others to commit to your agenda.

- *Cultivate allies.* Do not waste time trying to convert doubters who will not see your point of view. Develop strong supporters and allies.

- *Results.* Be outcome oriented, even if sometimes you have to get mad.[6]

Carl Mays, a nationally recognized speaker and personal coach as well as president of Creative Living, Inc., has listed three steps to success:

1. Find the thing you truly love to do, then do it. Success comes in loving what you do and having a burning desire to do it well.

2. Specialize in some particular area of what it is that you love to do. Through study and experience, become proficient in that particular area.

3. Importantly, be sure that the thing you do does not lead to your success only. Your desires and goals must not be selfish. Real winners concentrate on Win–Win situations. There is plenty of success to go around. You do not have to hoard it.[7]

These qualities for building success are highly applicable to fundraising, and when coupled with a set of steps specific to the profession, they may provide some insights that you can adapt to your own list of success factors and how to achieve them:

1. *Do not try to be an overnight hero.* Choose your activities for maximum effect. Know your organization, what shaped it, and what it will take to reach programmatic and fundraising goals.

2. *Build on what you know and what your job has handed you.* Use your knowledge to approach current and new situations, understand your organization's funding patterns, look ahead for new sources of funds, and seek better ways to reach goals.

3. *Ensure that your organization's mission is reflected in your fundraising methods.* Those who give gifts will seek congruency between what is said and done.

4. *Think strategically.* Be factual in analyzing strengths and weaknesses of the organization, and develop a plan that capitalizes on strengths and addresses weaknesses.

5. *Build on success.* Build on your first success and continue building on each subsequent success. You can use each achievement to bolster your confidence and knowledge for reaching the next peak.

6. *Be patient.* Teach others what time it takes to accomplish certain steps and goals.

7. *Educate others, particularly your CEO and board.* Again, this takes patience and is a gradual process. Provide them with information in small increments and let each piece build on the other.

8. *Sharpen your own skills.* Become a better manager, a leader at your appropriate level (perhaps leading from the middle rather from the top), a team player, and do not hesitate to get appropriate training, education, or mentoring in your quest.

Success is subjective, and it often depends on the perceptions of others. Ultimately, it is up to you to determine what success factors are important to you, and to match these to the expectations of your organization, your responsibilities, and the people whom you serve.

When you observe those who have succeeded over the long term in the field of fundraising, what you first see is this extraordinarily diverse group of individuals who seem to have little or nothing in common. Educational backgrounds vary, introverts and extroverts succeed, size of institutions and infrastructure may be complex or simple, fundraising education backgrounds differ widely. Certainly salary is no measure, and is widely inconsistent.

But look deeper, and what you find are a set of values and behaviors that are reliable barometers of success. What successful fundraisers hold in common is a passion for their cause, a belief in the values of their organizations, a sense that it is the outcomes of fundraising that count, not the activity of fundraising. They are individuals who stay focused, who have a high degree of flexibility and a high tolerance for ambiguity. They love people, working with people, supporting people, coaching and teaching people. Finally, they are people who go to work every day knowing they are making a difference in the world and in their institutions. It is these professionals who maintain a high quality of work and their own professional balance.

The applicant for a fundraising job was asked, "What is it that you do well?" She responded, "I think clearly, I write expertly, I like people, and I talk well!"

Is there anything else you would want?!

EDWARD C. "ED" SCHUMACHER M.Ed., is the managing partner and primary trainer for Third Sector Consulting. He has worked successfully in the nonprofit community for 35 years as a consultant, executive director, development, and staff member of a national organization. He has worked for many years as a volunteer and served on many boards. He teaches for The Fund Raising School and is an adjunct faculty member of the University of Washington Graduate School of Public Affairs, a workshop leader at the Graduate School of Social Work, and an instructor in the University's Fundraising Certificate Program. His consulting and training work encompasses a diverse group of nonprofits including hospitals, social service agencies, independent schools, community institutions, and colleges and universities.

One's attitude is the only thing over which he has absolute, complete control.

W. Clement Stone

You have heard volunteers (too often these are board members) say, "I'll do anything for you except 'fundraise.' " There is a Yiddish word, *Shnorrer,* that describes a beggar or a moocher and, sadly, fundraising is sometimes placed in that category. These attitudes represent an astounding misunderstanding of what we do, how we do it, and especially, why we do it.

In almost 30 years in the fundraising profession I have learned six essentials for true success.

1. *Understand why people give.* I ask donors, "Tell me why you gave your last gift and how you felt after it was completed." Motivation ranged from, "I believe in their mission," to, "the need was so great, I couldn't resist." I most often hear, "I just wish I had more to give." So rarely do I hear people respond negatively that it cannot be measured. When you truly believe that raising money actually makes people happy (when it is done properly), you will be a winner in this profession.

2. *Develop your personality.* From a positive mental attitude to a great sense of humor (absolutely vital!), and even a good handshake.

3. *See yourself as a problem-solver.* Recognize that you were hired to solve problems, not ask your boss or your volunteers to solve them. Have a plan, share it with them, and say, "Unless you stop me, here's what I will do."

4. *Be entrepreneurial.* See your department as "your company." You are the profit center for your organization!

5. *Work by objectives.* See the goal and purpose in each thing you do, especially in your contacts with donors. Constantly ask yourself, "Why am I doing this?" If the answer doesn't blend with the strategies and objectives in your plan, do something else.

6. *Get out of the office.* If you see this as an office job, you are doomed to mediocrity. The winners in this profession spend their time with donors.

JAMES E. GILLESPIE, CFRE is president of CommonWealth, a firm that, since 1995, has been providing comprehensive counsel in the area of planned gift development programs and specializing in training, mentoring, and professional development. Jim was chief operating officer of the consulting division of Renaissance Inc. for 6 years and was a professional development officer for the previous 20 years. He served Junior Achievement and Tri-County Mental Health Foundation in Indianapolis, and was recruited to the Indianapolis Symphony Orchestra as chief development officer in 1985. These positions have provided a wealth of background in the youth/educational, social services, and cultural environments. Jim is a lead faculty member of The Fund Raising School, a unit of Indiana University's Center on Philanthropy. A frequent speaker and author, he also serves as Conference Chair for the 2001 National Conference on Planned Giving, held in Indianapolis.

PROFESSIONALS SAY . . .

If you do nothing else to prepare for a career in the nonprofit arena, learn to write well and how to read a balance sheet.

Linda Brimmer, Director of External Relations, Sigma Theta Tau International, Indianapolis, Indiana

Every life experience, both positive and negative, has helped me in developing my fundraising career. No experience in life is wasted but is useful for learning and growing into a better professional.

Joyce E. Helyner, Associate Vice President for Development, Taylor University, Upland, Indiana

CHAPTER 25

Creating a Personal Mission and Performing with a Passion

SIDEBAR BY MARGYE S. BAUMGARDNER

"To be successful in our work we must be fully convinced that we can influence the world around us."[1] Attitude has a strong bearing on ability to do the job. In order to do not only satisfying work but to exceed expectations, we have to believe in the missions of our institutions. And that mission must be congruent with our personal mission.

If pay and status are the major underlying impulses for engaging in fundraising, then we will not find fulfillment—not only because salaries are not outstanding, for the most part, but also because fundraisers are usually the people behind the scenes. Most fundraising professionals enter the field because it allows responsiveness to human needs; it is work that heals, educates, inspires, restores, preserves, or comforts.

Without a doubt, nonprofit organizations have their bureaucracies, administrative problems, and managerial dilemmas, but on the whole, the focus is on social concerns, on resolution of issues and problems, and on outcomes that benefit human beings.

When writing about organizational alignment and focus, John Gehrke stated that there are four essential elements in every nonprofit organization, and the first of these is mission and vision. Gehrke believes that there are internal and external perspectives of each element.

"Vertical alignment describes the staff's understanding of the organization's mission/vision. This alignment is attained when all staff members understand their individual role in the pursuit of the organization's mission. . . . Horizontal alignment references the organization's strategies that are used to serve others."[2]

This is a good illustration of the need to reflect, in a personal mission, the overall mission of the institution because that is what drives our willingness to serve and succeed.

Writing in *The NonProfit Times*, John McIlquham stated that otherwise brilliant professionals, particularly those with expertise in technology, may lack the spirit of what nonprofits are really about. "They don't understand the link between institution and mission."[3] If fundraising is an exercise in which skills are mastered while people become secondary, then the professional has forgotten the mission of the profession as well as his or her own sense of mission.

Commitment to a personal mission that is congruent with the organization's mission is fundamental to fundraising. This commitment, followed by actions that support public good and moral purpose, allows donors to trust us and our organizations. Scott Preissler, president of the Christian Stewardship Association, says, "The values of stewardship are prime motivators for fundraisers. I cannot stress enough the importance of connecting the exploration of one's career with a personal understanding of one's calling."[4]

How can a professional craft a personal mission, one that is suitable for fundraising and for the organization he or she serves? Some fundamental questions may help in this exploration.

First, an examination of a personal value system is important. Given the many causes that make up the sector, which ones hold values that can be shared by the professional? Although all nonprofit causes are worthy (with few exceptions, perhaps), a fundraiser should evaluate which ones have values that motivate his or her action, which are part of a personal belief system, and which ones provide the most energy when striving for a resolution of a problem or need.

Second, what outcomes are the most satisfying to the individual professional? Will the outcomes be focused on healing the body or the mind? On educating children, young people, or adults? On the aesthetic experiences of life? Examining what we wish to influence by improving, shaping, managing, or guiding the circumstances can be vital in seeking a job that brings satisfaction.

Third, what are the mundane activities that our more lofty ideals, those of our mission, require? Can we work with these details and functions in a way that provides satisfaction and fulfillment, and not get lost in the trivia of life while adhering to our personal mission?

When writing about the myths of success, Paul Huff quoted Martin Luther King, Jr., who said,

" 'If a man hasn't discovered something he's willing to die for, he isn't fit to live.' King was on a crusade—a cause that fired up the consciousness of a nation because it was something that really mattered. I'm not suggesting that we can or should create something worth dying for in our organizations, but I do suggest that defining our work in ways that make a difference in the lives of others can create something that employees will be excited to live for."[5]

At the end of a day—or at the end of a career—those who have a mission of service to institutions and causes can reflect and see that individuals and society are better because of their efforts. Not every profession offers potential for such deeply satisfying interactions.

During the Cultural Revolution in China, a famous pianist was imprisoned for 7 years. He couldn't practice at all during that time, but when he was released, he could play as well as ever. Why? "I practiced every day in my mind," he said, "and I knew what I could accomplish." His turn came, and he was able to exceed the limits he might have set for himself. The same could be said for those of us with a mission. It begins in the mind, if we have examined our motives and values, and extends to our actions. Those actions subsequently serve the mission of the organization as it, in turn, meets the needs and wants of a defined population as well as the non-profit sector.

FURTHER READING

Bolles, Richard Nelson. *How to Find Your Mission in Life*. Berkeley, CA: Ten Speed Press, 2001.

An exploration of the spiritual aspects of finding one's place in the world, from the author of What Color Is Your Parachute? *This is an inspirational gift for those who are new to the job market or who are reconsidering their place in it.*

SIDEBAR   MARGYE S. BAUMGARDNER

Few among us grow from childhood dreaming of a professional life as a philanthropic fundraiser. It is when we have the blessed opportunity to implement the mission and the vision of a worthy cause that our passion ignites.

Although many can be technicians, some grow to be visionaries and leaders when we truly grasp the enormity of the possibilities. Each day we patiently put the pieces into place, we establish the relationships, we hear and tell the stories of the people in need and how their lives are touched, we plan and strategize, we feel the privileged responsibility, and then the spark flames forth in us. A professional epiphany occurs, and that spark becomes a passion.

Fundraisers value the process, the journey. We listen to the inner voice that informs our ethical and creative work, which supports the vision we see so clearly for our organizations.

We draw our power and inspiration from the lives we assist, the learning and knowledge we foster, and the enrichment we nurture. Combining these with integrity, accountability, strategic thinking, leadership, and management skills, we can then share our vision and passion, and guide the ripples moving out everywhere.

Envisioning and embracing the possibilities of our organization's mission brings out the best in each of us, and it fuels the pride, energy, and dedication that becomes our passion. This breeds and secures success.

Our work leaves a legacy of many kinds of riches, and a personal fulfillment beyond any expectations. Our passion multiplies and elevates the fire in those who share the vision and who carry the legacy forward.

Pass it on!

MARGYE S. BAUMGARDNER, CFRE serves as the Southwest region director for the Juvenile Diabetes Foundation, with responsibilities in major gifts and planned giving. In her nearly 30 years in the field, she has been responsible for raising about $250 million, including service with the American Cancer Society and the Santa Monica Medical Center Foundation as its president and CEO. Additionally, she has consulted for national clients in the arts, education, youth, and animal and health services. Distinguished service to the National Society of Fund Raising Executives (NSFRE) earned her election to the office of president of the Greater Los Angeles Chapter in 1987 and 1988. The chapter recognized her as the Professional Fundraising Executive of the Year for the Los Angeles area in 1991.

PROFESSIONALS SAY . . .

Go with a cause and mission you identify with and have an affinity for. I know too many colleagues trying to raise money for causes they don't care about. I can't think of a situation more difficult or trying.

Gregory Long, Director, Outreach and Partner Relations, Quest International, Newark, Ohio

Early recognition of the values that define you as a human being, the ethics that guide you as a professional, and the entities that merit your duty will help determine and illuminate your career path. The three together will guide your selection of causes, your decisions about the manner in which you practice, and your priorities when faced with choices. Firmly planted within this concept is my definition of what we do as professional fundraisers, which is to facilitate the transfer of available dollars from willing donors to worthy causes.

Barbara H. Marion, CFRE, Senior Principal, Hayes Briscoe Associates, Petaluma, California

The Future of Fundraising: What Lies Ahead

SIDEBARS BY STANLEY WEINSTEIN
AND JASON CHANDLER

Joe Mixer, one of the founders of The Fund Raising School and a respected professional and consultant, wrote, "Complex forces are always at work in the charitable arena and their directions will continue to shape the course of fundraising and the growth of philanthropy."[1]

Fundraising is a dynamic field. Changes occur and are influenced by many factors—economic, political, technological, and cultural. Some changes are caused by demographics; others by shifting values in society that shape personal value systems. All of these affect how fundraisers do their work. Therefore, professionals must remain alert as to how the non-profit sector changes and must be adaptable as needed and required, both by the broader context in which they work and the individual variations within specific organizations. Most experts in the field believe that while the demands on fundraisers may become more challenging, the opportunities also grow.

Some predictions for the future of fundraising are relatively certain. Others aren't quite so predictable and depend on a variety of circumstances that are mercurial and ever-changing. Many factors that are bound to have an effect on fundraising are described as follows; while nothing about the future is certain, it can be said that these factors will affect fundraising to one degree or another.

The predicted transfer of wealth, as indicated by research conducted by Paul Schervish and John Havens,[2] will make greater opportunities possible. With this forecast, however, come accompanying challenges that include more sophisticated donor relationships, better information sharing and accountability, and well-trained fundraisers who know how to handle major gift prospects and donors. This transfer of wealth also is indicative of changing donor preferences in how they make gifts and what they require of the organizations that they benefit. The venture philanthropists will continue to select the organizations they wish to work with, or will create their own. They will expect clear outcomes and have expectations of good accountability and businesslike practices by the nonprofit. They will remain involved with the organizations to which they give, and a different working relationship will result, one that may not be the current norm for most fundraisers.

Public attitudes about fundraising will continue to affect the profession. Currently there is considerable attention paid to philanthropy—and therefore, to fundraising as well. Media widely cover philanthropic news, factual and heartwarming stories abound, and critiques as well as accolades are prevalent. It is the duty of professionals in the nonprofit sector to educate the public about the importance and value of the nonprofit sector and therefore of fundraising; it is also their duty to work and behave in such a way that fundraising is seen as a noble profession that aids the success of each nonprofit cause, which, in turn, builds a healthy community and society.

Changes in tax structures and charitable deductions will continue to shape fundraising. Although these depend on political whims in many cases, and cannot be predicted with certainty, the fundraising professional must remain current with tax implications that affect donors and must be knowledgeable enough to assure donors about the benefits and consequences of giving. Major organizations such as the Association of Fundraising Professionals and INDEPENDENT SECTOR can be of considerable assistance in this area. They provide information and serve as advocates for the nonprofit sector when tax issues are discussed in Congress or at the local level.

The demand for accountability will increase, as will the expectation of ethical behavior. During the 1990s, the sector was affected by some fundraising debacles, and these influenced the transparency of organizations. Justifying fundraising costs, issuing appropriate reports, placing the Form 990 on the Internet and making it available—all these were tasks that credible non-profits carried out in an attempt to assure donors of good stewardship of their funds. Without a doubt, the demands for accountability will continue, if not grow. Donors have become more sophisticated in asking for information on just how their funds are used, and what outcomes they can expect from their investments.

Increasingly, donations such as major gifts are being handled by others besides the donor. Donor-advised funds and other forms of indirect giving make it easier for some to be philanthropic, but they also remove the donor from direct interaction with the cause, and make it more difficult for some organizations, especially smaller and low-budget ones, to have access to major gifts.

A definite trend in philanthropy and fundraising is the attention on diversity in giving as well as asking by minorities, the inclusion of different and new population groups in the ranks of professionals, and cross-cultural communication. As was indicated in Chapter 13, there is ample professional opportunity for minorities in the ranks of fundraisers; frequently, organizations seek to diversify their staffs, and as fundraising extends beyond the traditional markets, it is necessary to have staff who can relate to the differences in culture and ethnicity. At the same time, current professionals must become better acquainted with the cultures of giving and therefore the implications of asking within and across these cultures. This, perhaps, is one of the most positive changes and challenges of the future of fundraising.

The sector will continue to grow, therefore making it necessary to increase the ranks of fundraisers. At the same time, expectations of fundraisers will also increase because of the needs of new organizations that enter a highly competitive field. It stands to reason, then, that there will be ample job opportunities for fundraisers, but that the work they undertake may also be more demanding. For those who are serious about fundraising as a profession, this will be a positive and exciting challenge, while the dilettantes will probably fade quite quickly.

As the accountability requirements become more stringent, watchdog groups increase their activity, and donors demand more information on how their funds are used, there will continue to be a focus on fundraising costs. Just how much money goes to the cause and how much is used for fundraising and administrative costs will be a serious issue that merits much research and information dissemination.

Along with demands for accountability and attention on fundraising costs will be increases in regulation and control. Governments, from federal to local, will at least consider legislation that prevents abuse of public trust and violations of ethical behavior. Most infractions of laws and public trust are now handled by possible revocation of the 501(c)(3) tax status, but it is inevitable that laws will be considered from time to time that affect how nonprofit organizations function and report those functions.

Continuing professionalization of fundraising is inevitable. Some of the trends and forecasts just listed will naturally make it necessary for fundraising to become an accepted profession and to be recognized as a valuable part of developing and maintaining a successful nonprofit organization. This means that fundraisers will require more continuing education (this was also evident in the 1990s) and will enroll in academic courses and degree programs in increasing numbers. The requirements by professionals for quality education and training will grow, and those providing learning opportunities will have to ensure that course and workshop content is relevant, factual, credible, verified, and appropriate.

The blurring of boundaries among the sectors will increase as nonprofit organizations engage in business ventures for nonphilanthropic income, and as for-profit organizations become involved in areas that were traditionally considered the realm of the nonprofit. Already this has occurred within health care and education, where some hospitals have changed to being for-profit entities, and some schools are run on a for-profit basis. This will continue to cause donor confusion and perhaps make it more difficult to explain the need of the nonprofit and the case for support.

Technology will continue to have a strong impact on how fundraising is done. Already it has affected the scope and professionalism of fundraising through use of software, communication capability, donor record keeping, prospect research, and fundraising via the Internet. The wise nonprofit organization will avail itself of technological capabilities for fundraising, and because of this, the requirements for knowledge and skill in technology by the fundraiser will also increase.

Privacy issues may well increase as a result of the growing facility of communication, research and record-keeping, as well as donor awareness that information is acquired about him or her, and is used in the relationship-building process. Although a limited number of court cases on this issue thus far have ruled in favor of the nonprofit, it is likely that privacy will remain a concern, both by the donor and the organization.

Disparity between the fundraising potential of large, well-recognized nonprofits versus small, grassroots organizations will be exacerbated as the numbers of nonprofits grow and the numbers of philanthropists at all levels gravitate toward the better-known or popular causes. This is already evident, as well-known organizations such as the Salvation Army, major universities, and Habitat for Humanity find it easier to raise money than the community-based, grassroots organizations that function on a small budget and with many volunteers.

Professionalism in fundraising will continue to be bolstered by the increased research base for practice. Organizations such as the Association for Research on Nonprofit Organizations and Voluntary Action (ARNOVA)[3] are a venue for researchers to increase knowledge on fundraising, which is then disseminated by education and training organizations and put into practice by professionals. This research provides credibility for fundraisers, particularly when faced with questions and criticisms. As Joe Mixer predicted, "The debate within the field of fundraising and outside in the larger public arena requires more information and understanding about the role of fundraising among both donors and donees. A solid conceptual base that illuminates the place, function, and values of fundraising will clarify many of the issues."[4]

Nonprofit organizations will continue to be sites for civic involvement by members of a community. Although neighborhoods have changed over time, and people no longer find their identity in such geographic areas, the nonprofit sector will be an avenue for involvement, whether in school-related activities, volunteering, participating in special events, or other activities that bring people together for common good.[5]

Bruce Glasrud, writing in *Fund Raising Management,* said that fundraisers must "start to prefigure the philanthropic temperament of our future society. From there, fundraisers must prepare new attitudes, methodologies, and technologies to cultivate the donor, receive the gift and maintain the relationship."[6] Certainly fundraisers must remain alert, flexible, willing to learn and change, and committed to the profession as well as the causes they are serving so that they can handle the challenges and opportunities of the future.

　　　　　　　　　　　STANLEY WEINSTEIN

In the future, resource development professionals will face numerous challenges. Among these are ever-increasing competition for philanthropic resources; changes in government regulation; compassion fatigue among some donors; increasing demand for services from the not-for-profit sector; changing demographics; and increasing time constraints facing volunteers. At the same time, fundraising executives are presented with several potentially high pay-off opportunities. These include the anticipated $12-trillion intergenerational transfer of wealth; advances in technology; a growing emphasis on collaboration; and a focus on outcomes . . . with a concomitant positive response from funders to measurable progress.

The mature professional of the future—a person committed to serving our neighborhoods, communities, cities, states, country, and world—must be flexible and dedicated to continued education. In two recent campaigns, our solicitation and volunteer training materials were in both English and Spanish. Several years ago, I would have thought a bilingual capital campaign unlikely.

We must recognize that we are not only the products of our changing environment; rather, we can be positive change agents. Certainly, it behooves us to stay close to—and to influence—the political processes and regulators who shape the not-for-profit sector's legal environment. To actually benefit from the inter-generational transfer of wealth, we must become more proactive in requesting planned gifts.

The ability to deal with change and commitment to continuing education are essential to success. Equally important are the fundamental underpinnings of success in fundraising—a genuine concern for each person we work with . . . and a passion for creating visionary institutions that respond to the most pressing human needs.

STANLEY WEINSTEIN, CFRE is principal of Baxter Farr Thomas & Weinstein, Ltd. He has spent 30 years in the nonprofit sector. He served for 9 years on the National Society of Fund Raising Executives' Board of Directors. His experience with Baxter Farr Thomas & Weinstein, Ltd. included work with a broad spectrum of social welfare, health care, arts, and religious and educational institutions. He founded the consulting practice in 1988. Since then, he has traveled extensively, facilitating board retreats and strategic planning processes, helping to initiate planned giving programs, and supporting endowment and capital campaigns for clients throughout the nation. Mr. Weinstein is the author of *The Complete Guide to Fund-Raising Management* published by John Wiley & Sons.

Fundraising has a brilliant future. There is an ocean of energy swelling up for philanthropic, political, and philosophical causes. There are several trends that will intensify as time goes by. Following are eight trends, listed in no particular order, that I, as a relatively new professional and graduate with a master's (emphasis in nonprofit studies, 1999) believe will be a major part of the future of fundraising.

1. Programs in professional schools and associations are popping up all over the place in order to help train fundraisers. They will continue to be champions of a greater emphasis on ethical and accountable fundraising.
2. Technology will continue to influence the future of fundraising. Fundraising software and online giving will allow for a more detailed strategic and methodical approach to raising money.
3. The Internet will facilitate the gathering and sharing of vital information. Even today, any fundraiser, with the right software, can access his or her organization's entire donor records system from any airport computer kiosk or personal palm pilot.
4. The future of fundraising will see more attention placed on matching the strategy to donor preferences.
5. The emerging global marketplace will encourage more international fundraising because companies will continue to engage new markets.
6. Nonprofits will look and function more and more like for-profits.
7. Fundraising professionals will achieve greater respect from the general population.
8. Successful fundraising will continue to be people asking people to help people.

These are a few of the trends I see influencing the future of fundraising, and as a young professional, I'm preparing myself to be ready for these trends.

JASON C. CHANDLER is senior associate director of development at the School of Medicine, Emory University. He attended the University of Tennessee at Knoxville, where he earned an English degree in creative writing. After graduating, Jason worked at the Fort Sanders Hospital Foundation. In 1997 he began his graduate work at the Indiana University Center on Philanthropy. Upon graduating in 1999, Jason accepted a position as the assistant director of corporate relations for Emory University in Atlanta, Georgia. Jason is now the senior associate director of development for the School of Medicine at Emory University.

PROFESSIONALS SAY . . .

Throughout the nation, the public sector role in the delivery of programs and services is under ever increasing scrutiny. Meeting the expectations of service recipients is shaping public sector goals as never before. As a result, governmental entities at the federal, state, and local levels are actively seeking individuals with the fundraising skills and experience necessary to develop partnerships with the private and nonprofit sectors. The intent is to develop service delivery systems that are measured by the effectiveness of the outcomes and not just the efficient use of inputs.

Eric Myers, Executive Director, Indiana National Resources Foundation

The future will look a great deal like the past in the sense that the most effective fundraising is based on relationships. Clients I have worked with or am currently serving have found the truth in this. It is extremely difficult, for example, to shift from reliance on direct mail for operations to capital campaigning with all that implies in terms of personal solicitation and sequential fundraising (i.e., from the top down and the inside out). If the donors only have a stamp and envelope relationship with the organization, they can not be easily shifted to a personal one. Invitations to "visit our site" or a request for a personal visit from a development person are easily declined, in part, because many mail donors prefer keeping their distance. I doubt that we will see the day when the top 10 to 20 percent of donors needed for 80 to 90 percent of the goal are going to give the levels of gifts needed via indirect Internet contact or direct mail. Even the much publicized venture philanthropists give because they get involved in very personal ways. In fact, as I read the research from Silicon Valley and elsewhere, involvement has been the key. They find a need and attempt to fill that need by the same process they made their fortunes—intense attention and dedication to achieving an objective or goal—with or without a fundraising executive or consultant. They approach the situation just as Bob Payton describes philanthropy—voluntary action for the public good. That hasn't changed since Alexis de Tocqueville first observed it. When everything else is stripped away, the best and most effective fundraising has been, and will be in the future, that which is built on relationships, beginning with those who serve on governing boards and extending as far as possible into the constituency of those served and those who care about those served.

Robert Pierpont, CFRE, Chairman, Pierpont & Wilkerson, Ltd, Garrison, New York

There is no doubt that we are in the midst of a huge largely technical revolution in the way we raise funds for our organizations. But no matter how sophisticated our tools, the need to continue to build relationships between ourselves and organizations will always be paramount.

Nat Irvin, II, President, Future Focus 2020, Executive Professor, Future Studies, Babcock Graduate School of Management, Wake Forest University

Notes

Introduction

1. Quoted in *Accent on Philanthropy II,* Washington, D.C.: Philanthropic Service for Institutions, 1983.
2. Margaret A. Duronio and Eugene R. Tempel, *Fundraisers: Their Careers, Stories, Concerns, and Accomplishments* (San Francisco: Jossey-Bass Publishers, 1997), p.1.
3. James M. Greenfield, *Fund-Raising: Evaluating and Managing the Fund Development Process* (New York: John Wiley & Sons, Inc., 1991), p. 192.
4. Eugene R. Tempel, Sara B. Cobb, and Warren F. Ilchman (eds.), "The Professionalization of Fundraising: Implications for Education, Practice and Accountability," *New Directions for Philanthropic Fundraising,* No. 15 (Spring 1997), p. 1.
5. Robert L. Payton, *Philanthropy: Voluntary Action for the Public Good* (New York: Macmillan Publishing Co., 1988), p. xvii.
6. Quoted in James Gregory Lord, *The Raising of Money,* Cleveland: Third Sector Press, 1987.

Chapter 1

1. The term *third sector* is often applied to the nonprofit sector. This term is disputed by some scholars who, while not questioning the concept of three sectors—business, government, and nonprofit—do question the label *third.* Another term frequently used for the nonprofit sector is *not-for-profit.* Nonprofit organizations are allowed to make a profit, but it is not for personal gain of board members, stakeholders, or employees.
2. Robert L. Payton, *Philanthropy: Voluntary Action for the Public Good* (New York: Macmillan Publishing Company and the American Council on Education, 1988).
3. Some scholars believe that three sectors are limiting in nature, and that there is a case to be made for adding a fourth, and perhaps even a fifth. "The sectors of society include not only the government, business, and nonprofit sectors but also the personal (expanded household) sector. The nonprofit sector is the fourth (and, if necessary, fifth) sector, not the third sector. Either the membership sector (member-serving nonprofits) is recognized as a significant part of the nonprofit sector more adequately, or it should be seen as a fifth sector." This was written by David Horton Smith, "Four Sectors or Five? Retaining the Member-Benefit Sector," in the *Nonprofit and Voluntary Sector* quarterly, vol. 20, no. 2, Summer 1991, Jossey-Bass Inc. publishers. Dwight F. Burlingame of the Center on Philanthropy at Indiana University concurs with this thought.
4. Lilly Cohen and Dennis R. Young, *Careers for Dreamers and Doers: A Guide to Management Careers in the Nonprofit Sector* (New York: The Foundation Center, 1989), p. 3.

5. Lester M. Salamon, *America's Nonprofit Sector: A Primer*, 2nd Edition (New York: The Foundation Center, 1999).
6. *The Nonprofit Almanac In Brief—2001: Facts and Figures on the Independent Sector* Washington, D.C.: (Independent Sector, 2001).

Chapter 2

1. Jeanne Harrah-Conforth and John Borsos, "The Evolution of Professional Fundraising: 1890–1990." In Dwight F. Burlingame and Lamont J. Hulse, eds. *Taking Fundraising Seriously* (San Francisco: Jossey-Bass, Inc., 1991), p. 31.
2. Barbara H. Marion, "The Education of Fundraisers," *New Directions for Philanthropic Fundraising, The Professionalization of Fundraising,* No. 15 (Spring 1997), p. 72.
3. Scott M. Cutlip, *Fundraising in the United States: Its Role in America's Philanthropy* (New Brunswick, NJ: Transaction, 1990; original work published in 1965), p. 3.
4. Cutlip, page 43.
5. Harrah-Conforth and Borros, p. 27.
6. Henry A. Rosso, *Rosso on Fundraising* (San Francisco: Jossey-Bass Publishers, 1996), p. 113.
7. Thomas E. Broce, *Fundraising,* 2d ed. (Norman, OK: University of Oklahoma Press, 1986).
8. Rosso, p. xi.
9. Eugene E. Brussell, ed., *Dictionary of Quotable Definitions* (Englewood Cliffs, NJ: Prentice-Hall, Inc., 1970).

Chapter 3

1. Peter Block, "Safe Return Doubtful," *News For a Change* (June 2000).
2. Ethel A. Cullinan, Ph.D., "Notes to Newcomers," *AHP Journal* (Spring 1992), p. 43.
3. Cheryl Bernstein Gurin, "Finding the 'Fun' in," *Advancing Philanthropy* (Spring 1998), p. 48.
4. Thomas J. Billitteri, "Growing Ranks of Fundraisers Haven't Increased a Key Measure of Giving," *The Chronicle of Philanthropy* (October 21, 1999), p. 14
5. Kim Klein, "Make Fundraising Your Career," *Grassroots Fundraising Journal* Vol. 17, No. 1 (February 1998), p. 4.
6. Marina Dundjerski, "American Fundraisers Are Said to Ignore Technology and Demographics," *The Chronicle of Philanthropy* (April 4, 1996), p. 26.
7. Irving Warner, "Fundraisers Who Don't Know What They Don't Know," *The Chronicle of Philanthropy* (March 10, 1992), p. 41.
8. Jeanne Harrah-Conforth and John Borsos, "The Evolution of Professional Fundraising: 1890–1990." In Dwight F. Burlingame and Lamont J. Hulse, eds. *Taking Fundraising Seriously,* (San Francisco, CA: Jossey-Bass, Inc., 1991), p. 33.
9. Irving Warner, "How to Change Fund-raising's Public Image," *The Chronicle of Philanthropy* (April 20, 1993), p. 43.
10. Bill J. Arrison, "Selling Is My Game," *The NonProfit Times* (September 1994), p. 42.
11. Robert F. Carbone, Ph.D., "The Meaning of Profession," *NSFRE Journal* (Spring 1988), p. 26.
12. James C. Dean, "What Makes a Profession?" *Management* (November 1995), pp. 28–30.
13. Clyde P. Watkins and Susan T. Redfield, "Philanthropy Today," *Getting Started: A Guide to Fundamentals,* National Society of Executives, Chicago Chapter, 1988.
14. Kathleen S. Kelly, "Four Organizational Roles of Fundraisers: An Exploratory Study," Paper presented at the Association for Research on Nonprofit Organizations and Voluntary Action, 27th Annual Conference, Seattle, November 5, 1998.
15. Gonser Gerber Tinker Stuhr, LLP, 400 East Diehl Rd., Suite 380, Naperville, IL 60563. *Bulletin,* April 1995.
16. As quoted in *Accent on Philanthropy II* (May 1983), p. 16.

Chapter 4

1. Peter F. Drucker, "The Age of Social Transformation," *The Atlantic Monthly,* vol. 274, no. 5 (November 1994).
2. Peter F. Drucker, *The Effective Executive* (New York: Harper & Row Publishers, Inc., 1967).
3. Robert L. Payton, "A Tradition in Jeopardy," in Charles T. Clotfelter and Thomas Ehrlich, eds. *Philanthropy and the Nonprofit Sector in a Changing America* (Bloomington: Indiana University Press, 1999), p. 492.
4. Margaret A. Duronio and Eugene R. Tempel, *Fundraisers: Their Careers, Stories, Concerns, and Accomplishments* (San Francisco: Jossey-Bass Publishers, 1997).
5. Robert L. Payton, Presentation made to the Executive Leadership Institute, July 1998, Indianapolis, IN.
6. James M. Greenfield, *Evaluating and Managing the Fundraising Process* (New York: Wiley, 1991), pp. 192–193.
7. Susan E. Tifft, "Asking for a Fortune," *Working Woman* (November 1992), p. 68.
8. Kathleen S. Kelly, *Effective Fundraising Management* (Mahwah, NJ: Lawrence Erlbaum Associates, Publishers, 1998), p. 69.
9. Holly Hall, "Wanted: Big-Gift Fundraisers," *The Chronicle of Philanthropy,* vol. XI, no. 13 (April 22, 1999).
10. Holly Hall and John Murawski, "Fundraising: Hot Career or Hot Seat?" *The Chronicle of Philanthropy,* vol. VII, no. 18 (June 29, 1995).
11. Eugene R. Tempel, "Preparing the Next Generation of Fund-Raising Professionals," Occasional Papers, Bentz Whaley Flessner, Vol. VI (Spring 1998).
12. For detailed information please see the 1999 Profile of NSFRE Members.
13. Lilya Wagner and Mark Hager, "Board Members Beware! Warning Signs of a Dysfunctional Organization," *Nonprofit World* (March 1998).
    Lilya Wagner and Jamie Levy, "The Dysfunctional Organization: Should You Be a Whistleblower?" *Fundraising Management* (November 1999).
14. Thomas J. Billitteri, "Keeping the Best on Board," *The Chronicle of Philanthropy* (September 21, 2000).
15. Billiteri, "Keeping the Best on Board."
16. INDEPENDENT SECTOR, Ethics and the Nation's Voluntary and Philanthropic Community: Obedience to the Unenforceable, 1991.
17. Marilyn Fischer, *Ethical Decision Making in Fundraising* (New York: Wiley, 2000).
18. Fischer, p. 21.

Chapter 5

1. From a TRW advertisement, 1985.
2. From a speech by John Gardner, the Miriam and Peter Haas Centennial Professor of Public Service in the Graduate School of Business, "John Gardner on Life," printed in *Stanford Magazine* (March 1994).

Chapter 6

1. "HR Update: News that Works," *HR Magazine* (November 2000).
2. Indiana University also offers a dual master's degree program in nonprofit management and philanthropic studies.

Chapter 7

1. Harland G. Bloland and Rita Bornstein, "Fundraising in Transition: Strategies for Professionalization," in Dwight F. Burlingame and Lamont J. Hulse, eds., *Taking Fundraising Seriously* (San Francisco: Jossey-Bass, 1991), p. 114.

2. Lilly Cohen, "Educating and Training Managers for the Sector," in Lilly Cohen and Dennis R. Young, eds., *Careers for Dreamers and Doers* (New York: The Foundation Center, 1989), p. 54.

3. Bloland and Bornstein, pp. 116–117.

4. Robert F. Carbone, *Fundraising as a Profession: Clearinghouse for Research on Fund Raising.* The University of Maryland College Park, College Park, MD, 3112 Benjamin Building, MD 20742 (September 1998).

5. Margaret A. Duronio and Eugene R. Tempel. *Fundraisers: Their Careers, Stories, Concerns, and Accomplishments* (San Francisco: Jossey-Bass, 1997), pp. 134–136.

Chapter 8

1. Margaret A. Duronio and Eugene R. Tempel, *Fundraisers: Their Careers, Stories, Concerns, and Accomplishments* (San Francisco: Jossey-Bass, 1997).

2. James M. Greenfield, *Fund-Raising: Evaluating and Managing the Fund Development Process*, 2d ed., (New York: Wiley, 1999).

Chapter 10

1. Guy Kawasaki, "Life Lessons from 32 Truly Remarkable People," *Bottom Line Personal Interview* (January 1, 1996), pp. 11–12.

2. Henry Wadsworth Longfellow, *A Psalm of Life* (1839), st. 7.

Part Four

1. Kevin McCarthy, The On-Purpose Person. Pinon Press, 1992 (407-657-6000 to order direct).

Chapter 11

1. *Accent on Philanthropy*, II, Washington, DC: Philanthropic Service for Institutions, 1983.

2. National Society of Fund Raising Executives, *1999 Profile of NSFRE Members*. Alexandria, VA: NSFRE (renamed AFP in 2001).

3. Richard B. Chobot, "Compensation for Fundraisers: Closer to the Whole Story," *Advancing Philanthropy* (March/April 2001).

4. Anne Preston, in Lilly Cohen and Dennis R. Young, eds., *Careers for Dreamers and Doers: A Guide to Management Careers in the Nonprofit Sector* (New York: The Foundation Center, 1989).

5. Kathleen S. Kelly, *Effective Fund-Raising Management* (Mahwah, NJ: Lawrence Erlbaum Associates, 1998), p. 83.

6. Kelly, p. 85.

Chapter 12

1. Oliver Wendell Holmes, *The Autocrat of the Breakfast-Table* (1858), ch. 4.

2. Holly Hall and John Murawski, "Fundraising: Hot Career or Hot Seat?" *The Chronicle of Philanthropy* (June 29, 1995), p. 21.

3. Holly Hall, "Wanted: Big-Gift Fundraisers," *The Chronicle of Philanthropy* (April 22, 1999), p. 1.

4. Hall, p. 46.

5. Hall and Murawski, p. 23.

6. James M. Greenfield, *Fund-Raising: Evaluating and Managing the Fund Development Process*. 2d ed. (New York: Wiley, 1999).

Chapter 13

1. Marilyn Fischer, "Respecting the Individual, Valuing Diversity," in Dwight Burlingame, *Critical Issues in Fundraising* (New York: Wiley, 1997).
2. Emmett Carson, "Philanthropy and Minorities," presented at "The Future of Philanthropy In a Changing America," The American Assembly and The Center on Philanthropy at Indiana University (April 23–26, 1998), p. 1.
3. Stephen G. Greene and John Murawski, "New Faces in Fundraising," *The Chronicle of Philanthropy* (March 21, 1996), p. 37.
4. The increase may be due partly to the sample selected, which included 800 minority members.
5. Greene and Murawski, p. 38.
6. Margaret A. Duronio and Eugene Tempel, *Fundraisers: Their Careers, Stories, Concerns, and Accomplishments* (San Francisco: Jossey-Bass, 1996), p. 27.
7. Quoted from Project Presented to European University, Barcelona, www.stephweb.com/capstone/htm.
8. The quotes in this chapter have been acquired through personal interviews.
9. Holly Hall, "Black Philanthropy: A Focus on Careers and Building Endowments," *The Chronicle of Philanthropy* (June 3, 1999).
10. Kathleen S. Kelly, *Effective Fund-Raising Management* (Mahwah, NJ: Lawrence Erlbaum Associates, 1998), p. 86.

Chapter 14

1. Barbara Kellerman and Larraine R. Matusak, eds. *Cutting Edge Leadership 2000* (University of Maryland: The James MacGregor Burns Academy of Leadership, 2000).
2. Note that *foundation,* in this context, defines a 501(c)(3) organization that is a separate entity but exists solely for the purpose of providing support for the parent organization. This type of foundation should not be confused with the grant-making type.
3. Walter Kiechel III, "The Leader as Servant," *Fortune,* May 4, 1992.
4. Mary Lippitt, "How to Influence Leaders," *Training and Development* (March 1999).
5. Max De Pree, *Leading Without Power: Finding Hope in Serving Community* (San Francisco: Jossey-Bass, 1997), p. 3.

Chapter 15

1. Clayton J. Lafferty and Alonzo W. Pond, *The Desert Survival Situation* (Plymouth, MI: Human Synergistics, nd).
2. Lafferty and Pond.
3. "Computing Your Innovation Style," *Training & Development* (December 1992), p. 11.

Chapter 16

1. The total number of nonprofits, all 501(c) organizations, is 1.2 million.

Chapter 17

1. Nongovernmental organization (NGO) is the international, generally accepted term for nonprofit or not-for-profit organizations. Another term that is sometimes used is civil society organization (CSO).
2. Kathleen D. McCarthy, Virginia A. Hodgkinson, and Russy D. Sumariwalla and Associates. *The Nonprofit Sector in the Global Community* (San Francisco: Jossey-Bass, 1992), p. 1.
3. Leslie M. Fox and S. Bruce Schearer. *Sustaining Civil Society: Strategies for Resource Mobilization* (Washington, DC: World Alliance for Citizen Participation, 1998), p. 13.

4. McCarthy et al., 1992, p. xiv.
5. Nicole Lewis, "Have Expertise, Will Travel: U.S. Fundraisers Abroad Find Hot Job Market, Big Challenges," *The Chronicle of Philanthropy* (July 13, 2000), p. 39.
6. Lester M. Salamon, Helmut K. Anheier, and Associates. *The Emerging Sector Revisited, a Summary* (Baltimore, MD: The Johns Hopkins University Institute for Policy Studies, Center for Civil Society Studies, 1998), p. 4.
7. Masha Gessen, "The Rebirth of Russian Charity," *The American Benefactor* (Spring 1997).
8. "Foundations Gave $639 Million More to International Causes," *NonProfit Times* (February 2001).
9. Debra E. Blum, "Corporate Giving Rises Again," *The Chronicle of Philanthropy* (August 13, 2000).
10. Holly Hall, "Spreading U.S.-Style Philanthropy to Eastern Europe May Be Mistaken, Fundraisers Are Told," *The Chronicle of Philanthropy* (March 22, 1994), p. 24.
11. Lewis, p. 41.
12. Lewis, p. 42.

Chapter 18

1. Clare N. Harman, "Lighten Up," *Association Management* (October 2000), p. 88.
2. Adapted from Bill Mengerink, "Burn, Burned, Burnt: The Conjugation of a Fund Raiser," *Fundraising Management* (April 1990).
3. With thanks to the unknown person who wrote this inspirational bit of verse.

Part Five

1. François Marie Arouet Voltaire, 1694–1778, *Candide* (1759), ch. 30.
2. Thomas Carlyle, 1795–1881, *On Boswell's Life of Johnson* (1832).
3. Joseph Conrad, 1857–1924, *Heart of Darkness* (1902).

Chapter 19

1. "The Executive Search, An Interview with Rick King, Kittleman & Associates," *Advancing Philanthropy* (Spring 1998), p. 37.
2. "How to Recruit Top Talent in Today's Tight Job Market," *The Chronicle of Philanthropy* (2001).
3. Caprice Lengle and Richard C. Struck, "A Journey Worth Sharing," *Advancing Philanthropy* (Fall/Winter 1998), pp. 4–6, 8.
4. Alexander Pope, *An Essay on Man* [1733–1734], Epistle II, 1.
5. "The Executive Search," p. 37.

Chapter 20

1. Roger Ailes, "The First Seven Seconds," *Success* (November 1988), p. 18.
2. *Interviews That Win Jobs* (Garden City, NY: Benci-Ventures, Inc., [Suite 312, 661 Franklin Avenue], 1994).
3. *Interviews That Win Jobs*, p. 37.

Chapter 23

1. "How to Recruit Top Talent in Today's Tight Job Market," *The Chronicle of Philanthropy*, Recruitment Advertising, 1255 23rd Street, NW, Washington, DC 20037; Phone: 202-466-1230; Web site: http://philanthropy.com/jobs.
2. Dickey.
3. Kelly Beamon, "Nonprofits Seek Expert Fund-Raisers," *National Business Employment Weekly* (April 8, 1995), p. 29.
4. Dickey.

5. Mark Gibson, *Hiring the Right Staff: The First Time* (Cleveland, TN: Life Care Centers of America, 2000). Some materials used from Richard J. Pinsker's book, *Hiring Winners,* with appropriate credit given.
6. As quoted from *Accent on Philanthropy II* (Washington, DC: Philanthropic Service for Institutions, 1982).
7. Katharine Graham, "How to Get Power the Old-Fashioned Way," From a speech delivered at the 1984 Matrix Awards luncheon held by Women in Communications.

Chapter 24

1. Walter Doyle Staples, "Winning Big," *Bottom Line* (October 30, 1991). As Canada's acclaimed author on the subject of human potential, Doyle is also author of *Think Like a Winner!* from Pelican Publishing.
2. Paul Huff, "Debunking the Myths of Success," *Training & Development* (August 2000).
3. Margaret A. Duronio and Eugene Tempel, *Fundraisers: Their Careers, Stories, Concerns, and Accomplishments* (San Francisco: Jossey-Bass, 1996), pp. 175–196.
4. James C. Dean, "What Makes a Profession?" *Fundraising Management* (November 1995).
5. John Schwartz, *Anatomy of Philanthropy: A Personal Account* (New York: Wiley, 1994).
6. Adapted from Tom Peters, "Success Secrets From a Master," published in *Communicator* (October 1994).
7. Carl Mays, *A Strategy for Winning* (New York: Lincoln-Bradley Publishing Group, 1991), p. 245.

Chapter 25

1. Michael R. Mauds, "On Confidence," *Fund Raising Management* (September 1998), p. 30.
2. John Gehrke, "Organizational Alignment and Focus," *Advancing Philanthropy* (Spring 1998), p. 39.
3. John McIlquham, "Beware of the Technopeasant," *The NonProfit Times* (February 1994), p. 8.
4. Scott Preissler, Letter to Lilya Wagner dated November 20, 2000.
5. Paul Huff, "Debunking the Myths of Success," *Training and Development* (August 2000), p. 60.

Conclusion

1. Joseph R. Mixer, *Principles of Professional Fundraising* (San Francisco: Jossey-Bass, 1993).
2. John J. Havens and Paul G. Schervish, "Millionaires and the Millennium: New Estimates of the Forthcoming Wealth Transfer and the Prospects for a Golden Age of Philanthropy," Report Released October 19, 1999, Social Welfare Research Institute, Boston College.
3. Association for Research on Nonprofit Organizations and Voluntary Action, 550 W. North Street, Suite 301, Indianapolis, IN 46202-3162, Phone: 317-684-2120, Fax: 317-684-2128, e-mail Exarnova@iupui.edu, www.arnova.org.
4. Mixer, p. 250.
5. Robert D. Putnam, *Bowling Alone: The Collapse and Revival of American Community* (New York: Simon & Schuster, 2000).
6. Bruce Glasrud, "Fund Raiser Futures," *Fund Raising Management* (August 1999), p. 40.

Index